How To Die

And Survive

****

Book Two

Extending Our Interdimensional Awareness:
Next Concepts
For Living and Dying

KEYS TO
CONSCIOUSNESS AND SURVIVAL
SERIES
Volume 11

Dr. Angela Brownemiller

How To Die And Survive

****

Book Two

Extending Our Interdimensional Awareness: Next Concepts For Living and Dying

KEYS TO
CONSCIOUSNESS AND SURVIVAL
SERIES
Volume 11

Dr. Angela Brownemiller

Illustrated By
Angela Brownemiller

METATERRA® PUBLICATIONS

metaterra® publications

How To Die And Survive, Book Two

EXTENDING OUR INTERDIMENSIONAL AWARENESS:
NEXT CONCEPTS FOR LIVING AND DYING
KEYS TO CONSCIOUSNESS AND SURVIVAL SERIES, Volume 11

Copyright © 2022, 2021, 2020: 1998, 2000, 2005, 2010, 2015, 2018, 2019, Angela Brownemiller.
Copyright © 2022, 2021, 2020: 1998, 2000, 2005, 2010, 2015, 2018, 2019, Metaterra® Publications.

All rights reserved in all formats and in

all languages and dialects known or not known at this time.

Published in the United States by Metaterra® Publications.

Library of Congress Cataloging-in-Publication Data.

Brownemiller, Angela.

HOW TO DIE AND SURIVIVE, BOOK TWO

Angela Brownemiller.

1. Survival. 2. Evolution. 3. Consciousness. 4. Psychology. 5. Biology.

6. Ecology. 7. Future. 8. Spirituality. 9. Metaphysical. 10. Interdimensional.

11. Science. 12. Science Fiction. 13. Brownemiller. 14. Browne-Miller.

15. Dr. Angela.

ISBN-13: 978-1-937951-50-4   (Paperback on Amazon).

See Amazon.com for eBook (Kindle eBook) and AudioBook (Audible) versions.

Published in the United States of America for US and worldwide distribution.

Metaterra® Publications.

How To Die and Survive, Book Two
EXTENDING OUR
INTERDIMENSIONAL AWARENESS:
NEXT CONCEPTS FOR LIVING AND DYING

is dedicated
to defenders of
Free Will in all dimensions.

Speaking only for
the right use of Will
in the name of
and vision of
ever purest
ever highest
everlasting
Light.

. . . though I walk
through the valley
of the shadow of death,
I will fear no evil . . .
Psalm 23

Preface From The Heart

My wish for you is that you feel your strength and meaning, your love and joy, your peace and purpose, as you live and yes, as you move beyond this life, whatever this moving beyond may mean for you. We can be seeing views of the possible flowing in to us from here and beyond, in streams of Light, powerful openings to what is here for us to see and know.

My wish for us all is to soothe the pain and fuel the joy, to guide ourselves when we are lost, and share of ourselves when we can. My greatest hope is that we can ease our passages both through this life and into the seeming end of life, and that we can open for ourselves access to our rightful after lives, whatever these may mean for us.

The world here on Earth is not an easy place. Beyond the glitter and material distractions, we see there is great beauty, joy, and love, yet also longing, loneliness, pain, even fear. We as individuals and as a species, as members of all life on Earth, know that our days may eventually be limited, whether soon or long into the future. We can hear the call of potential extinction out there. Whether it be our own or other species being called, the pace is quickening, the preciousness of life is all the more clear.

We can forge a way for ourselves to hold ourselves, our spirits, in high regard. We can touch the Light, and see the precious spirit of life each of us carries. We can know what this is and what it may mean to survive, both here and beyond.

Angela Brownemiller

7

BEFORE YOU BEGIN

Readers, note that this book, ebook, and audiobook, as well as the other *How To Die And Survive* books, ebooks, and audiobooks which follow this book, and all the books in this *Keys To Consciousness And Survival Series*, are provided for educational and informational purposes only. These books, ebooks, and audiobooks do not provide medical advice or professional services. The information provided should not be used for diagnosing or treating a mental or physical health condition, problem, or disease. Always seek the advice of licensed professionals such as your doctor or another qualified health provider regarding a medical or psychological condition. Never disregard professional medical advice regarding physical health, or professional psychological advice regarding mental health, and never delay in seeking this. If you think you may have a medical or psychological emergency, call 911 or go to the nearest emergency room immediately. Thank you.

How To Die And Survive, BOOK TWO
TABLE OF CONTENTS

> *NOTE: The following chapters and sections as listed here in How To Die And Survive, Book* <u>*Two*</u> *are numbered in sequence proceeding from the previous How To Die And Survive book, Book* <u>*One*</u>*, where the basics of this material are presented. What follows builds upon those basics.*

LIST OF FIGURES

How To Die And Survive, Book Two
LIST OF EXERCISES

PART VIII

SPECIAL NOTE
TO READERS OF
How To Die And Survive
BOOK TWO

Welcome Readers. On these pages, you are stepping into what some will call science fiction, what others will say is a twilight zone, what still others will say is the place we can and do go when we die. However you choose to see this *How To Die And Survive* material, you are opening doors to a world of possibilities.

On these pages, you are seeing more about how things work in your daily life. And, you are also going places BEYOND usual daily life via your imagination, your mind, your spirit, your consciousness, your SELF.

LEARNING TO DIE AND SURVIVE

Take this where you would like to take this. Teach yourself *How To Die And Survive* while living here on Earth in a biological body. Get to know what minor and major in-life and seeming end-of-life transitions, and even seeming endings and deaths, may look like, feel like, be like. Get to know what it means to "make it through," to "come out on the other side," to *die and survive*.

Where we may not believe we can go, we can imagine what it is like to go there. We can train ourselves, our minds, our spirits, our souls to move BEYOND, to go where we may have

been told we cannot go, or where we may have been told only certain people can go.

These certain people may be self-named leaders or seers or believers who say there are controls on who gets into the afterlife. Yet, I say that the right to *die and survive* belongs to all of us, that we can learn to *die and survive*.

REACHING BEYOND BOUNDARIES
TO SURVIVE

And then there is the limit, the boundary, that has been set all too often, the one that says there is no there there, that when we die, that is it, we are done, gone, over. There are many who tell me, even write me and insist, that we cannot and do not die and survive. I appreciate and accept their views. If you choose to close the door on the possibility that we can *die and survive*, I accept this. We each must decide this for ourselves.

I choose to develop an ever expanding awareness of what it may be like to leave the biological body when it expires *and then survive*. I choose to develop and share training for consciously moving through in-life and even seeming end-of-life transitions and deaths. I choose to detail what it means to experience survival BEYOND.

There are many of you out there who, like me, have had near death and perhaps even actual death experiences of your own, and or of others you are in contact with. For those of you who have seen BEYOND, stepped BEYOND, floated BEYOND, momentarily or for minutes or for hours, or for lifetimes, maybe even eons, you are also welcome to the journey this book shares.

We are all together in on this concern for our survival options.

WE CAN TEACH OURSELVES TO SURVIVE

I understand that my giving the books in this set the title, *How To Die And Survive*, is in itself a pretty far out description of the contents of these books. On the pages of these books, you are embarking on a journey beyond given boundaries. You are opening doors to possibilities. Where we may not believe we can go, we can imagine what it is like to go there. We can train ourselves, our minds to believe, to learn, to teach ourselves, HOW TO GO BEYOND, and thus *How To Die And Survive*.

Welcome to a world of imagined and actual possibility. Can we actually survive death? Is there actually an afterlife option out there? I say yes.

THIS BOOK

This book, *How To Die And Survive: Book Two*, follows very specifically the foundational concepts and exercises presented in the previous book, *How To Die And Survive, Book One*. This second *How To Die And Survive* book, *Book Two*, delves ever more deeply into matters of interdimensional awareness, travel, and survival.

Certainly, many Readers are ready to jump right into this second book where these interdimensional survival concepts are deepened and intensified. It is nevertheless generally recommended that Readers also move through the foundational concepts and exercises in the preceding *How To Die And Survive* book, *Book One*, to not only prepare themselves, but also to prepare their mind-brains, for these ever more far-

reaching concepts and processes.

Also note that these *How To Die And Survive* books are volumes in the *Keys To Consciousness And Survival Series*. Readers are encouraged to see the other books in this series for more on the matter of the consciousness as a life form, one that can develop itself to live on.[1]

So, welcome to *How To Die And Survive*, the reality, the potential, the option we can develop for ourselves and for our species.

Your right to know the following interdimensional survival concepts is clear. These are simple, even logical, explorations our minds, our personal consciousness-es, can take.

TAP INTO YOUR LIGHT

Form your own ideas and concepts related to energy patterns and arrangements. For example, form your own definition of light with a lower case L and Light with an upper case L. Then, tap into the light, into the vision, the understanding, the ***idea of Light***, coming in from higher dimensions of yourself, of your universe, of your reality.

Let this feel for Light filter into your awareness. Take your actual power back by seeing what is actually here for you, by tapping into the inspiring, transformational, and catalytic

---

[1] The *Keys To Consciousness And Survival Series* by Dr. Angela Brownemiller can be found on Amazon.com and DrAngela.com. See recommended reading list in the Appendices section of the present book.

forces available to you, to your mind, to your consciousness, to your actual SELF.

SEE and fuel this LEAP in your awareness, in your consciousness, even in your energy structure. This is the LEAP that you can make to survive profound changes, shifts in reality, ends of cycles, any of the many in-life and seeming end-of-life transitions, even what are so-called "deaths."

After all, the meanings of endings, even of deaths, even of *after lives*, are what we understand and define these as being. These *How To Die And Survive* books offer an innovative and inspiring array of *concepts for living and dying*: offering new ways of understanding ourselves and our lives; detailing progressive practices for sensing, generating, and expanding our interdimensional awareness, our psychological knowledge, our consciousness itself, and our survival skills.

The concepts and exercises in these *How To Die And Survive* books begin quite simply and carefully build toward some very esoteric understandings. On these pages, we can begin to overcome limits to old models of what we are, who we are, and where we can be and go.

Ultimately, this is an exploration of the tremendous potential of your own consciousness, of your actual SELF, to survive.

Join us for the journey of your lifetime, of all your lifetimes....

KEYS TO
CONSCIOUSNESS AND SURVIVAL SERIES
Foreword

Just as the fish itself did not discover water, we ourselves have perhaps inadvertently demonstrated the obvious, which is that we cannot entirely, absolutely, know what all it is "we" are immersed in, nor even what all it is that "we" are.

Ultimately, the question of the hour, the question of our times, the question of our reality, is regarding this thing we call our consciousness. Do we identify with our consciousness, is it *of* us, is it *us*, is it *more* than we are, or is it simply a *side effect* of life?

The question as to whether the amorphous consciousness is itself *derivative* of biology, or is itself *independent* of biology (and perhaps even independent of *what any intelligence can entirely discover of itself from within itself* and its tools), will reveal itself to be irrelevant. This stunning shift in understanding will happen once we recognize that our elusive consciousness can at any point be redefined, or redefine itself to itself—or even shift into (or back into) independence of biology, stepping out of evolutionary, synaptic, and conceptual controls, into existence independent of Human science, religion, philosophy, even of the Human brain itself—much like a grown child leaving home.

As they depart, we can speculate that our consciousness-es are in a sense like our children, in that they are apparently born from us—a speculation no artificial or machine intelligence (as

yet incapable of actual procreation and actual biological parental ties) can do unless consciously programmed to be able to do.

Our children, once they consciously leave home, their consciousness-es in tow, can grow up to consciously be who they already are.

Get ready, even the Human Consciousness is going to break free of the definitions and confines of its biological host bodies here on Earth. It's been a nice visit but the time will come to go—

...or at least to be able to come and go, back and forth, at will.

Dr. Angela Brownemiller

Dr. Angela®

DrAngela.com

AUTHOR'S NOTE

This book presents this author's basic, and primarily metaphorical, interdimensional awareness, consciousness, travel, and survival material and technologies, and related understandings. This is simple yet complex material, easy to take in and yet potentially powerful in effect. Readers have a right to such knowledge. Readers also have a responsibility to apply such knowledge with care and with the highest of ethical intent.

This is more than a book. This is itself a portal, an opening into a journey of the mind, heart, soul, spirit. When read in sequence and with great concentration, the following chapters and their exercises may produce an alteration in the Reader's state of mind and awareness. Understand that such shifts in awareness can be valuable in psychological and spiritual growth, and can range from obvious to easily assimilated to confusing to challenging. Should a Reader find the solitary study of this text confusing and or disorienting, seek a fellow Reader and/or a trained psychological or spiritual guide.

If you are indeed reading this, you are most likely a Human being living on planet Earth. This is the evolutionary level of life form for which these words are written.

Other Readers, should there be any, will feel free to interpret the messages transmitted herein according to respective levels of location, and or of belief and understanding, and, again, with only the highest of ethical intent.

LEAP Lev20	LEAP Form	LEAP Description
One	Embracing	*Accepting, feeling ready for, fully moving into,* the concept of shift (or death) out of a dimension, or phase or stage of life or mind, or out of the physical body itself.
Two	Quickening	*Raising the presumed or actual energetic vibration or frequency* of one's *aware consciousness;* pulling together the *conscious focus* to ever more *consciously move* into another dimension and/or to *ever more consciously move into and through* a major transition in life, or a physical death.
Three	Willing The Exit	*Focusing the Will* in such a concentrated way that the exit from the dimension or phase of life or physical body is energized, facilitated.
Four	Leaping To The Next Dimension	*Moving the consciousness in such a manner that it shifts, LEAPs,* out of its current or present focus and format or dimension of its reality, generally occurring after its exit from the dimension, or phase of life, or if biological, from the physical body it has been in.
Five	Elevating-- Ascending	*Moving the consciousness in such a manner that it ascends* into what may be experienced as higher frequencies, higher realms of Light, or higher dimensions of its/the reality.
Six	Catharting Beyond	*Using the energy released by shifting, breaking, LEAPing,* out of a dimension or phase of life or physical body to move well beyond the realm of existence, or format, being left.
Seven	Meta- scending	*Realizing the effects of transition or death, and or ascension and interdimensional travel,* without appearing to have a phase of life or a physical body die. The understanding itself LEAPS.
Eight	Achieving High Metaxis: : The META- LEAP	Achieving the highest possible range, or dimensional span, of oneself. An *intentional inter-dimensional shifting, an energetic reformatting, the essential LEAP-ing,* the META-LEAP, without depending on actual physical death to propel.

BASIC
LIGHT-ENERGY-ACTION-PROCESSES (LEAPs)
Keys to Interdimensional Travel: Eight Levels

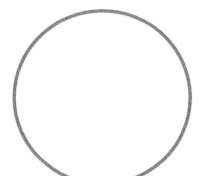

PART IV

How

To

Get Out

Reminder: The Part, Chapter, and Exercise numbers in this book, *How To Die And Survive: Book Two,* are numbered in sequence to follow those Parts, Chapters, and Exercises in the preceding book, the first of these *How To Die And Survive* books, which is *Book One*.

22
LEAVING THE BODY

> Now Cassim had forgotten the magic
> word. He had had his mind on the
> gold. The more he tried to think of the
> magic word, the more frightened he
> became.... The gold was no good to
> him if he couldn't get out of the cave.
>
> "Ali Baba and the
> Forty Thieves"
> *1001 Nights*

On the pages of this book, we will be exploring states of mind that can be developed to improve one's experience of changes and transitions in daily life -- and also in dying processes, and also in what we may want to call after life transition processes. This is about becoming ever more aware of how you move through transition processes such as changes, endings, and deaths -- about how you survive these.

Leaving a situation or a state of mind is in a sense leaving a body. This body is a pattern of biology or behavior or emotion or perception. Indeed, we can think in terms of how we move through a change as being similar to how we move through leaving a situation or a body. So, where this book talks about leaving or being out of the body, this is both an imaginary process, an example we can apply to daily life, and also perhaps a very likely process. You decide.

33

YOU MAY OR MAY NOT SOMETIMES FEEL YOU ARE OUT OF YOUR BODY

You will likely be, to some degree, aware of times when you (your focus, your center, your SELF) have moved out of your physical body. Yet, this awareness may be vague for many individuals.[2]

Although we (our attention, our focus, our center, our SELVES) quite frequently move slightly or more than slightly in and out of our physical bodies, even in daily life and dreams, we may not notice we are doing this.

Many people report that they are somewhat aware of times when they may be partially or entirely out of their physical bodies. Some say they have had out of body sensations or perceptions while dreaming, some say even while walking around, facing danger, undergoing surgery, and in other situations.

And apparently, many people who are physically dying, or perhaps even physically dead, may not realize they have moved away from or even entirely left their physical bodies, or that they already have died physical deaths.

Some instances of persons who have died physical deaths, or at least have been close to medically dead, are reported to include experiences of disorientation and even confusion.

---

[2] Refer to opening chapters in *Volume 3* in this *Keys To Consciousness And Survival Series*, titled, *Unveiling The Hidden Instinct.*

Preparing in advance for this profound transition can help ease and navigate this passage. (Therefore, Readers are offered the material in these *How To Die And Survive* books, as well as in the other books in this *Keys To Consciousness And Survival Series*.)

You can develop the associated **body exit awareness** in advance of your temporary or even actual physical body exit. This is advisable, as it allows greater **aware consciousness during profound transition**. Minor and major transition experiences can be greatly eased and ever more consciously navigated.

ONCE YOU ARE "*OUT*"

Many intense life changes may feel like profound events, challenging transitions, major endings, even deaths. We frequently hear people saying they feel like they are dying when undergoing an emotionally or physically difficult time.

Once you have undergone your exit from the flesh of your present life, you will know this, at least on some level. The more awareness you bring to this passage, this transition, the more you can be consciously engaged in the process. Now begins one of the greatest adventures in all in-life and seeming end-of-life transitions and deaths.

These *How To Die And Survive* books are dedicated to details that can assist, even nourish and protect, you in your journeys and adventures to SELF. These are what can be called *transition awareness training exercises*. The exercises and teachings in these books must be practiced with a commitment to use these and

teach these only in circumstances of the highest intent and the right use of Will. Never use this knowledge against your own or others' well-informed and fully Free Wills.

Your understanding of the concepts and exercises offered in these *How To Die And Survive* books will evolve as you consider and reconsider them.

NEEDING THE PHYSICAL IS NATURAL

Even after getting out of your physical body, you may find that you are tempted to cling to it. You may cling to your physical body as if you need it to survive. This is natural. You have needed your physical body to survive (physically) while living in the physical plane on 3-D Earth. Yet, there comes a time when it is necessary to leave the physical body as aware, as consciously, as possible to save the wealth of spirit, the riches of soul, you have acquired while in that body—perhaps even to save your personal consciousness, your actual SELF.

Even if you understand this and exit your physical body, your emotional body may not want to let go. It therefore pays to further examine this *getting out* (of an old or not so old problem pattern, or of a time-to-move-on stage of life, or of a physical body itself).

Keep in mind that all minor and major changes involve shifts in, or endings of, patterns. In essence, in changing or leaving any minor or major pattern, there is transition out of that old form of that pattern. Patterns themselves have become repeating patterns to maintain their existence as patterns. In

this sense, patterns may actually resist their own transitions and deaths.[3]

EMBRACE THE
UNKNOWN

There generally does come a time when there is nothing to do but leave the old life, perhaps even the old physical body and its old emotional body. You will know this juncture when you come to it, although you may try not to see it, not to recognize that you are there.

At this juncture, you may find yourself resistant to dying, even nostalgic for the past, no matter how troubled a past it is. You may naturally want to hang on to the familiar, both the familiar physical body and the familiar emotional body the physical body has developed.

NOTE: Nothing in these How To Die And Survive books, or in any of these Keys To Consciousness And Survival Series books,[4] suggests actual suicide. Not at all. Rather, these books encourage a fully

---

[3] For an in-depth examination of **how patterns themselves may resist dying,** refer to the book, *Seeing The Hidden Face Of Addiction,* also by this author. See reading list at the end of this present book.

[4] Refer to the Recommended Reading list in the Appendices at the end of this present book, where many of the volumes in this *Keys To Consciousness And Survival Series* are listed. Note that the first *How To Die And Survive* book is *Volume 4* in this series, and this present book, the second *How To Die And Survive* book, (*How To Die And Survive: Book Two*), is *Volume 11* in this series. See also the collected *How To Die And Survive* exercises as a progressive training, in *How To Die And Survive, Book Three.*

informed mind and an increasingly aware personal consciousness in preparation for all the minor and major in-life and seeming end-of-life transitions we (as individual persons and as a species) may face.

Even if you have released all or most of your attachments to the familiar (attachments and their ties, cordings, as discussed in the previous *How To Die And Survive* book, *Book One*), you may still prefer the familiar to the unknown. This preference is often found even among those who have endured much emotional and/or physical suffering. Many tend to prefer known suffering to entire unknowns. Is this our emotional body bargaining with us?

*Understand the difference between hanging on to what is familiar even when it is not healthy, and moving forward to a **new form of survival**.* These are two different drives, although frequently co-mingled and confused. *The desire to hang on to the familiar no matter what can camouflage itself as a survival instinct*, even sometimes leading a person to remain in a dangerously sick situation or condition, or a dangerously sick addiction to another sick system, longer than he or she has to.

Sometimes the individual experiencing this confusion remains resistant to leaving the sick system, resistant to transitioning or dying out of that dangerous energy arrangement. This resistance may last far too long. One's spirit or SELF may then lose energy and itself begin to fade away. This death of the spirit, of the personal consciousness, is not the death to seek. This is the death to avoid by ever more consciously undergoing constructive physical and emotional transition and death releases in order to save the spirit, the SELF of the personal consciousness.

It is therefore of tantamount importance that you, while living in the biological body, practice healthy, aware, positive, conscious transition and even exit processes. Again note that this is NOT about suicide, this IS about survival. Learn what it means to: rewire or even leave a sick and dying emotional or even biological system before it takes you down with it.

This is a matter of the actual SELF, the personal consciousness, conserving and preserving it SELF, its own energetic design, to move forward.

At a certain point, the energy you expend to hang on to the familiar is energy much needed by your personal consciousness for it to survive.

GETTING OUT ALIVE

Get out while you can still get out alive. One might say this another way: die while you can still survive. (Again and again do note: nothing in these *How To Die And Survive* books advocates suicide or anything like this. These exercises and concepts are about preparing the SELF, the personal consciousness, to survive by recognizing the options and processes both here and BEYOND.[5])

So, yes, the idea is to know how and when to shift, to LEAP, to change, to transition, to get out while you can still get out alive. The involves understanding what it can mean to ever more *consciously navigate transition*, minor and major, in-life and even

---

[5] Refer to *Volume 10* in this *Keys To Consciousness And Survival Series*, titled, *Seeing Beyond Our Line Of Sight.*

seeming end-of-life deaths, and even perhaps the seeming *after*life domains.[6]

(The terms, *seeming* and *after*life, are used here, as what may *seem* to be an *after*life is actually not an after LIFE if the life is still there. Of course, this may be an after-transition, or perhaps an after-physical life LIFE.)

So, you can consciously leave a sick and dying system, a dangerous energy arrangement, while you can in order to get out alive. Sounds obvious, sounds easy. Yet, this dictum is not so readily appreciated by a troubled and heavily corded person.

There are many tugs and pulls tying that person, cording that person, to the troubled physical and or emotional system. These ties and cordings do not just readily let go. The heavily corded person is frequently being pulled on, not only by her or his own cordings and ties, but also by external forces and factors, ties and cordings coming from physical and emotional bodies of others, and more. (See the in-depth discussion of cording and attachment in the preceding *How To Die And Survive* book, *Book One*.)

If you are feeling this sort of situation – if you are being caught in a dangerous system or energy pattern, even perhaps being addicted to this dangerous system or energy pattern, you know what this can feel like. You know how strong are the ties (attachments and cordings) to this system and its patterns. Until you see the truth about this situation, the truth about

---

[6] See two other books in this *Keys To Consciousness And Survival Series: Volumes 8 and 9*, the *Navigating Life's Stuff* books.

your potential survival, your programming may be telling you to fool yourself, to lie to yourself, and *you may be living the lie the programming is telling you to live.*[7]

ALLOW YOURSELF TO REALIZE

Once you allow yourself to realize the need for shedding a problematic, draining, and or even dangerous pattern of emotion or behavior, a problematic energy arrangement, you must let yourself out of, shed, this pattern, this arrangement of your energy.

Here you may find others leaving with you. Or, you may find others putting up strong resistance to their own, or even to your own, leaving of this dangerous pattern and its energy arrangement. Just as you may cling to the familiar, the people around you may not want you to change away from what is familiar. There are many ties and attachments that may be resisting the shedding of a particular pattern or energy arrangement of a particular emotional body network.

CLEAR THE RUNWAY

Daily life offers many opportunities to learn about these issues. In fact, daily life is the best place to begin to learn about *How To Die And Survive* the changing or leaving of a troubled situation or pattern, of a problem social, emotional, or physical system. All that is presented in this book can be applied to the

---

[7] See details on this matter of a personal program, maybe even an addiction, tying you to itself, holding you caught in its pattern, in the book, *Seeing The Hidden Face Of Addiction*. See readings listed at the end of this present book.

issues of being tied to troubled patterns and systems. Yes, many of these troubled patterns and systems, with conscious awareness, can be changed from within, and other of these must be exited to either change them -- or to leave them, to avoid or stop their effects and holds on you.

Think of the biological death process as a metaphor for other changes and endings. These are all transitions. Learn about transition while living in a biological body, in daily life. There are stages of change in all transitions. Learn to see these stages as you undergo these. Remember that death is a metaphor for change, and change is a metaphor for death. Seeing this helps prepare for later seeming end-of-life transitions.

 The point of seeing this is to help clear your own personal runway, your own path to *transition survival*.

CONSIDER POSSIBLY
CONFLICTING PULLS

Remember that there are going to be phases, what are frequently described as three phases, of what at first may appear to be your death: basic physical death, then emotional body death, then possibly mental body death.[8] Physical death has its own stages, is quite frequently perceived as more challenging than emotional death.

However, it is the emotional body itself that can also undergo quite challenging exit processes. And, emotional sensations such as pulls of unfinished business, along with a general sense of lack of preparation, as well as fear of the unknown, feelings

---

[8] Refer to *Volume 10* in this *Keys To Consciousness And Survival Series*, titled, *Seeing Beyond Our Line Of Sight*.

such as frustration, anger, sadness, and depression, and other challenging emotions can make leaving the physical body all the more difficult.

Detaching from the physical frequently involves feeling powerful tugs not to detach coming from the emotional body. Furthermore, where physical pain may become a reason for wanting to leave the physical body, emotional pain regarding the idea of leaving may work in the other direction. Sometimes the emotional and the physical body agree and move in the same direction. Other times, the conflict is powerful: stay versus do not stay.

LOOK AHEAD

Being aware of these issues well before dealing with physical death can be helpful.

It can even be useful to look ahead, walk yourself, or think yourself, through various daily life exit stages and phases. Imagine or design your own transition processes if you wish.

Then, also think of the possible death processes, and then even after-life scenarios, you might wish to find. Begin to think in terms of where you are going. You can generate for yourself before you die, a clear picture of where you want to go or be after your transition or death, a clear definition of the BEYOND, your BEYOND.

When you generate this clarity, even if you may later amend it, you give yourself a sense of direction and purpose to hang on to right through all your changes, transitions, and dyings. **You give yourself the idea that you have a place to go, that this**

place is your territory, that you, your SELF, can live on to go there, that you can choose to *die and survive.*

ENVISION YOUR REALITY

Here is where you, your increasingly aware personal consciousness, can design within itself, within its own territory, its own place to be and go. **You can imagine yourself creating your own post physical death reality, as this is not really post death -- as, if you live on, you of course have not died.**

YOU, WITH YOUR AWARE CONSCIOUSNESS, CAN BE THE ARCHITECT OF YOUR OWN PLACE TO BE AND GO. AS YOU WILL AT SOME TIME LEAVE YOUR PHYSICAL BODY, YOU CAN FIND YOUR <u>SELF</u> OUT THERE, IN THE REALM OF YOUR CONSCIOUNESS.

GET TO KNOW THIS REALM MORE AND MORE NOW. EXPLORE THE EXIT POSSIBILITIES YOU CAN OFFER YOURSELF, EVEN DESIGN FOR YOURSELF, NOW.

Your personal consciousness can design its own SURVIVAL PATHWAY. And, your personal consciousness can develop TERRAINS within itSELF, within the realm of your personal consciousness. This realm of YOU is already here, just get to know it better and better every day.

Always remember not to let anyone tell you that you cannot get there from here. This statement reveals the deep programming to believe in severe limitations. This "there" this book is talking about is already "here," as it already exists within your SELF.

Your personal consciousness is a vast territory, and this is your domain.

You can move your mind, your SELF, into anywhere your consciousness can access from here (anywhere you can conceive of in your mind's eye. *Your interdimensional reality is yours, is the territory of your own personal consciousness.*

SEE AND KNOW AND MAP

Just understand and envision, begin to map, your journey. Grow familiar with your intended destination. Envision increasingly clearly, with the understanding that you are always continuing to focus and refocus the lens of your inner vision.

Begin in advance of travel to allow your awareness to explore, to map, to get to know, what it is designing for itself, the path you are designing. You will see this is the path you are already on. Begin in advance to get to know the vehicle of SELF you are already traveling within. In essence, your vehicle of SELF is you, your SELF itself.

ENVISION SURVIVAL

Envision. Allow your mind's eye, even your imagination, to explore the non-physical dimensions of your SELF, of who and where you already are. Begin to practice your exploration and definition of territories not mapped on physical plane maps, whether of Earth or of off Earth locations. Begin to map the world BEYOND this life, which is a world you also already live in. (See *Volume 10* in this series, where the

45

CONTINUUM OF CONSCIOUSNESS where you live is defined and explained.[9])

You can begin to plan your own survival, to define for your SELF what it means for you to *die and survive*. You can practice planning your *survival pathways.* Experience the practice of, or even actual planning of, your expansion, your transition, your movement further into your own realms. Do this even here and **now**.

Plan in order to generate your envisioning. Even imagine you can take steps to plan the death of a body of behavior you have outgrown, even of a life you have outgrown, even at some time of your physical biological body. Learn what you want to know later: **now**.

*Get to know what your own **survival pathways** may look like, how these will feel, how you will sense these. Open your eyes to what may be openings, forks, and the windows, other portals of opportunity.[10] These are everywhere.* Identify the best openings or portals into *your personally envisioned transformation.*

You will find this process easier than you expect if you remain focused on your intent, your vision of your own journey and destination. This is an ongoing learning process:

This is
the continuing focusing of your

---

[9] The title of this book is, *Seeing Beyond Our Line Of Sight*. See reading list at the end of this present book.

[10] Refer to *Volumes 8 and especially 9* in the *Keys To Consciousness And Survival Series*. These are the *Navigating Life's Stuff* books.

internal lens.

LEAVING THE BODY

In some cultures now disappearing from the face of the globe, there are socially acceptable means of leaving the body. Not all of these methods involve the taking of drugs, the using of morphine pumps, the pulling of life support system plugs, or the administering of forms of so-called euthanasia.

Some indigenous peoples have traditions allowing an individual who wishes to, at the right time, peacefully leave the physical body for good. These ancient traditions allowed a person to quietly (or formally in ceremony) decide to do so and then to lie down and die, taking one or a few twenty-four hour periods to accomplish this.

So-called "modern" Humans seem to have forgotten that this SELF-willed-exit with no outside enabling is an option. Still, even "moderns" frequently, albeit subconsciously, practice this option as a sort of temporary leaving during their dream, near death, and other out of body states. Body exit and return processes may be more common than we realize. We may be engaged in these processes much of our lives.[11]

---

[11] Readers are encouraged to see the first chapters of *Volume 3* in this *Keys To Consciousness And Survival Series*, which is titled, *Unveiling The Hidden Instinct*. These chapters discuss various forms of out of body experience.

Then there are those who find themselves caught in a death wish cycle. There are those who unfortunately may harm themselves, even lead to their own deaths, by continuing to wish they would die.

There is significant responsibility in choosing to leave the physical body. There is also often overlooked responsibility in allowing oneself to mistakenly or carelessly exit from the body. (Note: This in no way suggests that persons experiencing illnesses or accidents are to be held responsible or perhaps blamed for their conditions, and or for their deaths.)

Generally, we already know healthy ways to conduct temporary and even ongoing body exits, although we may not realize we do.

Leaving the body is actually quite simple. To do so, you must know the keys—the ways out—and the ways back in. And, you must know how to release your own attachments, your own cords, to your own body.

*(Note: The previous **How To Die And Survive** book, **Book One,** discusses the severance or detachment from the network of cords. Here, we focus on the actual getting out. Also note, regarding the exercises that follow here below in this chapter (**Chapter 22** of **How To Die And Survive, Book Two**), see **Chapter 12** in **Book One** of **How To Die And Survive**, which defines the VERTICAL AXIS and provides basic exercises regarding the VERTICAL AXIS.)*

EXERCISE #22.1
FLOATING OUT

Lie or sit very still. Look at one of your hands. Imagine that you see your hand lifting out of itself, finger by finger, as if a ghost of your hand is leaving your hand.

As this ghost leaves, close your eyes. Follow your hand's ghost out of your body. Let your whole SELF follow. Float out bit by bit until you find yourself floating several feet above yourself. Linger there and look back at your body a while.

Visualize two very fine silvery cords attaching you to your body, attaching to points of your choice on your body, such as one hooking to your forehead area, the other to your heart area.

Form a triangle between yourself and these two points on your body. Hold this image a while.

Then, following the path by which you exited, gently slip your consciousness back into your body.

EXERCISE #22.2
GETTING OUT

*Stand up (if you choose to and can do so, otherwise sit or lie down). Focus on what we can call here your **vertical axis**, which runs up and down your body in the direction of your spine. This is your **vertical axis** whether you are standing or sitting or lying down.*

Place your right hand on the very lowest part of your abdomen. Pull all your attention to the area of your body behind your hand. Hold this focus a while.

Then, place your left hand over your belly button, and pull all your focus there as you lift your right hand off the lower abdomen. Hold your focus at this second point a while.

49

Then, proceed to climb your vertical exit ladder in the same fashion, placing your hands as follows:

Right hand over area just below center of rib cage. Hold your focus here a while.

Left hand over area at center of chest, at the level of the heart. Hold your focus here a while.

Right hand over throat. Hold your focus here a while.

Left hand over forehead. Hold your focus here a while.

Right hand over top of head. Hold your focus here a while.

*Left hand extended out (**along your vertical axis**) over top of head. Bring your right hand up there to meet your left hand. Hold your focus here a while.*

*Now move your focus, your personal consciousness, far, far above the highest reach of the hands you have extended over your head. Suck more of your consciousness into this point. Pull all of your consciousness to this high point on your **vertical ladder**. Hold. Hold. Hold yourself out there. . . .*

You are out!

Feel what this exit is like. Understand how you have arrived out here. You can follow your vertical axis out whether or not you have a physical body.

Now, please, you must climb back into your body, back down the ladder you climbed to exit, step by step, hand by hand, slowly, with focus.

ON KEYING OUT

The following exercise, KEYING OUT, is a central part of this *How To Die And Survive Technology* being presented in these books.

Readers are encouraged to see additional in-depth discussion of these and related concepts and processes in other books in this *Keys To Consciousness And Survival* Series such as: the previous and first *How To Die And Survive* book *(Volume 4)* where detailed concepts and exercises including those regarding attachment identification and release are presented; also *Unveiling The Hidden Instinct (Volume 3)* where exercises presenting more advanced keys to interdimensional awareness and survival are offered; and, *Navigating Life's Stuff, Book Two*, where definition and description of the PATTERN TERRAIN "out there" are presented.

EXERCISE #22.3
KEYING OUT

*You can temporarily, or at the right time permanently, unlock your SELF from your physical existence, from your body. To do so, you must press what we will call here the **exit triggers**, as they are a sort of combination lock. Here, you will practice this keying out with your hands. Eventually, you will know how to do this with only your mental focus serving as your hands. Any physical touch will then be unnecessary to do what this book describes as: **keying out**.*

Now, use your two pointer fingers. Press firmly but not at all hard on each of the following points in the order listed below:

1. *Breathe in and hold. At same time: Left hand finger presses in back, at the bottom, the base, of back of spine. Right hand finger presses in lower front, opposite the left hand. Hold. Release. Then exhale.*

2. *Breathe in and hold. Arms crossed. Finger of each hand presses outer side of upper arm at center of upper arm. Hold. Release. Then exhale.*

3. *Breathe in and hold. Left hand finger presses in front at base of throat. Right hand finger presses in back on spinal cord opposite left hand finger. Hold. Release. Then exhale.*

4. *Breathe in and hold. Pointer finger of each hand presses on its own side of lower back of skull, above top of neck. Hold. Release, then exhale.*

5. *Breathe in and hold. Both pointer fingers gently press in on very center of forehead. Hold. Release. Then exhale.*

6. *Breathe in and hold. Both pointer fingers very gently press in on very top center of head. Hold. Release. Then exhale.*

7. *Breathe in and hold. Pointer fingers press on each other at the point as far as the fingers can reach above the top center of your head. Hold this pressing a moment....*

8. *Feel a door click open as you pull these two fingers apart. Like water flooding out of an abruptly opened dam, exhale and LEAP out beyond those fingers.*

9. *Float or race out of your body to a place anywhere nearby that you choose. Stay there a while. Feel this experience.*

52

10. *Feel what it is like to be <u>out</u>. Get to know the accompanying sensations. There will be a time when you elect to move on and not to return to your physical body. But for now, for this exercise, and for much of your exploration and development, it is best that you come back. So...*

11. *Collect yourself back into your hands above your head. Then put yourself down on top of your head, ready to re-enter your body. Begin to will your SELF back into your physical body and you will come back.*

12. *Come back in. Place your right hand on top of your head and gently press there. Keep your right hand pressing there and place your left hand over your lower abdomen. Press there too. Hold. Breathe deeply....*

13. *You may need to hold for quite a while. This depends upon the degree to which you convinced yourself that you were able to key out of your body during this exercise. You may want to have someone press with his or her palms on the bottom of your feet, or hold your ankles, to help you move all the way back in to your physical body.*

14. *Note: if coming back in seems to involve more, then: Some of you will want to step back in the same way you stepped out, moving your SELF back down into your body via your vertical axis. Reverse Exercise 22.2 (GETTING OUT) for this. This will therefore be STEP BY STEP GETTING BACK IN.*

23
RELEASING THE OLD MATRIX —
ENERGETIC SHEDDING

> Distilled for purification are
> these juices of the Soma....
>
> Hymn in Praise of Indra
> *The Veda*

Moving through changes in life can be easy, or somewhat challenging, or quite difficult. Changes vary, and times vary. Our readiness varies. Our support systems, if any, vary. Our better and better understanding of, and even practicing of, transition processes can help us navigate the minor and major transitions we encounter.

One thing we will come to know is that change is always taking place. Any minor or major change involves some form of letting go. Get to know what letting go feels like, and how to navigate this letting go. Letting go is a shedding of something, perhaps of an energy arrangement, perhaps of a body of emotions or ideas or cells.

For example, think about physical death. Shedding the biological body is described as dying, and of course is a form of dying. We can expand our understanding of moving through in-life as well as seeming end-of-life and also so-called afterlife transitions. In so doing, we can expand our access to our own territories.

BEYOND THE BIOLOGICALLY-BASED SELF

When it comes time to die a physical (biological) death, we are aware of this self we have come to believe is who we are. This is the sense of self we have generated while living in a physical (biological) body.

For some of you, this biologically-based self may be anticipating and or already undergoing the experience of physical dying and death. This self may be anticipating or even experiencing some dying on the physical and emotional levels.

Yet, this biologically-based self is now more aware of itself as it thinks its existence is threatened. This self may tell itself it may be dying. Various sensations, what may be experienced as emotions, may arise. These emotions may range from what may feel to be hesitation and or confusion and or concern and or fear and or anguish, perhaps even on to acceptance, even relief, even great awe. The emotional body is being moved away from the biological body, yet its cords may be working to remain attached. (This sort of conflict in itself can be confusing for the dying person.) The emotional body undergoes intense experiences of the biologically based self at this time.

While the biologically-based physical body and the biologically-based emotional body may be dying, the biologically-based self, not the actual SELF, may be seeing itself as dying.

There may be an arising sense of the actual SELF emerging. The biologically based self may only vaguely sense this presence as dying proceeds.

BUT WHO OR WHAT MAY BE DYING?

Here we must ask, what and who may be dying? Is this dying of the self what is really taking place? Is this biologically-based self all there is? Can we have a say in the process? Can we have a say in whether or not we can *die and survive*?

As these *Keys To Consciousness And Survival Series* books suggest, we can learn, evolve ourselves, to be able to sustain ourselves, our actual SELVES. We can learn to know ourselves as far more than only biologically based beings. (For more on this matter of our not being only biologically based, see the *Foreword* to this *series* at the front of this and other books in this *series*.)

Who and what is this biologically based self that may be dying? While living in a biological body in the physical plane, we tend to think of our self as what our biological body and biological brain tells us is our self. Yet, many discover that we are far more than a biologically based self, far more than what our biological brain has generally indicated that we are.[12]

We are (each of us is) the actual SELF that can learn to sustain itself, can learn to reach BEYOND its biological basis. There is far more here. Labels for this "far more" aspect of the SELF include terms such as higher self, and spirit, soul, and consciousness. Here, in this book, this is called the *personal consciousness,* and the *SELF (capitalized).*

WE ARE FAR MORE THAN

---

[12] Refer to *Volumes 5 and 6* in this series, the *Overriding The Extinction Scenario* books.

BIOLOGY-BASED BEINGS

We are far more than this self our biological brains have come to define for us. (See deep review of this matter of what our biological brains are telling us, and even restricting us to, in the early chapters of *Volume 3* in this *Keys To Consciousness And Survival Series*, titled *Unveiling The Hidden Instinct*.)

When contemplating and or approaching (and or already undergoing) physical dying, we may experience the self in ever more accentuated ways. Our biological brains may be telling us that the self is dying along with the biological body. Our minds may be saying (or wanting) something different.

Here is where we can become increasingly aware that our biologically-based self is not our full or actual SELF. **After all, if there is a SELF that can survive physical death, wouldn't it make sense that the actual non-physical SELF is the one most likely to *die and survive* physical death? Yes.**

These *How To Die And Survive* books, along with all the books in this *Keys To Consciousness And Survival Series*, are suggesting that **we have the option of re-defining, re-developing, further evolving, this self, this actual SELF we have developed.**

We have the option of understanding we are more than this self we have come to believe we are, that our biological brains tell us we are. We can reach BEYOND what and who we are programmed to believe we are.[13] This BEYOND is

---

[13] See discussion of this reaching BEYOND in other books in this *Keys To Consciousness And Survival Series* such as *Volume 3*, titled *Unveiling*

where we find the actual SELF. THIS BEYOND IS WHERE WE ALREADY DO LIVE.

You see, we actually don't even need to die and survive -- once we realize that we can survive as the SELF WE ACTUALLY ARE, THE SELF WHO IS NOT TIED TO ONLY THE BIOLOGICAL BODY.

We can discover the SELF we actually can be and already are: the SELF that is consciousness-based, and can train itself to ever more consciously survive separation from the physical body and brain.[14]

DISSOLUTION OF BIOLOGICAL SELF NEED NOT BE DYING

The dissolution of what we have grown to think of as our self, which is the biologically formed sense of self, is such a critical part of physical dying that it warrants great attention. Think of the dissolution of the biologically defined and formed self as a shedding.

In physical dying, you must shed your biologically-based self to move on. As you lose the physical body when you die, your shedding of the physical body will naturally take place. This is a major transition, of course. When you go into this major transition of physical death, you are moving into a new place. Various parts (of what you may have come to feel is who and

---

The Hidden Instinct, and *Volume 10,* titled *Seeing Beyond Our Line Of Sight.*

[14] See related diagrams in other books in this series, especially *Volume 3,* titled, *Unveiling The Hidden Instinct,* and also the two *Overriding The Extinction Scenario* books, *Volumes 5 and 6.*

what you are) are being shed. While this may seem to be dying, this is actually, when you realize this, having your actual SELF survive.

There are things you usually cannot take with you, such as your biological body and brain. You are generally entering a place where you cannot carry these things. This is like entering a house where shoes are not allowed. You take them off, shed them, to gain entry. Shedding the biology-based self allows the actual SELF to enter the realm BEYOND, beyond this physical plane. We can begin to *See Beyond Our Line Of Sight*. (See the book by this title, *Volume 10* in this series.)

SHED TO DIE

All deaths are a shedding. Other books in this *Keys To Consciousness And Survival Series* discuss the importance of:

(1) being consciously aware enough to spot (to sense) windows of *energetic opportunity;* and, even before that,

(2) being sensitive enough to know when you are at an *energetic fork* in your road, in your life path, *in your living and your dying transition pathways -- and also in your survival pathways*.

Recall that there is usually an energetic build-up to your coming to a fork or a window; there is usually a real need for shedding.[15] And on some level, you know, you just know this.

---

[15] Refer to the *Navigating Life's Stuff* books, especially *Navigating Life's Stuff, Book Two,* for more on sensitizing to this movement in transition. See reading list at the end of this present book.

Remember: luggage, heavy baggage, at times even unnecessary baggage, makes it difficult to travel. So, this is about lugging the old biologically-based body and self, and its attachment cords, when it is time to be able to travel, to move or shift to a new energy arrangement.

We begin to see that the importance of various forms of, and levels of, *shedding* is true in all in-life and seeming end-of-life transitions, not just in physical dying. Note that: *No matter what level of transition you are in, it is easy to miss seeing that you need to shed your skin until you are either deep into the process of shedding, have completed the process, or are well into a new life and looking back on the much needed shedding that you stumbled into.* The more aware you are while in this shedding process, the more effective it is.

The pressure to shed tends to sneak up on you. Whether it is the skin of an old behavior, or of a troubled life, or the biological skin of a biological body, it may take a while to notice and then to really admit that the skin has become far too tight — that you have outgrown it the way a snake outgrows its own skin.

RESISTING SHEDDING CAN BE NATURAL

It can be a natural tendency, prior to understanding transition and death, to avoid (and or even struggle against) many sheddings. However, you can get more out of the shedding process by recognizing when you are at its threshold and using wisely the energy that collects at the **threshold of shedding**. This is true in all in-life as well as seeming end-of-life sheddings.

NOTICE
RESISTANCE TO SHEDDING

Of course, it is good we do not want to die. We must do whatever we can to live here on Earth in these biological bodies as long and as well as we can.

And then of course, in daily life we frequently find the need for some minor or major change. Yet, we may resist. It is natural to want to hang on to, stay attached to, what is known, even where there may be an obvious need to let it go, an obvious need for some form of change. We see this often in the physical realm where even in-life transitions, changes, may be challenging or difficult.

Our relatively obvious material plane resistances to change can serve as models of resistances to change BEYOND. These resistances are perhaps more subtle. Yet these can be present, and even can affect our survival.

Moving into new dimensions, into the BEYOND, is major change for many who feel this is their first experience of this. We will find changes in our realities out there. Our sense of change in environment, circumstance, even identity, will also exist as we begin to move or LEAP into the BEYOND, into other dimensions of self and of actual SELF, on less visible and seemingly invisible levels of reality.

Biologically-based minds do not want to change—not very much. Even when minds think they want to change, and convince themselves they have changed, they may cling to, cord to, old thought patterns, old energy circuits, old forms of logic, old definitions of reality.

This is due, in large part, to the literal wearing of actual grooves, deep neural pathways, into the physical (biological) brain. Over time, as the same thought pattern is again and again expressed by the brain, the molecules which carry this mental process from brain cell to brain cell and into the nervous system erode a river bed for themselves, a groove through which their movement is increasingly easy, increasingly habitual, increasingly automatic.

This is why some philosophers have even suggested that the surest way of removing old thought processes and conditionings is physical death. In physical death, the brain — with its physically burned-in programming — is shed, and eliminated.[16]

OPTIONS AT DEATH

It is clear by now that you may be able to exercise various options, not only during your in-life transitions, but also during your seeming end-of-life event we tend to call death, which is actually physical death rather than all death. These options may continue on into the afterlife "life" as we continue to survive.

The power of your physical death is perhaps determined in two ways:

---

[16] As neurophysiologist and cybernetician, Warren McCulloch, once suggested, the surest way to erase one's programming is to die a physical death.

1) In terms of the degree of energy your own Will collects and preserves through the physical dying process (or for that matter, during any transition);

2) In terms of the degree of sovereignty or Free Will your Will collects and preserves during the dying process (or for that matter, during any transition).

Figure 23.1 is titled, "Options at Death." This figure diagrams just some examples, some options and option pathways you have at death. These pathways are designated along three basic death paths, ranging from the less conscious, less aware and more powerless, entangled or weak deaths -- to the more conscious, more powerful, unencumbered, and strongly aware deaths. Note that the term "intentional" here refers to being conscious. Note also that the term "conscious" here does <u>not</u> refer to being medically conscious, as the personal consciousness we are talking about is not reliant on the physical body to survive.

Study this death path chart in Figure 23.1. Work at interpreting it for yourself. Internalize this information. You may want to remind yourself of these options someday. Note that you have many options at death. Figure 23.1 only suggests some of these.

(Again note: nothing in these *How To Die And Survive* books suggests suicide. Not at all. This is about survival. In fact, what is being presented here is thinking that can help preserve the actual SELF, to help the actual SELF be able to both *live and survive* and *die and **survive**.*)

The levels of energy and awareness you pump into your shedding processes can have great influence on the effects of

these processes. You can harvest a great amount of your own energy and SELF from your own in-life and even seeming end-of-life transitions and deaths.

The more consciously energetic and directed your shedding, the more clear your process is. When consciously focused, you can be highly aware as you move toward and through a greater and more directed transition process -- and then if desired, a death release. You can find your personal consciousness more aware and powerful at the end of the process, and more able to consciously move on into the next phase of your life, into your survival.

EXERCISE #23.1
TRACING YOUR DEATH PATH

Study the death paths mapped in Figure 23.1. With a pencil and piece of paper, draw and label the death path you think you may at some point want to follow. Use components of the paths diagrammed in Figure 23.1. Invent your own components and even design your own path if you wish. Discuss (with yourself in your mind, or aloud with another person) your reasons for choosing or designing your path as you have done. If it helps you with this exercise (as with all the exercises in these books), you are welcome to use your imagination here. In your discussion, touch on the following topics as best you understand these:

- *Emotional death.*
- *The release of attachments and cords.*
- *The old consciousness matrix.*
- *The strength of the consciousness.*
- *Energy involved in shedding.*
- *Increasing the concentration of one's Free Will.*
- *Variations of mental death.*

- *Giving over one's mental energy, even more so, one's PERSONAL CONSCIOUSNESS, to another power, OR:*
- *Choosing to further retain one's mental energy and PERSONAL CONSCIOUSNESS to further evolve it — to further SURVIVE.*
- *The option we have to have our personal consciousness DIE AND SURVIVE.*

EXERCISE #23.2
ENERGETIC SHEDDING

Close your eyes. Visualize a grid, or something like what you see when you look at graph paper. It may look something like this (a square with a grid in it):

Now, pour yourself into this grid, into the lines of this grid.

Imagine that you are this grid. Build tension into the structure of this grid, as if this grid is trapping your energy. Tense your entire body as you identify with the tension in this grid. Hold the tension at its peak.

Now, light up the lines of this grid. Then release this grid.

Deconstruct this grid: dissolve the lines. Transmute the energy that was held by this grid, allowing it to dissolve and dissipate into your own idea of highest Light.

Repeat this exercise several times, each time increasing the level of tension at its peak.

Feel the increase in the level of energy released when you dissolve your grid. This grid represents your old energy arrangement and matrix.

Your personal consciousness itself is escaping the biological matrix that housed it—it is releasing its actual SELF in order to survive, in order to DIE AND SURVIVE.

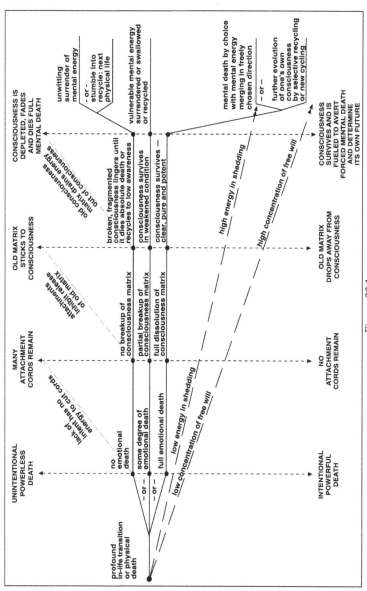

Figure 23.1
Options at Death

<u>24</u>
FINDING YOUR SELF
AND THEN BRIEFLY
DISSOLVING THIS SELF
TO MOVE
THROUGH THE MEMBRANE

> When upon thee Death fast approaches,
> fear not, but know ye are master of Death.
> Relax thy body, resist not with tension.
> Place in the heart the flame of thy Soul.
> Swiftly then sweep it to the seat of the
> triangle.
>
> Thoth
> *Emerald Tablet XIII*

Long before physically dying, in other words while still living in a biological body, it is good to learn (or re-learn) what you may want to "know" later. It is useful to be forming an idea of what you want to (again) find once you (again) die a physical death, or better stated, once you (again) leave your physical body and move on.

In forming the idea of moving on, you can begin to generate your own view, your own design. You can begin to get to develop and expand the territory of your own personal consciousness.

If your personal consciousness can learn to design and expand the territories of itSELF that it already also exists within, these territories can be far easier to know and navigate later.[17]

After all, we already live both here and BEYOND. We already live both within our biological bodies, and BEYOND these bodies, as we are not only biological beings, we are members of the Human Species of Consciousness.[18]

Note: As you have been doing with these *How To Die And Survive* books, continue to see this discussion as both symbolic and useful in daily life, and also useful in later transitions, such as those in physical death, and those in possible afterlife situations.

YOU MAY FIND
YOUR SELF "OUT THERE"

You may see that, after floating out of your old vessel (physical body), time feels different. You may find that, for an indeterminate amount of time, you are adjusting to the change, to the moving away from the physical (biological) definition of yourself and of time itself.[19]

Your biological body or vehicle is fading or dropping away, as is your emotional body which is attached to your biological body.

---

[17] Refer also to the *Navigating Life's Stuff* books, *Volumes 8 and 9* in this *Keys To Consciousness And Survival Series*.

[18] See the *Overriding The Extinction Scenario* books for more on this, *Volumes 5 and 6* in this series.

[19] Refer to *Volume 3* in this *series*, titled *Unveiling The Hidden Instinct*. See reading list at the end of this present book.

You are sensing these changes. With all this, you also sense you are becoming aware of an un-weighting sort of sensation.

You may sense (or even feel you can see) yourself, floating. You may feel a little like a helium balloon connected to your previous life, your biological life, by a string (or perhaps by an entire web of cords) to the people and emotions that were part of your biological body's life.

As all this is happening, you may find yourself checking out your new reality, even scanning the environment you find yourself in and within, looking for some sense of what appears to be a stream or spot or speck of Light. (Note that other books in this series have defined this environment you are scanning as the PATTERN TERRIAN.[20]) Be aware of variations in your environment, in this TERRAIN. For example, sense varying areas of density. See where what appears to be Light reaches in, is present.

FURTHER SENSITIZE

Note that, when you see or sense these specks or areas of Light, you may feel drawn to this Light. As you feel drawn, begin seeking to clarify the Light you sense is there. Sense what this is you feel drawn to, as this sensing is a *key awareness* you will want to carry with you as you move BEYOND.

---

[20] See in depth definition and discussion of this PATTERN TERRAIN in other books in this *Keys To Consciousness And Survival Series*, such as the first and second *Navigating Life's Stuff* books (*Volumes 8 and 9*) and also *Unveiling The Hidden Instinct* (*Volume 3*).

Furthering your sensitization, forming new awareness levels, is key as you move within and through nonphysical environments. Begin fine-tuning your awareness now, while still living in a biological body with a biological brain.

In this timeless time passage, you may feel as if you are floating onward. It may not yet be entirely clear you have left your physical body, or for that matter your emotional body. Your experience may feel quite new to you, yet also somewhat familiar.

Slowly, you may grow increasingly aware you are in another space, an ever more non-physical space. This non-physicality is you, your non-physical SELF, continuing to exist as you leave your biologically defined self. Now you begin examining your new "other-worldly" terrain, the PATTERN TERRAIN you find yourself moving through. Here you will sense all kinds of elements such as openings, windows, streams, various portals and pathways.

DETECT OTHER FORCES AND FACTORS

You may find yourself feeling pulled in directions not entirely clear to you yet. Be aware when you feel pulled, as these pulls may not be your own directions. You may not be pulling your SELF: other forces and factors who are not you may be pulling you.

Know that you can further sensitize yourself, your actual SELF, to the elements of, even presences within, your PATTERN TERRAIN. (Again, refer to other books in this series for more on this TERRAIN, such as the *Navigating Life's Stuff* books.)

When you find yourself sensing characteristics of the PATTERN TERRAIN, be aware of your SELF, and of your sensations. For example, become more aware that you are sensing density, and Light, your idea of Light, and openings, pathways, forks in the road or pathway you are on, and other elements and presences. Sense the subtle variations in the atmosphere you are moving into and through. This is a sensitivity that is useful in daily life, as well as in afterlife possibilities.

FIND YOURSELF BEYOND

As you find your SELF sensing your environment, you realize that *it is YOU sensing your environment*, that therefore you ARE, that therefore you exist. You realize that you have found your SELF out there BEYOND physicality, that you have survived. You are still here. Know that you have been able to *die and survive* as the SELF you actually are.

Actually, your non-physical SELF never died your physical death. The nonphysical SELF can survive.

MOVING IN THIS NON-PHYSICAL REALITY

Out in non-physicality, movement in this PATTERN TERRAIN is not what movement appears to be in the material plane. We can call this movement here in the interest of simplicity. Movement implies mov*ing* which is more understandable to physical plane beings as the changing of location from one place to another. However, when there is no physical body being moved or relocated, this movement takes on another nature.

75

Sense your SELF being aware. Recall the old dictum of Descartes, "I think, therefore I am." Here, we can say I SENSE, THEREFORE I AM, MY SELF <u>IS</u>.

Sense the variations and textures of the non-physical environment you find your non-physical SELF floating within and through. Sense the appearance of what appears to be more and less Light, perhaps even areas where Light appears to be flowing in. Sense openings, windows, spaces where Light and perhaps other energies can flow in.

You are still learning to read your new realities and their characteristics and even presences. Be aware, stay aware. Be discerning.

The openings and windows you sense are present appear to be places where you can enter and exit the space you are in. You will either continue to float, or you will move through (perhaps float through) one or more of these windows. These windows appear to be openings or portals into other spaces or expansions of your present space.[21]

Again note that many of spaces you are in exist within your personal consciousness. So these spaces are your awareness of the reality you are defining for your SELF, the reality your actual SELF is defining for you.

Note that there are also other spaces out there, BEYOND. Some of these spaces are at times even reaching into the physical

---

[21] For more on these openings and windows, these portals, that can be found in moving through this space BEYOND, see *Navigating Life's Stuff, Book Two*.

plane. These other spaces may not be spaces you have sensitized to, become aware of, within your own personal awareness.

Begin to differentiate between what is territory of your own personal consciousness, and what is not. Begin to differentiate between what is the PATTERN TERRAIN of your own personal consciousness, and what is the PATTERN TERRAIN not of you, not of your SELF.

SEEING MEMBRANES OF PORTALS, OPENINGS

Moving the SELF, the personal consciousness, through a window into another space entails *a crossing, something like the crossing of a membrane.* Think of this membrane as the skin of a next space. This skin is something like a cell wall in that it is semi-permeable, only allowing through some of what seeks to pass into or through it.

If you are feeling aware you are crossing this skin or membrane, this is your actual SELF crossing this membrane. If this membrane is within your own territory, you are in charge of choosing whether you allow your SELF to move or expand through that membrane.

If this membrane is the skin of a territory that is not OF you, then notice if you are being allowed into, or even pulled through, this membrane. Begin to sensitize to subtle variations here. If you feel pulled into something, examine the pull. Become aware of whether this pull is from your SELF, or from outside of your SELF. If from outside, pause rather than be

77

pulled, and discern the nature of the source of this pull. You may or may not choose to be pulled.

MOVING THROUGH WINDOWS

It is useful to think in terms of portals, or openings to pathways, as being windows. Our moving through windows is often taking place. We can become more aware of these transitions in daily life, as well as BEYOND daily life.

Although each window has its specific characteristics, the basic requirement for passage through the membrane, the cell wall of that window, is a reorganization or dissolution of the being's existing energy arrangement.

Where this movement is through the window into life BEYOND physicality, or into a particular space BEYOND physicality, we can learn to become ever more aware of this movement.

This awareness itself is key in understanding transition, movement through situations, spaces. You can consciously navigate your movement even after the death of the old biologically based self, the one you formatted during your most recent lifetime in the physical plane. (Note that if you happen to be a Reader whose last life was not in the physical plane, the material in this book is still highly applicable, as sensing one's *dying and surviving*, discerning one's movement or expansion into and out of any TERRAIN (physical or beyond physical), involves the ever refining of the awareness—the increasingly inter-dimensional awareness.

RECOGNIZE PRELIMINARY

AND EVENTUAL DISSOLUTIONS

Moving from the physical body into the BEYOND, is one form of *dying and surviving*.

As detailed in other books in this series, the first death in the physical death process is the basic death, that of the physical body. The phases of this first death can be quick, or long and drawn out. When this death is complete, there still remains the emotional body death. This second death can be as complex and even as challenging as the first death, the physical death.

EMOTIONAL BODY DEATH

Eventually, the physically dead individual must die the second death, the emotional death, leaving behind emotional connection, and any related cording to both the physical and the emotional planes, and moving on.

This *letting go* is a critical and challenging process for many a soul. Yet, we can easily prepare ourselves. We can be consciously developing our personal consciousness, our actual SELF. We can be doing this throughout our day to day life, as well as in our seeming end of life or physical death process, and on into our afterlife.

MENTAL BODY DEATH

Of course there is the other option, the choice *not* to continue to be the SELF. This is a full mental body death. This is the entire dissolution of the actual SELF.

Of course this is an option. We can of course choose to die and *not* survive as a personal consciousness, and instead to move into the oneness or into other compelling energy bodies and presences. Of course, when dying this way, dying a full mental death, our energy moves on as it blends back into the encompassing energy field (or into some other energy field).

However, keep in mind that you have a right to choose <u>to</u> accept this option, OR to choose <u>not to</u> undergo this full mental body death, to instead die and SURVIVE as your actual SELF.

So, let's look at this notion of mental death. While this form or level of death has many meanings to many people, here let's just say that after the death release of the physical body, and then after the death release of the emotional body, there can remain more of us to either die and be released or to continue on, to *die and survive* as a *personal consciousness*. In this book, we can call what of our own SELF may be able to live on, to *die and survive*, our own personal consciousness, the locus of our actual SELF.

Now, for some Readers what comes to mind when we say *mental body* is the cognitive thoughts and functions of the biological brain. However, here, in this book's (and in the previous *How To Die And Survive* book's) discussion of *dying and surviving*, we are not talking about the mental functions and memories of the biological brain. After all, once the biological body has died, the biological brain will likely have done so as well.

Here, we are reaching BEYOND to connect with what houses the personal consciousness, and in essence with what IS the

80

personal consciousness. For the sake of this discussion, we will call this the personal mental body, the actual SELF.

OPTION TO SURVIVE

Therefore, *dying and surviving* does not involve the dying of the mental body, of the personal consciousness, of the SELF. *Dying and surviving* is the identification of and remaining aware of, present with, the actual SELF during transition.

This *survival* can remain an option, one we can be aware of during our transitions, even during the physical death transition.

OPTION TO DIE

All too frequently, we are told to, or pulled to, merge with another energy or presence, as if this most powerful presence seeking to absorb us and our energy is always a positive option. We do have a right to choose whether to be absorbed and thus fully die. And, if we do choose to be absorbed, to die and not survive, we do have a right to choose by what energy or presence we choose to be absorbed.

DO NOT MISUNDERSTAND MENTAL DEATH

Because it is frequently misunderstood, mental death warrants an additional note here. Many teachers suggest that mental death is desired, that the so-called "highest" beings die mental deaths; and, they say that very few spirits are "evolved enough" to succeed in fully completing this third death and, in so doing, crossing the threshold beyond the "death cycle." It is also said that most fail at this death and therefore must recycle

involuntarily and without selectivity again and again until someday they will finally succeed.

However, this is not a full understanding of mental death. A full mental body death is the death of the personal consciousness, of the actual personal SELF. You have a right to survive, which means you have a right to continue to exist as your own personal consciousness, as your actual SELF.

Your choice regarding the death of your own personal consciousness, of your actual SELF, is yours to make. It is important to remember this when you move through your physical and emotional death releases.

You do not have to release your own personal consciousness in a mental body death. This is not required. This is not necessarily more divine or higher or more advanced.

When it is time for you to experience your own physical and emotional body death releases, you can then choose to die and survive of your own Free Will.

As Figure 23.1 indicates (in its lower right hand corner), there are various pathways available. Your personal consciousness can survive and fuel itself to avert forced mental death. You can always return to the oneness later, at any point. So, why do so, why be pulled to do so, if you prefer to continue to survive?

So many of us have not been prepared to know we have this option. We have not been prepared to consciously navigate death to allow ourselves this option. We have not been allowed to know we can die and survive.

SENSITIZE TO WHAT
YOU MAY FIND ON YOUR PATH

You will likely want your transition and death processes to be conducted in the manner, and with the outcome, that *you* choose. These are, after all, your own transition and death processes. You have a right to know that you do not have to die a full mental death just because you are presented with or pulled toward that option. You have a right to choose whether or not to die and survive, no matter what energies, pressures, or belief systems may tell you otherwise.

Note: Once out of your old body or pattern, you may experience a competition for your energy, a sort of competition for what some might call spiritual real estate. If when you are in transition, you sense pulls on your energy, on your SELF, pulling you to be absorbed by some other energy pattern rather than to remain your own, be aware. Always remember that you can continue to hold onto your SELF and not die, and not surrender yourself to a presence that may seek to acquire you. This is always your choice, not the choice of the presence that may be pulling on you to join it. Knowing what this is may be the best preparation for encountering it. Knowing you have the option NOT to die, that you can die and SURVIVE, is the best defense.

Figure 23.1 suggests just some possible paths that may be available in surviving, in preserving one's personal consciousness—in evolving Free-Will-promoting die and survive options. Let's say you elect the path leading to the survival in the lower right hand corner of that diagram. Once well into this Free Will path, and up to the point of freely

83

determining whether to turn your energy over to a higher or other power, or to continue to evolve it for your actual SELF, you have yet another process to conduct: you must dissolve at the membrane of the next reality, the next dimension.

The essence of you must dissolve at the membrane of your new reality to fully enter your next Kingdom, and then reassemble to survive.

EXERCISE #24.1
CLARIFYING
YOUR ESSENCE

Spend quite a while attempting to find the essence of you. What are you without your feelings, your friends and family, your history, your commitments? Sense the core, the basic character of your personal consciousness' energy. Get to know this inner and true nature of your actual SELF. Strip down to your pure unencumbered personal consciousness. Hold there.

EXERCISE #24.2
DISSOLVING AT THE MEMBRANE

Now, be in the center of this core essence of you, of your actual SELF. Direct your essence to spread out, becoming even less dense than it has already become, by focusing on it. Dissolve to minuscule bits of yourself. Know that each bit is all of you. You are not broken into pieces here. Each bit is whole. Contemplate this state of being for a while. . . .

Now, have all your bits approach a wall of clear skin. The skin appears to you to be the wall of a giant bubble. You must get into the bubble through its pores.

Be just one of your tiny bits representing your entire SELF, your purified personal consciousness. Move toward the membrane. See the

opening, the pore in the membrane, that you will take your essence through. Approach the pore in the skin.

Get right up in front of this pore. See that this pore has a membrane across it too. This membrane is thinner than the skin around the pores. **This special membrane is a sieve-like barrier, only allowing bits of your essence through, bits that are unformatted, that carry no grid or matrix from the previous dimension.**

See yourself as stripped down of all projections, matrices, grids, attachments, old ideas about your SELF or reality. Clarify and purify, as if you are a drop of water un-muddying itself, a Light changing from murky to crystal clear.

Feel crystalline and sharp in your essence. Sharpen. Sharpen your essence.

Sharpen and refine. Hold a while as if perched on a high mountain ledge, or on the outside window sill of a very tall building. Sharpen your essence and perch. Hold this perch. Take a soft breath in and hold it in as you perch, balancing your crystal clear purified essence before the special membrane. Hold your breath a little longer. Then, suddenly, feel as if you are melting. Relax and release your breath. Melt until you are almost nothing.

Slip, like a very clear, very tiny, microscopic river, right through the membrane or pore of the skin of the next dimension of your personal consciousness. As the river of you crosses through the membrane, feel as if you are being combed through and through.

Know that your arrival on the other side has occurred when the combing sensation ceases.

Congratulations. You have made it through to the other side. Collect your SELF here. YOU have continued to survive.

SEE MEMBRANES

Sieve-like membranes across openings, pores to other dimensions of your reality, are all around you. Once you train your eyes to see them and your SELF to sense them, you will be amazed at how many there are. This can be true in daily biological and social life, and also in the ongoing afterlife.

You may wonder why more individuals do not just slip through the membrane, the boundary of the next place, by mistake. Yet, few beings slip through without choosing to. As this book continues to explain, you have a choice here. You can choose your direction and path all along the way.

(Note: You may feel as if you are being pulled through against your will. Again, knowing that you have a choice is the best defense. You do not have to be pulled through, into a space you choose not to go, by an energy you wish to resist. ... Some Readers point out that there may be openings to dark environments which do, from time to time, manage to kidnap beings and cause their apparent disappearances. Readers, such kidnapping is not ascension. We deal with this matter in another volume.)

When you or someone you are close to is about to cross over to the other side, to another dimension of him or her SELF, you may notice, out of the corner of your eye, a membrane coming into focus in your vicinity. Sometimes long gone friends and family appear faint and semi-material just the other side of the

membrane, as if they are waiting to coach you (or whoever is in transition) through to the BEYOND.

Notice how detached they are. Notice what and who is there, and how these beings appear. Sense the authenticity of these presences, even ask these presences if they are who they appear to be. Notice any form of response or reaction to your question.

This is not surprising. Your arrival into the next dimension of your SELF is greeted with far more detached anticipation than your heavily corded departure from your physical plane.

Listen with the ears of your SELF, of your expanded awareness.

You will hear the welcoming applause. This is you, as you have *survived*, and you know this now.

25
RETAINING THE CONSCIOUSNESS

> …. The place between thine eyebrows,
> the place where the memory of life
> must hold sway. Hold thou thy
> flame here in thy brain-seat until
> the fingers of Death grasp thy Soul.
>
> Thoth
> *Emerald Tablet XIII*

Your life on Earth as a biological being is a great learning experience. Getting to know yourself, your daily life physical plane self, and also your actual SELF, is valuable survival knowledge.

A highly trained being, practiced in these *How To Die And Survive -- Life, Death, And Survival Technologies,* may be able to leave the physical vehicle quite consciously and in full awareness, to fully preserve the continuity of consciousness while moving from the physical plane to the "after-death" and "after-life" states. Again, these terms are not intended to be precise representations of what can take place when you *die and survive.* These terms are ideas, concepts, allowing us to develop aspects of ourselves and of our survival options that are there for us to develop.

Let's be clear here: If there is no death, then the term after-death is not accurate. Perhaps it is best to consider the after-physical-

death state as a *state of living, of surviving*. And, if life continues after the death that does not occur, then in a sense there is no AFTER life, there is only ongoing LIFE.

You can move ever more consciously through transition and seeming death, and do this relatively well, whether or not you have received intensive training. You can stay aware of your SELF and your personal conscious. You can remember that all your emotions are part of an emotional body that you are shedding. The YOU that survives is clear.

APPRECIATE CONSCIOUSNESS

Also remember that the *thread of awareness*, the *thread of your awareness*, is an energetically woven fiber. This precious and vulnerable thread is what you have of yourself, of the SELF, once you have unraveled your biologically-based self from your actual SELF, from your personal consciousness.

KNOW THE DIS-ASSEMBLING

Your awareness can guide you through the dis-assembling and re-assembling you will do as you move through layers, membranes, into new domains.

There will be passages when you are dis-assembled, unbundled. In your unbundled state of many minuscule bits, you are the ball of yarn unwound. You are the weaving pulled off the loom: the grid, warp, and weft, indistinguishable. You are your SELF in its most unwound, disassembled state. Yet your SELF can be aware of itself and can hold it SELF together. (I have discussed in depth this *conscious cohesion, and its role*

90

in our survival, in other books in this series, such as *Volume 3, Unveiling The Hidden Instinct.*)

At this point, if you sense you are so unwound, just stay present. Time is not the issue here. This situation can change almost on the spot. This is an awareness function. Medically conscious awareness does not entirely matter here, as is the case in all phases of conscious dying, both before and after physical death.

Note: This conscious awareness is not biological. You need not be biologically, medically, conscious for this awareness. This is the *actual awareness of the actual SELF* we wish to generate. This is your non-biological consciousness that you can have survive when you leave your physical body. (See the Foreword to this book for more on this matter.)

KEEP IN MIND WHAT SURVIVAL IS

Keep in mind that conscious awareness is key in dying and surviving, Always strive to be consciously aware of your SELF when you are in transit, both in your physical life, and BEYOND in the so-called after-life. Note that there may be times in transit, times when you feel you are dis-assembled or otherwise vulnerable. Stay aware of yourself so as to steer away from predators who may seek to absorb you.

You need not be absorbed. You need not die. You simply must maintain your sense of your SELF, of your personal consciousness as its own life form, in your travels both here and BEYOND. Keep in mind that you can continue to exist as a personal consciousness, that this is what and who you are.

This is how you can indeed die and survive. This will sustain you in your transitions.

Once you find that you have made it into the BEYOND, you can know that you have conducted an *aware interdimensional transit*, or a dying as some may say it is. You have done this consciously, no matter how conscious the physical body you left was when you left it. Already this has been a great adventure. Yet, there is still more to this great adventure. Dying and surviving is an ongoing process, just as living in a biological body is.

CONSCIOUS DYING

Think a moment about the importance of conscious dying. As valuable as conscious dying is said to be, it takes concentration to understand exactly what it is that is of value. Why is this understanding so difficult to come by? Because consciousness itself is elusive and slippery. Your consciousness cannot be contained; it has no boundaries. Consciousness cannot be bottled and sold; it is not in itself a biochemical compound or a hallucinogen. Consciousness itself is not a physical item.

Although many things affect consciousness and many individuals claim to be able to measure the effects of these things on consciousness, consciousness itself cannot be measured. Consciousness is not measurable in terms of "brain size" or brain waves or other electrical measures such as synaptic potentials, or "I.Q." (intelligence quotient), or "E.Q." (emotional quotient), or other measures.

Third-dimensional characterizations of consciousness do not fully characterize *inter*-dimensional consciousness because

non-physical inter-dimensional consciousness is not a third-dimensional "material plane" item, even though it appears to register some of its effects in 3-D.

Your personal consciousness is your reach beyond the particular dimensions in which your physical and emotional bodies live. Your personal consciousness is larger, more expansive, than what you may know it to be, or have been told that it is.

CONSCIOUSNESS IS NOT ALWAYS ATTACHED TO THE PHYSICAL BODY

It is frequently mistakenly assumed that persons who are medically diagnosed as either "senile," "brain dead," or "comatose" are not very, or not at all, conscious. This is an understandable material-plane error in perception. The consciousness of beings who appear to be "semi-" or "un-conscious" is not being expressed to any great degree, or to any degree at all, through the physical vehicle, the physical body. This does not mean that the consciousness is dead. The consciousness of that individual may linger nearby or be far away.

Know, with full resolve to really know, that your personal consciousness, your actual SELF, can be, or become, what is neither physical nor emotional. Think in terms of retaining your consciousness through the shedding of both the physical and the emotional cord networks, through the dissolution of the biologically-based *consciousness matrix,* and through the crossing over or through the membranes, layers, and boundaries into the BEYOND. There BEYOND, you will form

your non-biologically-based consciousness matrix for your actual SELF.[22]

THE BIOLOGICAL BODY IS NOT THE SELF

Your biologically-based self may hold your actual SELF from full access to itSELF, and thus to its own survival processes. Keep in mind, the biological body is, and even its cells are, programmed to die. (See the *Overriding The Extinction Scenario* books in this series for in-depth discussion of this death programming.) However, you as a personal consciousness are NOT designed to die. You can survive once you understand who you are and what survives.

Know that, if you try to take into the BEYOND your biologically based self, or anything with you that is not pure you, that is not your SELF, your pure core personal consciousness, you will be held back, perhaps even dragged down, fragmented, weakened, confused, perhaps lost.

You cannot get there from here if you go as anything but who you really are. *You must go as your actual SELF to SURVIVE.* So reveal your SELF to yourself. See, know, your essence to survive.

EXERCISE #25.1
RETAINING YOUR CONSCIOUSNESS

Find yourself passing through the membrane, or even the pores of the skin, of the next dimension of your SELF. Remember, you have

---

[22] For details on the importance of this process, see *Volumes 5 and 6* in this *Keys To Consciousness And Survival Series*, the *Overriding The Extinction Scenario* books.

become many bits of your essence to do this. You have disassembled and reassembled your SELF to pass through boundaries and membranes.

As you pass through the pores in the membrane, feel your entire consciousness housed in, stored in, each reduced and purified bit of your SELF. You are your whole self in each bit of yourself. Contemplate this form of your SELF for a moment. There you are again and again and again!

Now, be with one bit of your SELF. Move that bit of yourself through the pore in that membrane you wish to move through.

Now, move all the bits of yourself through this layer or membrane, into the next place you wish to be.

You have no body and thus no physical eyes here, so use your inner eye, the one you trained while still in a physical body, to see every bit of this process. See each bit of yourself being combed by the fine sieve of the membrane. Feel every minor sensation involved in this combing process. Continue into next exercise.

EXERCISE #25.2
CLUSTERING YOUR CONSCIOUS BITS

See each bit of yourself arrive on the other side. Recognize each bit of your SELF. Gravitate all these bits toward each other. Have your bits begin to cluster. Have your bits greet each other quite consciously. You are consciously re-assembling now.

Yes! Consciously! You are still conscious! You are still here!

HELLO ACTUAL SELF, YOU HAVE SURVIVED.

26
REBUNDLING:
DANCE OF CREATION

> It is a strange awakening to find sky
> inside you and beneath you and
> above you so that your spirit is one
> with the sky....
>
> Thomas Merton
> *Entering the Silence*

Be immensely patient with your SELF.

This *How To Die And Survive Technology* is a lot to take in. All this *survival and death technology* is so profoundly simple, yet so profound.

Here, you are learning about navigating not only daily life transition, but also about navigating movement into and within boundless infinity. Your mastery of transition, change, death, survival, and travel will unfold within you as your personal consciousness grows in its awareness of itself. You are becoming ever more aware of who you truly are, and of who it is that can truly survive. Hint: It is you who can survive, as you know.

At the right time, and only at the right time, your instinctive longing for the incredible journey into the glistening BEYOND,

into YOUR BEYOND, will begin to invite the dissolution of your old biological webs.

You will eventually manage to dissolve into whole bits of yourself and transport your essence, your purified personal consciousness, across the membrane.

ASK THE QUESTION

But will you ever pull yourself back together again? This is the most significant decision you will make on your journey. Come to know now that you can, at the right time, have this option.

Will you re-assemble, re-bundle these minuscule bits of your SELF? Will you spin a new personal consciousness matrix out of what you have taken through the membrane? Will you be your actual SELF again?

By asking this question at the point in your journey when you have just managed to cross the membrane, you have accomplished something tremendous: you are on "the other side" and you are still conscious, or you would not be able to ask yourself such a question! You, your actual SELF, have survived!

DANCE YOUR CREATION

Now is your opportunity to choose of *your own Free Will* whether to:

- Disperse the bits of your SELF, your pure core personal consciousness, into the particular dimension and location

within dimension that you have come to, thereby dissolving your SELF for good; <u>OR</u> ...

- Rebundle the bits of your SELF, your pure core personal consciousness, and remain your SELF, and journey on through the Cosmos as your SELF, as long as you choose to survive.

We will return to the pros and cons of the first of the above two options in later chapters of this book. Here, we will concern ourselves with the second of these options: re-bundle your consciousness, survive as your personal consciousness, as your SELF.

Once you have clustered the bits of your SELF on the new (new to you) side of the membrane, in order to actually rebundle, you must have your bits engage in the following steps:

1) Arrive at a common intent to rebundle.

2) Pull the cluster of bits of your SELF in tighter together.

3) Begin spinning each bit in what seems to be a clockwise direction at its base and a counter clockwise direction at its top.

4) Increase the spinning of these bits until a high humming is heard by each bit and among the bits.

5) Have the spinning bits form an ocean-like wave together by moving, oscillating en masse, up, up, up, and then rolling, rolling, rolling outward, and then coasting down, down, down.

6) Continue onward repeatedly making such waves, involving all your bits, as they are of common mind.

7) Increase the power and motion and speed of these waves.

8) As each wave rolls, begin to form a spiral at its center.

9) Have these spirals become increasingly powerful with a stronger and stronger suction force being formed within each successive wave.

10) Have this suction begin to overpower the wave, pulling more and more of the bits of the wave (the bits of you) into its center.

11) Have this suction eventually have all the bits pressing in on themselves so tightly that they compress and merge!

12) Become one with YOU, with your SELF, with your personal consciousness now rebundled, again.

13) As you do, see your SELF as a gleaming ball of Light. Call this your Light, call this YOU. You have realized you can *die and survive*. Welcome to your SELF.

EXERCISE #26.1
DANCING THE WAVE

Visualize your SELF as a cluster of bits of your pure personal consciousness. Now proceed through the steps listed above. You may want to have someone read these steps to you.

EXERCISE #26.2
ARRIVING AGAIN

When you have completed the last step, tell yourself: "I am my own personal consciousness rebundled, recoalesced." Feel the meaning, the essence of this statement. Feel your essence.

Congratulations. You have just completed the dance of survival and SELF re-creation. You have done another round of this process in order to continue to die and survive.

DANCE OF (RE-) CREATION

In this dance of creation, you are not the God defined by those who believe God created the Cosmos. You are you— and you have just re-created, re-bundled, your SELF! You have chosen to *die and survive.*

27
REFORMATTING THE SELF:
FREE OF CORDS

> Even if science—physical science or
> occult science—were to discover the
> necessary condition or means for an
> indefinite survival of the body, still, if
> the body could not adapt itself so as to
> become a fit instrument of expression
> for the inner growth, the soul would
> find some way to abandon it and pass
> on to a new incarnation. The material
> or physical causes of death are not its
> sole or its true cause; its true inmost
> reason is the spiritual necessity for the
> evolution of a new being.
>
> Sri Aurobindo
> *The Life Divine*

You wake up dead. Or do you? Once you would have thought
so. But now you know better.

There you are, having traversed the limits of the material plane,
having transformed to a most unbundled, evaporated, released
state, devoid of all that you most considered yourself to be
prior to this point, back when you were biologically-based.
And then you move into a re-bundled but still quite naked
personal consciousness, your actual SELF.

Now the challenge is to reveal to our SELVES the *key* for learning, acquiring, potential longevity (or perhaps even learning, acquiring, potential immortality) of the SELF, of the nonphysical SELF in the form of its personal consciousness. It is quite possible we do already carry this knowledge, this key, deeply buried within our consciousness-es, perhaps even locked away there.

Yet, why is this knowledge so deeply buried within us? To protect it? To protect us? Or to keep us from knowing that we can learn to *die and survive*.

We may want to ask how we acquired this deeply buried, yet quite blocked from our access, knowledge. Are we naturally programmed with it? Did we evolve this knowledge? Or was it implanted into us?

Have we blocked ourselves from knowing *How To Die And Survive*? Or, have forces or factors outside us implanted these blocks into us, to hold us as unknowing 3-D captives here in the physical plane?

Of course, the idea that if we live on, we will for a time or for all time (either is possible) be doing this living on non-physically makes sense to us, as our physical biological bodies do age. At a certain point, our physical bodies may not be the best vehicles for us. So, if there is the option of living on after physical death, it is likely living on non-physically.

We may find already within us, deeply buried within ourselves, the knowledge, the key, to our own survival. (For in-depth definition and discussion of these *keys to our survival*,

see other books in this *Keys To Consciousness And Survival Series*, such as *Volume 3, Unveiling The Hidden Instinct: Understanding Our Interdimensional Survival Awareness*. Also see books in the *Metaterra Chronicles Series*, such as *Revealing The Omega Key*, and *Detecting The Omega Deception.)*

What each of us who wishes to may discover is that we can still have and be our actual SELF, our own personal consciousness, as we move through dimensions of our reality, of ourselves. We can learn to ever more consciously transition. We can learn to consciously dis-assemble and move through membranes, dimensional boundaries ... and then, once on the other side, to re-collect, then re-bundle, and then re-format the matrix of our SELF, of who we truly are -- of who it is that can survive: YOU.

REFORMAT

We can call this *re-formatting* because time and again, on your great journey, you will be called upon (by yourself who seeks to survive) to dissolve old cords. This can involve dis-assembling your *self*, or at least *dis-assembling who you believe you are, or have been.* You will do this in order to unravel from the network of attachments and their cords that you have formed, and that has been formed around you.

Then you will seek to re-bundle and then reformat your personal energy arrangement without these cords. This will be your clearer and further purified personal consciousness matrix.

Reformatting may seem to be beyond all you have so far done.

We have discussed what is involved in releasing the old matrix, the old bundle of energy arrangements, the programming loops, patterns, attachments, cords, and connections to the interpersonal, physical, emotional, and intellectual worlds. We have discussed what is involved in crossing over and then re-bundling.

Once all this is completed, you have a further choice. You can either remain bundled but unformatted and have your consciousness naked and vulnerable, or you can *fashion a new consciousness matrix:* reformat or newly format.

You can build a structure around what has been re-bundled, out of the particles of your essence which have made it through the membrane because they successfully detached. You can call back to center, back into focus, and organize the particles of your SELF which have detached from their cords, their ties to the physical and emotional and intellectual particles they have left behind. (See the previous *How To Die And Survive* book for a close look at cords and attachments and their effects on us.)

The particles of your spirit that you will find "on the other side" will be those that have successfully made the full LEAP into another dimension of your SELF, of the realm of your personal consciousness. These particles of your SELF are the ones that increased their frequency of motion to LEAP into a higher dimension of YOU. These particles have entirely de-physicalized, de-materialized. As have you. Here you are. You have survived.

Now, in this new dimension, in this non-physical and non-emotional state, these particles must be reorganized, re-

coalesced, for you to continue as you. In order to survive long as even re-bundled components of your SELF, these particles (those bits of your SELF you choose to have survive) must re-join each other, forming a new non-biologically-based *personal consciousness matrix*. This new matrix format will serve to shield them. This matrix becomes your vehicle of travel, the carrier of your SELF.

Pull together and organize even these well-filtered particles very carefully, so that you take with you into your new life only the particles of your SELF you consciously choose, and only the ones which will fit your new format.

CONSCIOUSLY REFORMAT

This information regarding the reformatting of the SELF can also be applied in all stages of life, and then in any of life's and death's transitions. Once you begin to appreciate the concepts that your major transitions are all pattern deaths, and that you can reformat yourself any way you want to after your transition and death processes, you will gain power over the course of your life and of your afterlife, actually of your evolution. As you grow in this understanding, you gain an increasing say in the use of your energy arrangement, and of your personal consciousness matrix.

Remember that you are indeed continuously cultivating — manufacturing, generating, formatting, harvesting, and transforming — your energy arrangement, your actual SELF.

107

So long as you take responsibility for your energy arrangement, you can have a positive say in its arrangement and use, and thus its survival.

Understand your right to access and arrange your energy: You can access the energy flowing through you and through any dimension of your reality at any moment you choose. This is free energy. You help (re) generate it. You help (re) format it. You can preserve it, or if you choose to die, release it and contribute it into another's reality.

You have more right to your personal energy arrangement, to your SELF, than does anyone or anything else.

You have as much right to survive here and BEYOND as any other lifeform does.

APPLY ONLY
RIGHT USE OF FREE WILL

Yet, with your rights come your responsibilities. Energy is always arranging and rearranging. Your energy is always rearranging. In this sense, there are always at least minor dyings underway. To abandon these dyings, to be at any time willingly unaware, is a surrender of responsibility.

Always remember that each shift across a dimensional barrier, even to a new dimension of the physical reality in which you are presently living, is a LEAP. You must always be alert to the sensations that *accompany formation-shifting*— death. Do not let these sensations sneak up on you and take you over. The right use of your own Free Will is exercised by your alert consciousness.

108

Preserving your SELF involves preserving your Will, your Free Will. Both the SELF and its Free Will are best preserved when you are highly aware and alert.

RECOGNIZE FORMATION SHIFTING

Once your *dimension-shifting* is underway, you may sense that you are indeed traversing dimensions of your SELF. You may feel as if you are transforming, expanding, evaporating, or bursting in all directions.

As you dimension-shift, you may feel some fleeting moments of what seems to be compression. Know that the intense flatness, the compression you feel, is merely a passing state (unless you choose to stay in that compressed form). If you do find yourself in the midst of an intensely compressed experience, let time pass. This time will seem brief. After a while, you will see some Light beaming out of the dark. This Light may look like splashes of water or like pieces of broken glass. Imagine that you become one of those bits of water or pieces of broken glass. *Let yourself splash and shatter.*

Only when you have allowed whatever remains of your old matrix to shatter can you even consider putting yourself back together. Be determined not to reinstate old cords, old programs, old loops. Many of the old programs cannot be entirely reinstated without the cords they formed in the material world. But do be very careful not to reinstate old patterns—old patterns of victimhood, of aggression, of domination, of fear, or other patterns which may linger in your memory.

Some will call these karmic patterns. Some will say that this is the moment that karma can be rewritten, or that this is one of the prime moments in which the opportunity to rewrite karma is most available.

Yet, only a consciously aware SELF, a consciousness aware of its density, of its locale, of the extent to which its particles have actually dissolved particular chronic crystals and cords, can be careful to avoid reinstating even bits of old patterns and their cordings.

Pay attention. You will see what of you has been disbursed and how much of it you wish to re-collect, and how it can be re-collected. When re-formatting the SELF, take care. Pick and choose and arrange quite consciously. Now you are what you create yourself to be.

EXERCISE #27.1
REFORMATTING PRACTICE

Close your eyes. Imagine that you are dissolving. As you dissolve, find that what there is of you now is evaporating. As you evaporate, find that what there is of you now is dispersing, spreading out.

Disperse as far as you can imagine dispersing. Feel your consciousness dispersing.

Continue dispersing until you are told to reformat. When you are told to reformat, see and feel yourself snap back into your physical body.

Now reformat. Reformat in any way you choose. As you do, seek to preserve your unattached SELF. This is who survives.

Think of wild species, such as dolphins and whales, caught in fishing nets, then dying while entangled in the water. You do not want to be caught in nets and cords that have followed you from your previous life. These could drown you.

EXERCISE #27.2
REPEATING REFORMATS

Do the above exercise several times in a row, each time dispersing your consciousness further, then disentangling it from old cords, and then each time when pulling it back together, reformatting it with more awareness.

With each successive reformatting, try to detect and leave out more of any old bits of your SELF that carry old patterns, attachments, cords.

28

LEAPING TO THE NEXT DIMENSION: LEAP LEVEL FOUR

> Once upon a time, I ....
> dreamt I was a butterfly....
> Suddenly, I awoke...
>
> Now I do not know whether I
> was then a man dreaming I was
> a butterfly, or whether I am now
> a butterfly dreaming I am a man.
>
> Chuang Tzu

Humans living in their biological bodies here in the physical plane are understandably preoccupied with these bodies. They feed their bodies. They dress and decorate their bodies. They exercise their bodies, not entirely understanding that the exercise to which they subject their bodies is really a model for the exercise to which they desire to subject their spirits, their souls, them SELVES.

The symmetry attained by certain physical exercise is the balance they seek for their energy bodies and energy arrangements. The muscle strength they attain lifting weights is the strength they seek for their spirits. The endurance and stamina they attain in aerobic exercise is the endurance and stamina they seek for their personal consciousness.

The flexibility and agility they attain in stretching their bodies, moving to music, and participating in sports which require quick agile movements, is the flexibility, agility, and alertness they seek for sustaining themselves, for their survival during transitions and deaths.

What you do with your own physical plane body and self can be training for your own interdimensional consciousness -- and its survival.

Your own physical calisthenics mirror those *consciousness calisthenics* you seek.

You are preparing for multidimensional journeying and for the LEAPs you will take as you go through major transitional and dimensional shifts, sheddings, and dyings.

As defined and explained in the previous *How To Die And Survive* book, *Book One*, a LEAP is a movement from one format or dimension to the next. A LEAP is usually best and most efficiently brought about when consciously constructed. (For full definition and deeper discussion of the LEAP process, see also other books in this *Keys To Consciousness And Survival Series*, such as *Volume 3*, titled *Unveiling The Hidden Instinct*.)

Each LEAP is, of course, a transition, and thus a change in pattern, in this sense a seeming death. Each shift in dimension or in reality is a death LEAP. The more trained the dying being is, the cleaner and more potent the death LEAP.

You can master the LEAP. You can use it any time you wish, in any living transition or in any physical death, and then in any shifting well beyond any physical death.

EXERCISE #28.1
DIMENSIONAL EXPANSION

Close your eyes. Be a point, a single point in space. Feel that you have no height, width, or depth.

Now, stretch out this point into a row of points. Do this so that you are stretched out into a long thin line. Feel that you have only one dimension: length. Float this way a while.

Now, stretch the line out, spread it out, into a row of lines, or a plane, a big flat plane. Float this way a while.

Now pile many planes onto your plane, making them stack themselves, sandwich themselves into a cube. Feel that you now have length, width, and depth. Float this way a while, as a three dimensional object. . . .

Now, move this three-dimensional object that you are, this cube, through time, with its length, width, and depth each moving through time in its own different direction. Do this and see that you undergo an incredible expansion!

*You feel large and limitless, free of the confines, of the boundaries of the three-dimensional form of the cube you were trapped in. This is the **time burst** of the full fourth-dimensional energy expansion. This time burst signifies the LEAP into the dimensions BEYOND.*

Hold for next exercise.

EXERCISE #28.2
RAISING TO THE NEXT LEVEL

Now take that energy expansion, that time burst, that LEAP, and raise it yet another level.

Expand in some new way, a way you cannot exactly describe. Do not think about this too hard. Just let your mind review the nature of the mental shift, the LEAP across dimensions, that is needed to go:

> *from the idea of a point, to the idea of a row of points, a line or a straight piece of thread;*
>
> *from the idea of a line, to the idea of a row of lines, a plane or a flat piece of paper;*
>
> *from the idea of a flat 2-D plane, to the idea of a 3-D cube;*
>
> *from the idea of the 3-D cube, to the idea of a 4-D **time burst;***
>
> ***from the idea of the time burst to something yet another burst beyond that;***
>
> *and so on.*

LEAP TO THE NEXT DIMENSION

The LEAP into another dimension is at once incredibly complex and amazingly simple. This LEAP is complex because it involves the harnessing of many physical, as well as what may seem to be *meta*physical energies. It is simple because you have within you, buried deep within you, all the knowledge required to make such a LEAP both here in the physical plane and BEYOND. You carry the key to the LEAP. All that is required is the triggering of your memory. This is what we seek to do here. (For more on this KEY, see other books in this *Keys To Consciousness And Survival Series*, and also books in the

116

Metaterra Chronicles Series, such as *Revealing The Omega Key*, and *Detecting The Omega Deception*. See reading list at the end of this present book.)

You are already completely competent in the complete movement of your full personal consciousness, your actual SELF, from one dimension of your reality to another.

You already have the skills to LEAP out of your present dimension of reality—of your present phase of life, or your present physical body.

You are already expanding, elevating into another reality where you already do live.

You are already living within your own CONTINUUM OF CONSCIOUSNESS.

This is your realm, see it now.

Welcome home....

***

NOTE:

For more on this KEY, see other books in this *Keys To Consciousness And Survival Series*, and also books in the *Metaterra Chronicles Collection*, such as *Revealing The Omega Key*, and *Detecting The Omega Deception*. See reading list at the end of this present book.

For more on this ***continuum of consciousness***, see its definition and characteristics in other books in this *Keys To Consciousness And*

Survival Series, such as *Volume 10,* titled *Seeing Beyond Our Line Of Sight.*

PART V

How To Navigate

Transition, Death,

And

Elevation--Ascension

<u>29</u>

Options Here and Beyond:
Ascending, Then Surviving or Merging,
Or Re-descending, Recycling

> All those billions of men and
> women who have discarded their
> bones, their skin, their fat....
>
> Omraam Michaël Aïvanhov
> *The Fruits of the*
> *Tree of Life:*
> *The Cabbalistic Tradition*

Most of you reading these words have physical biological bodies. Therefore it is easy to believe you are physical biological beings. This makes sense. We have been evolved or been designed to live in this biosphere on this Earth.[23]

The question of the hour, of the millennium, of the epoch itself is, are we more than the animal species we have been evolved to be here on this Earth? Many belief systems and religions say we are. Do you feel you are?

---

[23] See detailed discussion of this evolution in *Volumes 5 and 6* of this *Keys To Consciousness And Survival Series*, the *Overriding The Extinction Scenario* books. See reading list at the end of this present book.

However each of us answers this question, the time has indeed come for us to explore what it may mean to survive physical death, *to die and survive.* If we may at some point have this option, it is good to do what we can to explore this now.

**The time has come
for us to prepare ourselves, evolve ourselves,
to be able to survive BEYOND.**

BEING OUT OF BODY

Some of you Readers have had out of body experiences (OBEs), near death experiences (NDEs), suspended or floating lucid dream experiences (OB-LDEs), and other experiences where you felt you were able to see or sense from outside your physical self. Many others have never had such experiences. You are all welcome to this discussion.

Of course, dying and then surviving, leaving the physical body behind and still existing, is by its very nature an *out of physical body experience*, as this is what this sort of survival would be.

Whether you feel you know about being out of your body first hand, or in some other way, you may have a sense or an idea, or an imagined picture, of what it may be like to be out of the physical biological body, and lingering, or even moving, around out there. This is useful, as this can assist you in developing the interdimensional awareness-es these *How To Die And Survive* books are offering.

Interdimensional awareness can be useful both here in the material plane, and beyond. Even in everyday life, every

moment offers you the opportunity to sensitize, to recognize subtle realities, to navigate unseen developments, spaces, and atmospheres. (See detailed discussion of this interdimensional awareness in *Volume 3* in this *Keys To Consciousness And Survival Series,* titled *Unveiling The Hidden Instinct; Understanding Our Interdimensional Survival Awareness.*)

MOVING THROUGH WITH AWARENESS

Many Readers tell me they are exploring the ideas in these *How To Die And Survive* books, even though they are unsure about whether they feel there is life after death. This is fine, as exploring these ideas is not only interesting, perhaps for some even entertaining. This exploring also prepares us for experiences with unfamiliar situations and unknowns we may have, both in daily physical life, and in dream life, and in after life settings.

It is good to have become somewhat familiar with these ideas and concepts discussed here, and with the sensations touched on in the exercises in these books. It is useful to have done this before being presented with any daily life out of body experience, (such as an OBE or NDE or OB-LDE as discussed in earlier chapters), let alone any *after life out of body* experience, such as surviving physical death.

PREPARING IN ADVANCE

We prepare in advance for situations and events we may encounter. We can prepare in advance for what it may be like to be moving around out there without a physical body. We

can prepare in advance for experiences out there, choices and options along the way.

For example, we can get to know what it may mean to feel vulnerable when out of a physical body. Moving through an in-life, or a seeming end-of-life, and even perhaps an *after* life, transition may leave you feeling vulnerable, as this new situation may be an unknown and unfamiliar environment.

This discussion is important to survival here and now as biological and social beings, as well as to survival post physical death, as beings who do not have physical biological bodies and brains. The more aware you are of what is going on while you are undergoing a change, ending, or any sort of transition, the more you have a say in how you navigate the transition. As you become more aware of the experience of minor and major transition, you can become ever more aware of your*self* in transition. You can better and better protect yourself.

You can also begin to sense any forces and factors, even presences, outside yourself who may be affecting you, even pulling on you.

You can begin to know when what is calling you is YOU, and when it is not you. This allows you to be able to ever more consciously choose to either surrender, become submerged into another energy, and therefore have your personal matrix, your actual SELF, *die* -- or to remain your actual SELF and *survive*.

THE CHOICE TO
CONTINUE TO ASCEND OR TO RE-DESCEND

Yes, once out, you have the opportunity to decide of your own Free Will to move on and ascend independently, or to merge with another consciousness. Or, as Figure 29.1 suggests, you can also choose to *re-descend*—to drop back into, *recycle* into, the dimension of yourself you have just left.

When you re-descend or recycle yourself, you are *cycling back* into the type of cycle or life pattern you have just completed.

There is not necessarily anything wrong with recycling yourself, especially when this option is consciously selected. Many beings try to learn by repetition, even if this repetition is of undesirable experiences. The truly unfortunate aspect of recycling is that the majority of this is done by mistake, without a conscious decision to re-experience a particular cycle for learning purposes.

Of course, the very fact that a being such as yourself may fall back into an old cycle "by mistake" suggests that being still is tied to the experiences of that cycle. Being tied to an old cycle may be the result of the inability to release attachment to—cording to—patterns, peoples, places, things, or events within that cycle. Or, this may be the result of these patterns, peoples, places, things not releasing that being, not releasing YOU.

Also note: It is important to emphasize the distinction between unwillingly falling back into an old pattern, and knowingly retaining attachments in order to pull yourself back into the same or a very similar pattern (such as a relationship, addiction, mood swing, or disease pattern) you have just left.

CONSCIOUSLY RE-DESCEND

Let's say you have already left your physical body. Once you are conscious of the reality that you are at a *post-death choice point*, that you can choose of your own Free Will, to either ascend or re-descend, you can manage to re-descend quite consciously—that is, if you so choose.

Whether this is about your leaving your whole physical body, or about your leaving just a part of your in-life, daily life, while still living in your physical body, this discussion can apply to your process. Just keep in mind that decisions to return and re-live are not always clean and clear of the old issues that drove you away from old patterns and lives.

Still, sometimes you will indeed find you have the option to recycle or re-descend yourself. Be aware that, quite frequently, this is not really an option per se. Rather, this is the tug and perhaps even still binding pull of cords and attachments which have not been left in the first place.

If you find yourself willingly or unwillingly pulled to journey back "down" and further explore a cycle or life you have left, do know that you may or may not be able to re-live that cycle or life *as who you once were*. Not all of your returns or recycles take on the same old form.

Still, if you do have the chance and do choose this, there may be the opportunity to learn by repeating an old pattern or life. If so, you may manage to learn more in this exploration by planning ahead, *by knowing what you are getting into*. To learn from this re-visiting or re-living of an old life or old pattern, you must:

1) Always seek to further know yourself.

126

2) Know that before re-entering a troubled cycle, you must seek to remove from yourself the patterning that acted upon you there.

3) Name cues, markers, you want your SELF to watch for in the event that you become so re-involved in the old cycle that you forget you are merely returning this time to study yourself there.

4) As you re-descend, watch which cords you re-establish. Watch how you choose, are drawn to, these. You may not need as many of the old cords this time. But will those old cords call you anyway?

5) See that the more detached you plan to remain as you re-descend into an old cycle, the more you can learn there.

6) Understand that re-descension involves becoming more dense again. As you climb down *the dimensional ladder*, try to remember your experiences in the higher, less dense, more Light realms.

7) Remind yourself continuously of what you have seen BEYOND.

REVIEW PROS AND CONS

Remain as conscious as you can at all times, at any point before, during, or even after your re-descension into an old cycle of life, an old dimension of your reality. This way you can always opt to cancel the re-descension and not further relive the old cycle even if you feel pressure to do so.

One of the positive aspects of *conscious re-descension* is that it allows you to take another look at your patterning, your programming. It allows you to move in very close in order to

examine the potential for further learning within an old way of being.

The first argument against re-descension is that, as noted earlier, this recycling is all too often not of one's own Free Will.

The second argument is that the recycling is, all too often, not done consciously.

Moreover, the third argument is that the recycling event itself can become a habit pattern which is difficult to break. When this happens, beings may even recycle themselves over and over again until they finally deplete their consciousnesses and wear away their Wills.

They may become trapped in the "no way out" paradox, without enough energy to ever again LEAP into freedom. It is at this point that absolute death may become the only escape. This is not surviving. This may even be surrendering the personal consciousness, the SELF, to a permanent graveyard of lost and diminished selves.

EXERCISE #29.1
IDENTIFYING CYCLES

Identify four or more cycles, patterns, parts of your life, or entire lives that you have experienced, or think you have experienced. Call each of these a cycle. Be creative here. Use your imagination if you cannot think of any large or small cycles you have lived through or are still living in.

Make a chart similar to the one below. This chart has four columns listed across the top, and then numbers listed down the left side. Across the top of this chart are these column titles:

The first column is: Identified Cycle Or Pattern.

Then, the second column is: Number Of Repetitions Of This Cycle Already Experienced.

Then, the third column is: Has Full Mastery Been Achieved, Or Are More Cycle Repeats Required?

Then, the fourth column is: Number Of Additional Repeats Of This Cycle That May Be Required/Desired.

Again note, down the left side of this chart are numbers for each row or cycle entry you may want here, such as 1,2,3,4, and so on.

For those of you with the print or ebook version of this book, you can see this chart here below:

Identified Cycle Or Pattern	Number of Repetitions Already Experienced	Has Full Mastery Been Achieved	Number Of Additional Repeats Of This Cycle Required/ Desired
1.			
2.			
3.			
4.			

Go ahead and list your cycles and patterns on this chart. Remember, every pattern is itself a cycle. For each cycle, list the estimated number of times you have already repeated it. Note whether or not you have learned what you want to learn from each cycle, whether you have mastered whatever it is you were learning from that cycle. You can also note whether you feel there is little or no learning that has taken place. Also note how many times you feel you may need to repeat this cycle to learn from it.

Never be concerned about making a perfect chart. The purpose of this exercise is to get to know your own life patterns and cycles, and whether these are being repeated. Even just jotting down notes about all this is a good way to become more aware.

EXERCISE #29.2
RECYCLING CONSCIOUSLY

Choose one or more of your in-life patterns and cycles. Imagine that you make a conscious choice to repeat it so as to finally learn all there is to learn from it. What would you do differently this time—now that you have made this conscious choice to learn?

How would you keep yourself conscious of the fact that you have made a conscious choice to repeat this cycle or pattern in order to learn from the experience?

*Can you feel the subtle, often unseen, energies involved in your making these decisions? Getting to know yourself on this **subtle energy and subtle awareness level** is part of survival both here and BEYOND.*

Figure 29.1

To Recycle or To Ascend?

131

30
THE IDEA OF RESURRECTING

> All this power which is inherent in Jesus—the endowment of life—and which enabled him to rise from the dead, is the very gift of eternal life which he bestows upon the kingdom of believers, and which even now makes certain their resurrection from the bonds of natural death.

> Paper 190
> *The Urantia Book*

Coming back to life, rising again, surviving, has long been a constant in our belief systems, stories, and themes.

There are so many *views* of death and dying, even of the possibility of resurrection. There may even be at least as many actual death, dying, and resurrection *options* available after the physical death transition. So many opportunities, changes, re-formations, and new formations may be open to us once we understand how to recognize, navigate, and survive through these.

Remember, these options are taking place within the realm of our personal consciousness. We create what we do and define there for ourselves, for the actual SELF who lives there.

THE CONCEPT OF RESURRECTION

The concept of resurrection is indeed found in many ancient and modern mythological and religious literatures. These ideas and descriptions open a possibility in the mind that a *survival behavior* similar in some way to being resurrected can take place. Resurrection is presented in such literature to suggest that resurrection of some sort has indeed actually taken place and therefore that it or something analogous to it can indeed happen in reality.

Of course, some of the belief systems that allow for resurrection say this is only for special groups or so-called chosen ones. Yet, we will always want to ask, why just the chosen ones, why not all who live? These *How To Die And Survive* books say that we all have a right to this knowledge, this option, this *survival technology* of resurrecting, of *dying and surviving*.

TRUE RESURRECTION MAY NOT BE PHYSICAL

Some resurrection beliefs and stories say that even the physical body can be brought back to life. However, where a physical body was not in good condition when it was left, why would it be healed simply because a resurrection is taking place?

Perhaps resurrection stories are more to suggest that the person, the soul, can live on, even without the physical body. Perhaps the message is that life itself can be re-bundled, re-formatted after physical death or after movement from one reality or dimension to another. This is certainly the message of these *How To Die And Survive* books.

In other words, the dissolution and then absolute final death of the soul or SELF or personal consciousness is not necessarily the only possible outcome of physical death. Moreover, the personal consciousness may be able to further develop itself in order to live on and, perhaps eventually should it choose to re-enter physicality, even develop for itself a physical body.

If the self, the actual SELF, can learn to live on, then we may say that some version of spiritual immortality is possible, that resurrection has taken place as there is survival.

Resurrection symbolizes rebirth, hope, and ascension into a potentially higher state of consciousness. If we think of the challenges and transitions in daily life, and the events of life in the traditional birth-to-physical-death life cycle, there are many resurrections such as resurrections following a traumatic divorce, following the loss of an important job, following a major illness, following a disaster.

Think of the sense of rising again following a feverish case of the flu, when a person stands again, feels whole again, feels comfortable in some way again. This person is, in a sense, resurrecting. This person *has made it through.*

Even rising up out of bed in the morning after a night's sleep is a resurrection of sorts. So, the death and resurrection process is something that we practice quite regularly.

One of the most prevalent symbolizations of resurrection is in the biblical story of the Christ who was Jesus of Nazareth[24], in

---

[24] This Jesus, described in the Bible, is described as Jesus of Nazareth, and Jesus Christ, who was an ancient Jewish religious leader, teacher,

which he was put to death, crucified, on a large man-made cross. And then, he was resurrected. This particular "rising from the dead" has been remembered and celebrated for centuries by a large portion of Earth's population.

The cross of this crucifixion is itself an important symbol, and a key to ascension concepts, which as this book says, are interdimensional. That cross symbolizes intersection: the intersection of dimensions—the multi-dimensionality of all existence.

That cross teaches us that life in the material plane, the third dimension, is intersecting with life in other dimensions. That cross tells us that death or the exit from the third dimension (the horizontal bar on the cross) is access to the dimensions beyond (the vertical bar on the cross) and access to what some have decided to call heaven.

We like to think of heaven as a place where all feels good, where all *is* good, where there is no pain or distress. Surely, the idea of heaven or any sort of after life would be wonderful and not too scary if we could assume it would be wonderful there, that there would be no energetic or other form of distress or pain.

---

and prophet said to have lived from 4 BC to approximately 30 AD. Other teachings, in other ancient and modern stories and beliefs, tell of a Christ who walked other lands both long before and after Jesus of Nazareth. The reappearances of this Christ through time may be part of larger cross teachings we are finding as we learn more about ancient teachings and messagings.

DISTRESSED PATTERNING IS A MESSAGE

Let's look at distress a moment. Pain is a troubled or distressed patterning. Why call this sort of pattern pain here? Because, this troubled patterning translates, when physical and emotional, into physical and emotional pain. Pain is always a message. Pain calls our attention and at times even calls us to act or re-act to the sensation of pain.

Distressed patterning is experienced in one form by physical beings living in the third dimension--and perhaps also in another form by physically dead beings if they are continuing to experience attachments and cordings that were established when living in physical and emotional bodies. Certainly we can understand this matter, that the distress that may be experienced after physical death may be experienced by those who have not entirely left the third dimension of reality because they have not released their cords. (See again the previous volume, the first *How To Die And Survive* book, *Book One*, for an extensive look at this matter of attachment and cording.)

Here the mythology of resurrection is valuable. It creates the possibility of a complete and clean transition out of this physical dimension, and a complete and clean severance of all cords back to this physical dimension. A resurrecting of the purified SELF, even of the healed body, or at least of the image of the healed body, symbolizes a liberation from old cords.

EXERCISE #30.1
SEEING SIMPLE RESURRECTIONS

Think of the times in your life that you have resurrected yourself. Try to come up with at least five examples. Include some very simple examples such as having a fever for a couple of days and feeling absolutely awful, and then feeling very cleansed and pure and relieved when you are well again. Also include some slightly more demanding emotional or physical experiences that you have encountered in your life -- such as consciously recovering from diseases, divorces, grievings, addictions, traumatic transitions.

Make some notes about these. Describe in a few sentences how your recovery, your transition out of those phases, can be interpreted as minor or major personal resurrections.

EXERCISE #30.2
RESURRECTING

Whether or not you participate in a religion that believes in resurrection, or in any religion, let us use the imagery of the Christian resurrection for this exercise.

Keep in mind that you do not have to believe in resurrection, or in the Christian religious doctrine, here. We are basically using imagery to train the mind, to focus, to visualize. We can use imagery and the sense of its energy in a particular way that will facilitate the death and elevation-ascension process being conducted by the mind, actually by the personal consciousness.

So now, see yourself on a hill, an abandoned hill, no people around.

You are on a cross, your arms strung out horizontally on either side of yourself, tied to a horizontal piece of wood which is attached to a vertical piece of wood. Your body is tied to the vertical piece of wood that intersects the horizontal wood, with your your feet tied together

there at the bottom. Higher up on this vertical piece of wood, your neck, shoulders, and torso are tied to that vertical piece of wood.

You are stretched out on this cross.

You go for days exposed to the weather and without food and water. Eventually your physical body weakens. It can no longer hold you.

. . .

You rise out of your physical body. You float higher and higher, expanding as you do. You detach the cords connecting back to your physical body. As you do so, you feel the frequency at which you vibrate raise, speed up.

You float even higher above your physical body and continue to look down upon it.

We will not parallel the journey of the Christian figure, Christ, and his resurrection here. We only use the imagery of the person on the cross.

You are still looking down on your body; you are not in any physical state. You access, you feel, a Light coming to you, a very high vibration of energy. You absorb that high vibration into your consciousness. As you do this, you feel yourself pull together.

You almost automatically pull your expanding perhaps dispersing consciousness back together to remember your physical form. As you do, you find the bits of your consciousness reassembling, generating the image or the shape of your physical form.

...

A major reduction in your vibration now occurs. Like a wave sweeping through you, you shudder. You shrink down from your floating SELF, but you do not touch the ground. You shrink down, forming this new SELF, the shape of which now appears physical, and which appears to be the physical shape you had maintained during your physical life that you have just left.

Now you float down and land on the ground in front of your dead, crucified, physical body hanging on the cross.

Realize that you are not as dense in your resurrected state as you are in your physical state. In your mind's eye, walk the planet this way for a little while. Note that only some of the people living in physical bodies see you. Only some eyes see your presence.

After a while, you become as dense and physical as the physical body you began with. Note the further reduction in vibration you undergo, as you slip back into your original physical body.

EXERCISE 30.3
RESURRECTING YOUR HEALING

Find yourself again in your body, on the cross, as at the start of Exercise #30.1. This time the cross is on fire.

Imagine for a brief moment your body is distressed, agonizing, suffering physically. Suffer until your only refuge is to escape your suffering body.

Whisk out of that body.

And now, while outside your damaged physical body, energetically form a non-physical version of your body, unencumbered by the pain

and torture of fire, unfettered by the assault with which it had been presented only moments prior.

Re-form your body, some distance away from the suffering body there on the cross. Stand in your reformed body and face the body on the cross. Stay there a while. . . . Look.

From your re-formed body, some distance away from the suffering burned body on the cross, you watch.

Now you see the burned body on the cross heal, return to a healthy state, and climb down from the cross.

This newly healed body now stands before you, the re-formed you. You stand there facing the newly healed body, looking from the reformed body you manifested.

Guide your reformed body back into your healed body.

Merge with yourself. Try to detect the instant in which the merging is complete.

Re-enter this dimension, this physical plane here on Earth.

31
DETECTING
PORTALS AND GATEWAYS

> "Let's pretend there's a way of getting through into it....Let's pretend the glass has got all soft like gauze....Why, it's turning into sort of mist now, I declare!"....And certainly the glass was beginning to melt away, just like a bright silvery mist.
>
> Lewis Carroll
> *Through the Looking Glass*

There may come a time when you are in a situation or environment that is quite unfamiliar. Of course, you may then recall that you have previously entered other situations that also felt unfamiliar. There may then be a resonance with such past experience, even if this feels to be a non-physical experience.

Exploring possible experiences that you may encounter when out of your body, either in the OBEs, NDEs, or OB-LDEs referred to in earlier chapters, or in the after life itself, involves allowing yourself to imagine, visualize, what you may find there and how you may navigate this, even if it feels largely unfamiliar.

SEE THE UNSEEN ENVIRONMENT

Take a very close look at the air or atmosphere around you. If you relax, and do not try too hard to see, you may sense or detect small openings or cracks in this atmosphere around you. These can be described as imaginary, yes, and this is fine, as these are openings in your perception of your reality. These are possible pores, windows, *portals,* ways into entirely new realms as discussed in earlier chapters.

These openings, these portals, are always around you. However, you may only really see them when you are prepared to do so.

RECOGNIZE PORTALS
AND POSSIBLE IDEAS ABOUT THEM

The openings or portals you sense around you can be seen as your gateways into other dimensions of your SELF, of your consciousness. On your journey through any reality, including the very reality in which you are immersed right now, which for many of you is daily life, there may be many openings or portals appearing to you. You may see these as something else, such as an opportunity or a new idea. This is up to you. However, you will from time to time sense, even if only vaguely, an opening to a new energy arrangement presenting itself.

Portals are difficult to detect in the physical plane until you learn to recognize them. Again note that some portals are distinguished as seeming material plane openings or opportunities (such as economic, interpersonal, spiritual, philosophical, or energetic opportunities). You may tend to think of these as "life choices."

Or, an opportunity may "open up" as a "way out" of a troubled cycle that you are trapped in. You perhaps do not take that opportunity. You perhaps do not travel through such a portal:

- If you are too attached to the troubled cycle you are in; OR
- If you are afraid of change; OR
- If you are afraid of changing or dying although you may realize that you must die out of your old cycle to move through a portal; OR
- If you do not know how to see the portal for what it is; OR
- If you do not feel confident in your ability to evaluate such a portal.

EVALUATE PORTALS

Whether or not your portals present themselves as physical plane life opportunities, or as non-material energy formations similar to *windows in the atmosphere*, you can use your discerning mind's eye to evaluate them. Know that:

1) A portal, for it to appear to offer a way to a higher, more conscious opportunity, must appear to have more Light coming out of it than is in your current environment. (See Figure 31.1, which pictures a star surrounded by rings of light, with the brightest light at the center). Of course remember that all that glitters is not gold, and discernment is essential all along the way.

2) When an opportunity or opening or portal offers Light appearing to be of the same or a lesser quality than the Light of your present atmosphere, do not travel through it without examing your reading of this portal. How are you seeing, sensing, what you are seeing, sensing? How

can you know that you are seeing, sensing? Is this seeing, sensing of your own Free Will? What do you do if you are unsure?

3) Look before LEAPing. Be in touch with the boundaries of your actual SELF, so you know that what you sense is of your SELF, is your actual SELF. Seek to know if another force is dominating your sense of your own boundaries, of who you are. When you gaze into the core of the portal, into the center of its opening, remember who you are: your SELF.

4) Know that these portal opportunities may be wonderful openings. So of course, do not close out all opportunities to be aware of, even to engage with, openings and portals, as some may be portals of positive opportunity.

5) Come up with a vehicle of transport symbol or icon for yourself, one you can keep in mind (such as the one pictured in Figure 31.2, which pictures a geometric diagram in front of a portal, with the geometric diagram symbolizing a *vehicle of transport*).

6) Give thought to your *vehicle of transport*. Of course you can change or develop this vehicle of yours over time, but do begin thinking about this now. Call the symbol you choose for your SELF to travel in, your own personal *vehicle of transport.*

7) Once you have your own vehicle of transport, take ownership of your vehicle; make it your own by knowing that it is yours. You then control your own vehicle of transport. Now, your vehicle of transport <u>does not fly you</u>

somewhere against your Will. This vehicle only travels where the Free Will of your personal consciousness sends it. Your vehicle of transport is powered by you, not by another force or presence.

8) So long as the Light of a portal you stand before is pure and clear, and so long as you feel no compulsion, suction, or hypnotic suggestion to enter, you can explore the possibility that this may be a safe portal.

9) Look for portals that meet the above criteria and that, upon close examination, reveal portals within portals within them, each portal indicating that your precious vehicle of transport WHICH PROTECTS YOU can drive your own SELF, your own personal consciousness, of your own Free Will and personal discernment, through.

10) Note that portals within portals are containing information. Where each portal appears to be exuding a purer Light than the one surrounding it, wait and examine, discern what you see and sense. (See Figure 31.3, which pictures portals within portals within portals, and your vehicle of transport appearing again and again before these portals). These are portals of escalated elevation-ascension, progressive infinite portal transports into the "highest" energy matrices, highest formations of what we can call realms of Light, of your Light.

11) Remember, any suction or hypnotization you feel is a sign that you are being deceived, pulled in without the agreement of your own Free Will. Your own vehicle of

transport does not transport you via another presence's suction.

12) Always be ready to turn away from the pull of an illusion!

REGISTERING RAINBOWS OF LIGHT

Images that can help understand and navigate may be useful. Visualize this concept: Pure white Light is composed of the combined seven colors or "rays," seven basic frequencies of Light.

There will be times during your journey into the BEYOND when the Light may register itself as a seeming perfect rainbow of seven rays. Such a seven-rayed Light prism may occur at very special portals, gateways to the highest clearest energy matrices or Light.

The rainbow can be the message, the instruction, the stairway to this Light. You can travel through what we can call the "rainbow realm," over the "rainbow bridge," and key into the Light by moving from the lowest frequency up to the highest frequency of color until you resonate at a high enough frequency that it will be but a small step into the clearest, brightest, of Light. If and when you encounter what appears to be a rainbow bridge or portal, use the idea of seven rays or colors as stepping stones.

Start vibrating low like red, then up to orange, then yellow, then green, then blue, then indigo, then violet. As you step up the frequency ladder, pull each of the lower color vibrations with you, as if you are collecting them.

You are not shifting frequencies upward; you are combing them and joining them from low to high until you are at full-spectrum white Light. The sum of the rays is far greater than all of its seven parts.

KNOW GATEWAYS
TO
GREATER FREE WILL

We want to always keep in mind that discernment continues to be important. Again, not all that glitters is gold. The matter of avoiding the lure of false Light will always be with you, will always be relevant. Aware discernment is key in survival both here in this life, and BEYOND.

PRACTICE DISCERNMENT

A consciousness such as yours desires this survival skill. There are times when clouded light may disguise itself as clearest brightest Light. Everyone is subject to being deceived. Discernment is the protection. If you are sucked into a portal *posing itself* to be one of those pictured in Figure 31.1, 31.2, and 31.3—while not really being one of these portals, you are not entering a safe space, you are not elevating-ascending, and you are not moving in the direction of greater Free Will.

Be aware of deceptive *suction gates,* dressed as gateways to higher realms of energy, of what appears to be Light. These suction gates seek to pull you, absorb you, into their realms, against your own fully conscious Free Will. They may seek to have you feel you are entering of your own Free Will when you are not. So, being highly aware, conscious, is what is best.

Suction gates can pull on, suck on, can even deplete, your own Will. As they do, your Free Will and your own personal consciousness may erode, *leaving a vacuum of vulnerability, a vacuum inside* your being. This is when you, your actual SELF, your personal consciousness, may be open to being kidnapped, trapped, enslaved. You can readily avoid this once you learn to recognize it.

Basically, do continue knowing that you do not have to surrender to a force or power or energy pulling on you, even if it presents, or even disguises itself, as higher light.

Do not relinquish the freedom of your own responsibility. Do not allow a false Light to program you. Programmed people are not free; they are being forced to become energy-production robots serving something else. Too many beings are trapped this way.

We may sometimes find ourselves in these situations, both in life and in death, perhaps even in after life. This happens when we are unprepared to see these situations, to detect them, to navigate them, and to protect ourselves from them. Understanding what both IN-LIFE TRANSITION SURVIVAL and SURVIVAL BEYOND are about (as explained in these *How To Die And Survive* books) can help prepare us.

What you do here, in your present (and, in your case, physical) dimension, has effects far beyond the reality you currently see and know. Look for ways to override your programming and patterning. *Problem patterns, whatever their symptoms, can trap energy.* Be careful how you use your energy, whether it is your

physical, your emotional, your financial, or your spiritual energy, or the core energy of YOU, or your ACTUAL SELF.

Try to see the patterns you are forming and feeding. Try to see the choices you make. Try to evaluate the patterns of energies and Lights to which you are attracted.

Will you commit to selecting only the portals that are gateways to your increasing freedom? Your personal consciousness can learn *to be free to SURVIVE*, **to increase the power of your own Free Will. Retaining your personal consciousness as you move through dimensions of your SELF is continuing to exist as your SELF. Your freedom to choose to survive BEYOND is yours to develop.**

You will know when you arrive at the threshold of spiritual liberty, of freedom of the Free Will of personal consciousness. Until you know, wait. Wait, because you have time.

EXERCISE #31.1
SEEING OPENINGS AND COMPARING PORTALS

Right now, with your eyes open, pretend that you see very, very large, openings, filmy mouths of caves, or eyes, or sides of bubbles at various locations in your environment. Realize that each of these is the opening to another realm, a passage, a walkway, yes, a portal of sorts.

Now, close your eyes and imagine that you see many, many, many more of these portals. You realize that each of these has a slightly different characteristic, a slightly different Light coming from it, a slightly different magnetic pull on you, a slightly different degree of and type of interest in you or attraction to you, a slightly different vibration.

Begin to think about the differences in experience that you would have should you choose to sample the crossing of the membranes into each of these various portals and the spaces beyond their membranes.

EXERCISE #31.2
FEELING PORTALS

Close your eyes. Reach before you, with both your hands, into the air or atmosphere. Begin to feel the space in front of you with your fingertips. Imagine that, or actually notice that, the atmosphere you are touching has great variations in energy and density. Sometimes these variations appear to be within an inch of each other or within a foot of each other or within a few feet, or further apart.

Notice that you can feel what your fingertips touch as well as what your fingertips perceive to be out in front of them, some distance away.

Where you find significant differences in the atmosphere you are scanning, begin to use your hands to detect the presence of a portal, an opening, to another dimension of your SELF, of your reality. When you think you have found one, stay with it. Or, if you do not think you have found one, just use your imagination, invent a portal, and stay with it.

Use your fingertips to feel the edges of that portal. Feel all the way around and then use your fingertips to feel the membrane of that portal's opening. Feel it very gently, delicately, as if you don't want to pop the membrane. Although this membrane appears thin and filmy, and weak, it is very strong and very selective as to what it lets through. Still, treat it gingerly and with great respect.

Hold for next exercise. Stay with this portal.

EXERCISE #31.3
RESPONDING CONSCIOUSLY
TO THE OPPORTUNITY OFFERED BY A PORTAL

Bow or nod your head downward, as if you are nodding or bowing in respect before this portal. See the portal as the mouth of an energy greater than yours. As you bow, check inside, check with your SELF, to be sure that you feel that this portal deserves your respect, your awe.

Is this a benign presence, or is this an illusion, a dark space wearing the mask of Light, a suction seeking to kidnap the energy you have generated by your personal consciousness, seeking to suck you in and take you over?

If you have hesitation while bowing, cease bowing in respect. Come back to face the portal and say, "No thank you, not today. I choose to go another way."

If, on the other hand, you feel great awe and respect for this benign energy, for this door to this potent energy that this portal represents, you may want to complete your bow and request permission to explore by stating, "I request permission to enter of my own Free Will."

Always remember that, if this is a portal into your own domain, you will learn to know this. Detecting when portals are opening into other domains, and what their purpose and intent may be, is part of exercising your increasing awareness--both in life and in after life.

Figure 31.1
An Opening to Light

Figure 31.2
Portal Vortex

Figure 31.3
Repeating (Infinite) Portal Vortex

32

PASSING GO:
VEHICLES OF TRANSPORT

> The impression of inertia is due to the powerful spans of energy that must be crossed within seconds of flight.
>
> In order to overcome high-frequency resistance levels, it is necessary to go beyond compound matter-energy "bondings" which are contained within electromagnetic "skins" and are impenetrable by the lower physical intelligence.
>
> J. J. Hurtak
> *The Book of Knowledge:*
> *The Keys of Enoch*
> 3-0-2:11, 12

You are now a long, long way into your brave adventure in transition and seeming death. And still there is more.

In moving through transition experiences, whether in-life, or seeming end-of-life, or possible after-life experiences, it is helpful to *form markers for yourself, signals from you to yourself that you have moved into or passed through particular phases or conditions of the transition you are traveling.*

161

You can place these signals into your consciousness, a little like bookmarks or street signs, to be available and retrievable later when you may want them.

Imagining, thinking about, even practicing, transition travel before being in various transition and death processes, can help you later recognize where you are and what you are experiencing. Having defined and then placed reminders or *notes in the consciousness* can provide you valuable signals to call on later, if and when you are feeling as if you have entered an unknown.

ABOUT GO

So, you have traveled a long way through both vague and clear situations, knowns and unknowns. You have held yourself together. You are still standing, so to speak.

Now it is time to pass GO, with full speed ahead.

As you move from one dimension of reality to another, from one format of your existence to another, you approach and then eventually pass a key point in your journey: We can call this GO. (See Figures 32.1 and 32.2. Figure 32.1 pictures a long tunnel which leads to a light there at the end of this tunnel. We can think of this light as GO, or the GO point. As you follow the line or pathway to this light, you move through progressive rings of light, starting at first with the darkest least light ring, and moving through increasingly lighter rings as you move toward the brightest light at the end of this tunnel. Figure 32.2 diagrams actual or imaginary steps toward this GO point and then BEYOND it.)

Of course, not all final destinations, not all GO points, are ideal and what you want to enter. Some are and some are not.

You can be aware of and avoid moving in directions, into openings, even into passageways and portals, you do not want to go.

Whether or not you enter a point called GO is up to you. Once you have consciously chosen of your own Free Will and discernment to enter a particular gateway or portal--or after you have fallen or have been sucked into it--is something you can be aware of, and even choose to avoid along the way before reaching this GO point, and then at this GO point.

Again, moving through and beyond this GO point may be your goal. This may be exactly what you have been looking for. GO may offer you the great relief you have been seeking. Just do be aware that this GO itself may not be what it presents itself as being. So, do discern, look closely. You can always say no to GO. All that glitters is not gold, both here and BEYOND.

The *level of awareness* you bring to such a journey, to the traversing of realities, of dimensions, of formats, has great bearing on how you come to this point called GO.

Passing GO is passing the point of re-bundling and re-creating your SELF and moving on.

PAY ATTENTION AT GO

Pay attention here at GO. Once you pass GO, turning back is very difficult. Once past GO, to return to the place from which you just came, to move backward, you have to unbundle the

163

SELF you have already re-bundled. You have to undo, reverse, your dance of re-creation.

You have to dissolve the new matrix you have already begun to manifest. You have to move again through the processes discussed in the previous and upcoming chapters, this time in reverse. And you can do this, if you choose. However, once past GO, the increased momentum deeper into the BEYOND, your or another presence's beyond, can make it more difficult to turn back.

GO

We do not call GO the "point of no return," because, as we note in the next and the previous chapters, many do choose to return, although they usually do not return in a form very like the one they have just left.

When you pass this GO point, you will know. You will feel as if you have pulled yourself back together after dissolving to move through a membrane. You will feel that the membrane you have moved through or crossed over is a one-way membrane. However, this is not really a one-way membrane, it only appears as such.

The work of crossing back through this membrane, if you stay conscious, *can* be done. It can even be fascinating and challenging. You may have a sense regarding what this is about -- as you may have done parallel in-life processes such as returning to a previous place, pattern, or perception, perhaps even a previous belief or home or relationship or habit.

Moving into a genuine GO is a particular moment in a transition process. Once past the GO point, you have fully arrived, you have moved through the GO point, the opening or membrane into the next dimension, the next reality. Once into GO, it may be important for you to look back and appreciate your passage through the membrane (as detailed in Chapter 24), to savor the experience (you have just had) of successfully moving through this semi-permeable membrane, this membrane that only allows more clarified, purified, essences to pass through its sieve-like wall.

We will discuss again the marvelous experience of passing through a membrane in Chapter 54, *Entering Metaterra.*

TRANSPORT
BEYOND

To be consciously passing GO and then to the realms beyond GO involves the *transport of your personal consciousness* in a special way. You can learn to transport your consciousness in a vehicle that your consciousness constructs out of energy and Light.

This is the *vehicle of transport* described in Figure 32.3, which pictures vehicles composed of two triangular Light structures, which together form a diamond shape. Study the details of Figure 32.3 where you see the horizontal vehicle as stable, the rolling vehicle moving into an unstable position, into the vertical position, where energy can move.

To operate this vehicle and to ride this vehicle into the BEYOND, study the practices described in Exercises #32.2, #32.3, #32.4, and #32.5. These exercises teach you how to enter

the idea, the symbolic, metaphorical, *Light vehicle*, to get it to move, to travel in it, to roll it, to spin it. Ultimately, this is the *vehicle of transport, the vehicle of the personal consciousness* that allows the personal consciousness to travel within its own *personal consciousness matrix*.

EXERCISE #32.1
ENTERING THE VEHICLE OF TRANSPORT

Visualize the figure in Figure 32.3. See the two triangles as balanced in such a way that the space between them is presently stable, horizontal. Imagine yourself climbing into this horizontal space, as if it were a ship. The walls of the ship are made of Light. You can get through those walls by climbing into the horizontal space between them and sitting there. Sit within that horizontal space and hold for the next exercise.

EXERCISE #32.2
TRIGGERING MOVEMENT
OF THE VEHICLE OF TRANSPORT

Realize how stable this vehicle of Light is while in the horizontal resting position. Now, imagine that someone has this vehicle of Light balanced at the top of a hill like a rock. Now, gently but nevertheless forcibly, this vehicle is being pushed down the hill. It rolls. Feel yourself roll, still in that central control room area which was horizontal, (but now is not), as the vehicle tumbles down the hill.

Continue tumbling, stay in this tumble, and feel how the energy changes as you roll while being in that space between the two triangles.

Continue this as you hold for the next exercise.

166

EXERCISE #32.3
FLYING THE VEHICLE OF TRANSPORT

The hill continues. You are rolling downward. At a certain point, you realize that each time that space between the two triangles of the Light vehicle is pointing at least somewhat vertically toward the sky, or in what you consider to be an upward direction, you feel energy sweep through you.

Decide that, on one of these tumbles, when you are pointing in an almost vertical direction, you will use that energy that sweeps through you and your vehicle to propel the vehicle upward so that you do not have to finish the downhill roll....

Here you come. You are now in the position that points vertically. The energy sweeps through you and your vehicle of transport. You fill yourself with intent to move <u>upward</u>.

Now, fly off the hill, but continue tumbling, rolling round and round, but into what you consider to be a <u>generally upward direction</u>. Fly further <u>upward,</u> still tumbling.

You have shifted the direction of your vehicle's motion by using the energy released when the space between the triangles is vertical. Hold for next exercise as you continue shunting <u>upward in an energetic tumble.</u>

EXERCISE #32.4
FLYING INTO HIGHER REALMS

Now, you begin to realize that you are tumbling <u>upward</u>, not just through your material plane atmosphere, but into other realms of density, less and less dense and more and more Light.

167

See, in the distance, a beautiful realm, full of very very bright Light. Aim your intent in that direction.

The next moment in which you again find your vehicle of Light balancing its control room in what you feel to be an upward or vertical direction, you feel the energy sweep upward through you. You aim yourself, aim your intent, to the beautiful realm you have selected. Imagine that you tumble upward very quickly toward this realm.

Now you find yourself in this next realm. The space between the triangles of your vehicle is now horizontal; you are stabilized. You pause there.

You will stay there as long as you choose. This is your vehicle, you can use it for transport. This vehicle works better when you purposefully begin to spin instead of getting pushed down a hill as if you were a top or the vehicle were a top.

Begin this spin of your own accord instead of using gravity to set it off. ... Experiment with this a while and then return to Earth, or to your starting dimension, which in your case currently is physicality.

CONSCIOUSNESS TO REMEMBER

Study a for moment Figure 32.4. This figure diagrams another form of transport or movement. Here, the two triangles forming the diamond shape with the space between the two triangles, the space which can be vertical or horizontal, engages in a more complex form of transport. Here the top triangle rotates counter clockwise while the bottom triangle mirrors this spin, rotating clockwise.

Now the space between these two triangles, your space, is experiencing profound effects on its energy. The power in that space between the two triangles, your power, your mobility, is enhanced.

Your ever more conscious movement of your SELF, of your SELF in your vehicle of transport, can take place. This is your key to travel both in your mind's eye, and in the pattern terrain where you do live, where your consciousness does live.

You can move yourself through changes and transitions here and BEYOND. As in Figure 32.5, you can consciously move from the destabilization of in-life pattern change, or what some may call seeming death, into the spinning climb of ascension, into the re-stabilization of liberation, all made conscious by knowing the operation of the Light vehicle.

This is some of the *How To Die And Survive Technology* you can choose to know, to remember always, even long after physical death. You can use this knowledge, the operation of this vehicle of your SELF, of your personal consciousness' vehicle of transport, in many dimensions, including in daily physical plane life.

Figure 32.1

Approaching Go

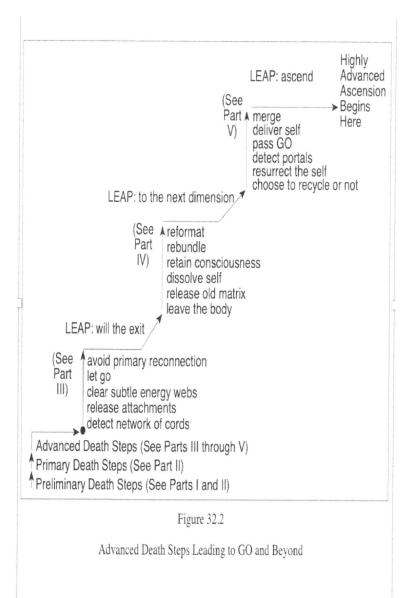

Figure 32.2

Advanced Death Steps Leading to GO and Beyond

Figure 32.3

Vehicle of Transport

175

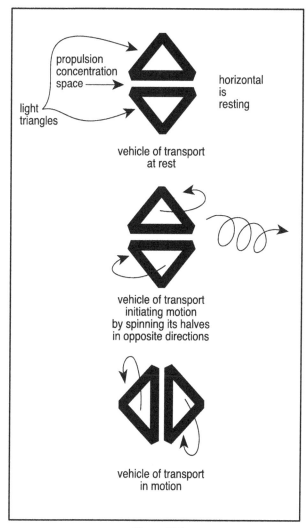

Figure 32.4
Operating Instructions:
Vehicle of Transport

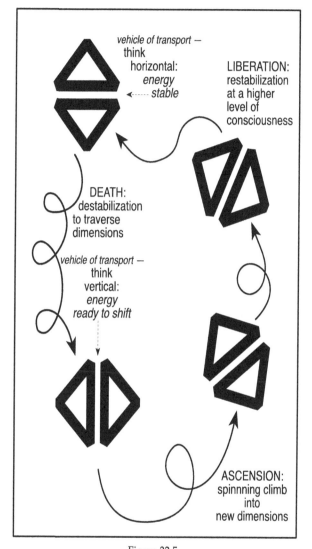

Figure 32.5

Vehicle of Transport
Through Death–Ascension–Liberation Spiral

179

33
DELIVERING ONESELF
INTO
ANOTHER DIMENSION

> I fled the Earth and, naked,
> climbed the weather,
> reaching a second ground
> far from the stars.

> Dylan Thomas
> *I Fellowed Sleep*

Change and transition, even in day to day life, can be interesting, exciting, challenging, at times difficult. Quite frequently we even resist change. Yet change is always taking place. In essence, we are all always in transition, on some level.

ABOUT SEEING ATTACHMENT

It is frequently seen that changing away from a troubled pattern is resisted, even when clearly the troubled pattern must be left in order to thrive, even to survive. Resisting change can be about the insistent resisting of the release of attachments and their cords.

It is misunderstanding attachment and its cording, and also remaining attached and corded, that can interfere with elevation out of patterns that are interfering with transition --

both in life, and in seeming end of life, and in possible after-life.

We are feeling attached to the self our attachments tell us we are, not to our actual SELF, as this actual core SELF is not defined by or directed by attachments.

Once you tune in to your actual SELF, your entanglements drop away, as your lower self is not who you are. The SELF that survives does not experience attachment and its cordings. So, unraveling your actual SELF from your lower self is not that difficult, as your actual SELF is already free.

Part of unraveling yourself from the web of attachments and cordings that you have woven or been woven into during physical and emotional life is seeing that the self entangled in these is not who you are. Survival is knowing that you are, in essence, your actual SELF. This is who can *die and survive*, as this is who does not die.

WHERE RELEASE IS FREEING, EVEN SURVIVING

Of course, attachments, cordings, are necessary in daily physical plane life as we generally form these for healthy reasons. It is when these attachments and cordings tie us to a situation, a pattern, a state of mind, a behavior, even sometimes to an addiction, that must change, that we may feel resistance. It is almost as if these patterns we grow attached to themselves resist our changing them.

There comes a time when survival may involve letting go. The idea of *dying and surviving* tells about this letting go to survive. Eventually, once we imagine we leave, or actually leave our

physical bodies, we sense this. Surviving major transition may involve knowing when to let go, where attachments and cords may impede movement into the next form or dimension of our existence.

Think again about the dolphin or bird caught in a fishing net and being pulled down. Entanglements may need to be released to survive. When we can liberate ourselves from our attachments, our entanglement in (physical plane) world experiences, whatever these might be--people, objects, foods, drugs, even pain, suffering—we can free our attention to focus upon something far more subtle, far more abstract, yet far more real, far more sustainable than worldly 3-D experiences.

Once we are fully liberated, a new kind of understanding or vision of truth can come to us. We can then see ourselves, our actual SELVES, as who we are, as part of a cosmic whole, part of the whole interdimensional Species of Humanity. (See the *Overriding The Extinction Scenario* books in this *Keys To Consciousness And Survival Series* for the definition and deep look at this definition of our species.)

PRACTICE
FOCUSING ON THE COSMIC WHOLE

Even before detaching, it is valuable to focus on this notion of the undivided whole, of this ground, this base, of cosmic eternal being. Such a focus trains the personal consciousness to utilize energies coming from the cosmic whole and coursing through the physical body or any other matrix of SELF we have constructed.

Focus on the energies coming in to you from the cosmic whole. By doing this, you can move the energy up and down and through your body to achieve high states of what some would describe, from the perspective of their Human existence, as bliss, love, and ecstasy.

Realize that these are but weak descriptive emotions when attached to material plane reality. This is not to say that your basic experiences in the attachment-prone physical world are valueless. The experiences that you collect and undergo in the physical dimension are excellent training for your travels beyond this dimension. Therefore, do not across the board suppress your material plane experiences. Learn from these experiences. Recognize the energy involved in these experiences.

Learn to harness the energy you cultivate and hold in the attachments and cordings you form while living in 3-D physicality. Recognize and harness this energy you cultivate, and then, at the right time, release it with care, allow it to fuel the LEAP discussed in Chapters 28, 35, 42, 29, and 56.

EXAMINE WHAT IS HAPPENING HERE

Not all involvement in third dimensional physical plane material reality experience is negative, unnecessary, and detrimental. Yet, we must become increasingly aware of how we are programmed to be tied to physical plane emotion and physical sensation. This programming has come to us in some way, perhaps through evolution, or via another source such as biological accident, or even perhaps via implant by intelligent

design. (Again, for more definition and discussion of this programming, see the *Overriding The Extinction Scenario* books.)

We must watch how we are caught in 3-D experience and emotion, even addicted to it by our programming. We must ask whether we are programmed to become enslaved to our very *programming to be enslaved to our 3-D definitions of ourselves*. Is there a deep programming within our biological brain to become automatically caught, even addicted, to behaviors, emotions, objects, even drugs? (Again, see other books in this series for more on this critical matter, such as *Volumes 5 and 6*, the *Overriding the Extinction Scenario* books.)

Simply stated, your addiction to your reality can kill you — not just your body but the arrangement, matrix, of your personal consciousness. You see, if you do not elevate-ascend, evolve, you stagnate. Stagnation winds down your energy. Stagnation can kill. Remember that a rigid addiction to your physical plane reality stifles the flow of your energy, energy which you could be using to generate the elevation-ascendence, the LEAP Level 5, soon to be discussed.

EXERCISE #33.1
DESIGNING ONE'S DELIVERY BEYOND

Reread the last exercise in Chapter 32. What did you do there? You imagined that you delivered yourself into another dimension of your SELF. You have seen, in the previous chapters, that there are many methods of doing this. Combine these methods or keep them separate. Your delivery of yourself into another dimension of YOU is your own process.

Now, fashion or imagine a delivery of yourself into another dimension of yourself. You may want to consult the exercises in the following chapters, as well as exercises in the previous chapters, to put together some series of activities or thought processes designed to deliver you, who you truly are, into another dimension of your personal consciousness. Or, you may want to pick one of the exercises and add to it.

Or, you may want to write your own elevation process. However you choose to do it, your assignment here is to begin to plan and practice your LEAP into another dimension of yourself. Be creative here. There are no wrong answers. This is in essence brainstorming, or perhaps we may call this consciousness-storming.

EXERCISE #33.2
DELIVERING ONESELF BEYOND

Now practice several times your delivery of yourself into another dimension of your own reality. With each practice, amend your method of deliverance to increase its degree of believability for you. Note what changes you choose to make and why.

34
MERGING:
BUT WITH WHAT?

> For, if energy can be released by the disintegration of matter—this is the most common method—it can also be released by fusion.
>
> Omraam Mikaël Aïvanhov
> *The Fruits of the Tree of Life:*
> *The Cabbalistic Tradition*

Let's revisit the important matter of merging.

Once out of the old system or program or pattern, you may feel the pull to merge with something more powerful than yourself. It is always good to look closely at what is calling you, to know whether this is the direction to go in order to survive as your SELF.

Yes, joining or merging into something else other than yourself, something that may seem to be a powerfully compelling or at least very attractive presence, may be desired. This may look like a great relief or even a beautiful option. Yet look before crossing into this.

As you merge, (should you decide to do so), think of this merging as both a surrender and an intercourse. It is a

surrender because you are giving up, either momentarily or for good, your sovereignty, the sovereignty of your <u>personal</u> consciousness, of your SELF, of your independent Free Will, in this merge. This is an intercourse because it is an engagement, one that moves toward a seeming temporary or permanent union.

You become one with that with which you merge by meshing energies, frequently by surrendering identity.

DISCERN, SENSITIZE IN ADVANCE, TO PULLS

When out of your physical body, look closely at what calls you. At this advanced stage of your journey into the BEYOND, this merging and intercourse act is most likely to be engaging you with something far more expansive and powerful, and appearing intensely more bright, Lighter than yourself.

The temptation is to merge. However, know what calls you, pulls you, to merge with it. Know that something more powerful than you may be beckoning you. Know that this power itself can pull you, and that this power itself can even appear benevolent.

This magnetic pull can indeed appear benevolent rather than just be the magnetic pull that it is. Of course, there may also be other forces and factors we want to learn in advance to discern regarding, as some magnetic pulls we will encounter may not only be not benevolent or not neutral, they may be predatorial or even malevolent. (Other chapters in this book, and other books in this series, discuss further this matter of discernment, and even of predatorial forces and factors).

CONSCIOUSLY SURRENDER

A giving over of your SELF, your personal consciousness, to this something is not necessarily an undesirable experience. This can be the most exhilarating of all your experiences. However, a giving over of your SELF, without determining carefully to what you are giving your SELF, may in some instances be dangerous. Hence, when you are about to merge, pause and ask what it is you are merging with. Even ask the factor or force (that is beckoning you to merge) who/what that force is. Identify your SELF as a distinct SELF with its own boundaries and its own Force of Will.

If you do choose to merge, merge consciously.

You can use the various methods of discernment discussed in other chapters of this book, applying your analysis of the Light to the Light or consciousness or intelligence with which you are preparing to merge. An understanding of the intercourse that takes place when you merge is essential here.

A FORM OF
WHAT WE CAN CALL TANTRA

You are about to mesh energies, to make a trade or exchange at a very high and very naked level. However, are you prepared, are you sensitized, are you aware, are you informed? This high-level exchange is in essence a very high level *integrative tantra*. You can begin to train your mind for this tantra while still in a physical body.

As you merge with anyone or any energy, understand that you are having intercourse with a force outside your own. When

you merge with what appears to be a Light, maintain your awareness during your intercourse with this brighter Light, with this far more expansive intelligence or life form or energy mass.

This can be the highest union possible, or this can be the highest union that an inexperienced being has yet to encounter. Again, teach yourself now, while you are still in a physical body, that *all that glitters is not gold.* Just because we are attracted or pulled to something does not mean it is going to contribute to our own survival and well-being.

ATTRACTIONS CAN BE DECEPTIVE

Attractions can be quite deceptive. You know this from your physical plane experience. Prepare to take this knowledge out to the realms of immaterial energies.

Once outside your physical body, you will want to be able to understand the profound tantra of an intercourse with what appears to be a higher or highest energy field or Light. You may wish to study now, while still in physicality, the Eastern traditions of "tantra," a practice which maps the subtle emotional or non-physical body, collects energy at various points in the subtle body, and then may move those energies in a way that elevates the consciousness, the spirit, the soul.

Tantra between physical partners is the exchange of harnessed, collected, and moved energies from one body to another and back, forming a circuit of energy. However, this *How To Die And Survive* book speaks of being in an *intercourse state with a far more expansive energy body,* rather than with another physical body. We speak of intercourse in order to inject a greater

190

degree of consciousness into the merging interaction, greater than simple surrender. Surrender tends to be part of a less conscious interaction with the energy mass.

When you are less conscious than the energy with which you are inter-coursing, you allow the more conscious energy mass greater discernment than you have and thus more power. And, once you move past the point of your surrender, you may be left with less discernment, less power to exercise *your own survival options*.

This can result in a death which is not survived as a personal consciousness. While of course, this level of high surrender, this merging, is your option, *the surrender of your personal consciousness is best done as consciously as possible*, as this becomes a decision that is frequently not entirely reversible.

Learn while still living in a physical body what it means to merge, what it means when the identity of your personal consciousness is surrendered to, lured into, pulled into, a larger force or factor.

When this is a divine energy body, what we believe is a benign and divine cosmic oneness, this may be a desired death that need not be survived. We may be returning to the Oneness from which we came. *However, discern well before taking this merging route, as you can retain the option to actually have your actual SELF choose to SURVIVE as your SELF, as your actual SELF, by not fully merging or fully surrendering.*

UNDERSTAND WHAT SURRENDER IS

Although there is always a degree of surrender in the act of energetic intercourse, the surrendering body or bodies can always retain awareness and participate consciously in the interaction, the merging, and the later separations of their energies (if the merging is not yet full and final). Intercourse, if done in a highly aware state, allows you to feel the energy with which you intend to merge, and then to decide how long or how completely to merge with this energy. You may know a bit about this based upon your experience with physical sex.

Understand that physical plane experience is only a place on a broader multi-dimensional spectrum. When you understand this, then your realization that you are part of a greater system, a larger, mostly non-material, cosmic whole, makes merging a completely different issue. *Again, remember to retain your personal consciousness as long as your personal consciousness detects that this is the best SURVIVAL option, which may be forever if you so choose.* And, as you do this on an individual level, also imagine how the Species of Consciousness of Humanity has the option to continue to *SURVIVE*, rather than to become extinct.[25]

USE INTUITION IN MERGING

Sometimes this intuition can be triggered by this sort of discussion. The triggering of your intuition, especially in the understanding of merging with energies in the BEYOND, must

---

[25] Again, see other books in this *Keys To Consciousness And Survival Series* defining and discussing in depth this survival matter, such as *Volume 5*, titled, *Overriding The Extinction Scenario: Detecting The Bar On The Evolution Of The Human Species.*

be initiated here and now, well before the possibility of such a merging presents itself to you.

See merging not as a once-in-a-lifetime event, (so to speak) but as a chain of events, which is at work again and again, at the same or more dense or less dense, more concrete or less concrete, and less tangible levels of reality. It is better to see a merging opportunity with which you are presented as one in a series of opportunities coming to you in your journey through the Cosmos.

So long as you treat merging as more of a conscious interaction (a conscious intercourse of energies) than a blind surrender, you can explore a series of opportunities to merge or not merge as part of your long ongoing elevation-ascent process, of your *dying and surviving* option.

Always, you must exercise discernment. Turn down some mergings, even if temporary. In inter-coursing, however momentarily: *withhold giving over your personal consciousness in order to separate after you have exchanged information with the other energy body or matrix.* Enjoy prolonged intercourse with but one or a few energies clear enough and pure enough to share in elevating you, *in extending your personal consciousness matrix.*

Be aware of the existence of predators, not only in the physical plane, but also out there BEYOND. You can set your own boundaries as you travel and elevate and expand out there, just as you can in 3-D life. Sense when your energetic boundaries are being crossed without your consent.

You can survive, emerge from mergings ALIVE, still independent (still a *personal* consciousness, still your actual SELF). You can emerge as YOU. Do this SURVIVING on an ongoing basis, or at least until you can discern to what you may be giving your SELF, and whether you your <u>SELF</u> ACTUALLY CHOOSES TO DO SO. You can know whether and when you choose for your SELF to merge for good, or instead, **to have your personal consciousness survive in order to DIE AND SURVIVE as your SELF.**

Each merging is in a sense a creation. You want to be certain that your personal consciousness is giving birth to an energy form it agrees with.

EXERCISE #34.1
EXAMINING THE ENERGY
THAT BECKONS YOUR MERGE

Now, write your own step by step procedure for determining the nature of a very large, very powerful energy form that you encounter outside of the physical plane. Use a step-by-step approach and do write this one out on paper if you can.

EXERCISE #34.2
TESTING YOUR DISCERNMENT

Now you will discern the nature of an energy form that has no characteristics you can see with your physical eyes.

Close your eyes. Imagine or actually locate a very large non-physical energy mass out there. (This mass may or may not be connected to a physical body.) Approach, with your personal consciousness, this presence, this energy matrix. But do not merge with it. Discern the nature of this presence by applying the steps you put together for

yourself in Exercise #34.1. Revise your steps if need be. Write your revisions down, if possible.

35
ASCENDING:
LEAP LEVEL FIVE

> I have beheld with the all-seeing
> eyes of mind the unseen things...
> and as I examined them, there came
> to me by slow degrees, but came in
> very deed, accurate knowledge of
> the truth.

> Hermes Trismegistus
> to his son, Tat
> *Aphrodite: 7*
> *Excerpt XXII Hermetica*

Take a moment to fix your higher sight beyond all that you know, all that you take for granted. Look BEYOND—beyond what you know as your daily life, your accepted reality.[26] Your mind's eye sees in its own way. You are aware of far more than you are aware of knowing.

You have glimpsed what is BEYOND so many times. Now, can you navigate yourself there? Can you expand, elevate-ascend, to these realms and dimensions of your reality, of your own personal consciousness? Yes, you can do this, you can *die and survive.*

---

[26] See *Volume 10* in this series, titled, *Seeing Beyond Our Line Of Sight.*

Yes, you *can* elevate-ascend to (and then, if you choose to, even through) the portals of whatever realms of the cosmic hierarchy that you define/develop for your SELF, that you see within your personal consciousness, that you choose to enter. At each portal, you must clarify and purify, shed attachments and cords to physical plane realities, to cross over the membrane, move past the boundary. And, once you cross through and over, you can choose to continue, to elevate-ascend again to the next realm.

Such elevation-ascension expansion is enabled by a focusing and directing of the Force of Will that you, your personal consciousness, can generate and maintain. Certain *elevation technologies* facilitate this process. We will discuss one elevation process here.

KUNDALINI IN DEATH

Let's call this concept Kundalini Death. This is the process of using the energy flow within your physical body, or parallel to what you would have in your physical body, as fuel providing the power to launch, to expand-elevate-ascend. All of the 3-D physical body activities, including sex, are training in the technical aspects of using energy or what is sometimes called "Kundalini." Kundalini itself is frequently misunderstood, or restricted to physical plane thinking. Here we reach beyond this view.

Certainly, many Human western teachings have emphasized the sexual aspects of Kundalini. Yet, Kundalini is much more than what Humans consider sexual. In fact, sexual energy itself is so much more than that generated between physical beings

who are physically attracted to each other. Human sex is practically child's play along the range of energy work the personal consciousness can navigate.

FEEL DEATH'S SEEMING SEXUALITY FOR WHAT IT ACTUALLY IS

First, let's take the physical out of the definition of sexuality. Then, let's address the issue of death's sexuality—sexuality at death. Quite often, books, tapes, movies, programs on death are said to either create a horror or a mystique around death, to wrongly glorify death. Interestingly, glorification is usually preferred to horrification. However, neither of these views is the intention of these *How To Die And Survive* books.

The intent here is to communicate that your death can be what you understand it to be—what you make it. You can have increasing say in whether and how you *die and survive* as a personal consciousness, as your actual SELF. In this sense, to present to you what some may interpret as being the seeming sexual aspect of death is far more than this. This is to open the door to the possibility that you can view your death as being a *directing of focus and energy*, **of Force of Will,** *through dimensions of your personal consciousness.*[27]

Kundalini is in essence a form of yoga—an exercise that involves the stretching, relaxing, and invigorating of the consciousness to heighten its awareness and help it access other dimensions of reality. Kundalini sex involves the control of one's breathing and the focus of one's mental energy such that the energy generated by a sexual meditation, stimulation,

---

[27] Refer to *Volume 3* in this series, titled, *Unveiling The Hidden Instinct.*

199

attraction, and interaction can be moved up and down the spine, or what this book, and the previous *How To Die And Survive* book, *Book One*, call the **vertical axis**.

Let's extend this concept here: Kundalini in death is not at all about sex. *This is about consciously moving energy up the vertical axis, which when in a physical body is up the spine.* Here, let's say that this energy can move up the vertical axis and then right out the top of the physical body matrix or lower form matrix, out the top of what may feel to be the person's head and brain. (Refer to the *How To Die And Survive, Book One* Figures, 12.1 through 12.8, and the exercises in that chapter, *Chapter 12*, for detailed definition and description of this movement up and out the *vertical axis*.)

In what this book is defining, this *dying and surviving* process, this expanded understanding of the *energy movement up the vertical axis* helps you to, at the right time, leave your physical body and travel to, expand to, realms far, far beyond your present energy dimension. These are your realms. Your realms are the realms of your personal consciousness. Many Readers still living in physical bodies are already moving to and from these realms.

EXERCISE #35.1
MOVING WHAT SOME CALL SEXUAL ENERGY

Tune in to yourself on an energetic level. Seek to generate in yourself something like a little sexual energy or the idea of this energy. Remember that what 3-D beings think is sexual energy can be transformed and experienced anywhere in your emotional or physical or even mental bodies and is not restricted to your biological sex organs.

Although physical stimulation is the most commonly recognized avenue of sexual (or any) arousal in physically incarnated Humans, this is not the avenue for the use of this energy in dying and surviving. Ways of generating what may still be for you something like sexual energy in yourself may include:

- *Excite or ignite, or power up just a little, your physical sexuality by imaging or fantasizing what you think of as a sexy encounter.*

- *Recall the experience and attempt to replicate the sensations leading up to this experience with no physical stimulation or sexual fantasy.*

If you are unsuccessful in generating some sexual energy within yourself, simply imagine that you have generated some sexual energy. Just imagine the signs or symptoms of this energy, whatever those signs may be for you. Suggested systems or signs of sexual energy are as follows:

- *Raised frequency of heartbeat and breathing.*
- *Raised body temperature.*
- *A general sense of physical and emotional excitement and anticipation.*
- *A feeling of an internal fire or glow, a feeling like a warm pleasure.*
- *A rippling of what feels to be energy up and down your spine or vertical axis as suggested here.*

Now, take any memory or hint or sensation of this anticipatory, exciting, energy and imagine that you put it at the base of your spine. Focus on its presence there. Remember, as is true for all exercises in these HOW TO DIE AND SURVIVE books, you can use your imagination to conduct this exercise.

201

Now, imagine that you move, or actually move, the energy up your spine. When this energy is nearing the high range of your vertical axis, or what may seem to be near the top of your physical body's head, reverse the exercise, moving the energy, almost step by step, or vertebrae by vertebrae, back down your spine or vertical axis.

Do not insist to yourself you need to do any more than you can here. Even working with this idea in your mind is doing this exercise.

Now, run this energy from what seems to be the base of your spine to the top of your head, and then back down, and then up and back down, and up and back down again many times. Continue to do this. Just imagine or visualize you are doing this as you continue.

*Move the energy up and down your spine again and again, more and more rapidly. Start to feel exhilarated as you do this. Start to feel, or imagine, as though there is an electrical energy moving, flowing, shooting up and down your spine, your **vertical axis**. Continue doing this into the next exercise.*

EXERCISE #35.2
USING ENERGY AS FUEL FOR LEAPING

As you make this energy more and more powerful by running it up and down your spine again, again, and again, prepare your mind for your launch into elevation-ascension. Continue moving the energy up and down your spine. As you do so, think but do not yet do this— think about what it will be like, to shoot this energy out the top of your head, along your vertical axis.

You can image here how it will be to shoot your energy so far away from your physical self, that your actual SELF LEAPs across many realms of your personal consciousness, across the many realms of

202

decreasing density and increasing Light you find out there -- into a very, very, very expanded, vaporous, brightly lit realm.

Keep moving your energy up and down your spine. . . . Get ready, you are going to let the energy burst out the top of your head.

Now move your imagination, your focus, up and down your spine, **then up, up, and up out the top of your head and you LEAP into the Light!**

Float out there in this Light for a while. Get to know what this feels like.

Return your focus to your physical body with this sensation in mind.

ELEVATION-ASCENSION

Elevation-ascension is simply the moving of the actual SELF, of personal consciousness, in such a manner that it expands along and through the CONTINUUM OF CONSCIOUSNESS. (This **continuum of consciousness** is defined and described in other books in this series, such as *Volume 10* titled, *Seeing Beyond Our Line Of Sight*.) This expansion is survival. *This non-physical continuum is where you already do live, and is where you can DIE AND SURVIVE.* Your continuum is your road map, your navigation plan, your expansion-elevation-ascension into what you may sense are higher frequency energy matrices, higher realms of what appears to be Light.

Clearly, what you have come to know in physicality as sexual energy can be transformed to so much more. The tantric kundalini death LEAP you are asked to imagine or design in your mind, and then practice or imagine you practice (in the

203

above exercises) *fuels your expansion into your own elevation-ascension survival.* Recognize that the energy and consciousness you bring, or imagine you bring, to your elevation-ascension processes can determine their outcomes.

With any intimate discussion of death being a taboo in many social circles, this sort of discussion of sexuality — which is also a taboo in many social circles — the sexuality of dying must be handled delicately. Nothing on these pages suggests that you must practice this concept on yourself, and especially not on others, in actual physical dying processes. This is an awareness that you can carry with you and tune into at the right time. Again, nothing in this book suggests you end your own physical life at this time.

The basic message here is that sexual energy is much more than the untrained physical body may see. What may in physical plane life be seen as sexual energy can fuel an efficient, profound, transition of any sort, from: in-life change, ending, and transition; to seeming end-of-life death; to possible after-life expansion and travel. What may be called sexual energy is only physically sexual for those who either choose to reduce it to physical-sexual density or who know of no other level of *transformative energy.*

An expanded awareness of the dimensions of reality beyond the physical plane changes a being's understanding of sexuality, of energy itself (and of all physicality, for that matter).

PART VI

How To

Discern And Cathart

36
DISCERNING WHAT BECKONS HERE AND BEYOND

> Be willing to change the timing or
> form of your holy understanding of
> Truth so as to climb the octaves of
> Jacob's Ladder through initiations of
> refinement.

> *Virtues, Laws and Powers*

Let's say (just for the sake of discussion here) that someday you wake up dead. At first, you are not aware of this, as you are perhaps simply floating out there, immersed in your environment. Floating. Floating. Time is not part of your awareness now.

You, your SELF, may not even be part of your awareness now, at least not immediately. However, you can find your SELF again, because if you are there, then you, your actual SELF, has survived.

Listen. You will hear your SELF calling. You can be *beckoning your SELF to your SELF*, to see you still exist, that you have died *and survived*, that you have not simply died. This is something you can learn to know long before you find your SELF out there BEYOND. You can prepare your SELF to both understand and navigate the BEYOND, to continue to survive.

207

JUST BE THERE

Just be there, feel yourself being there. You can become aware of yourself, of your actual SELF, as you become aware of what is going on. Becoming aware out there is key in surviving. Basically, knowing you *can* survive is key in surviving.

You have left your body, your biological physical body. If you are fully out, you have also left your biological emotional body, and of course also your biological mental body and its biological brain. All cords and attachments to these biological bodies have been let go, released. (Keep in mind that once you detach from your biological brain, *your non-physical higher mental body can survive*. This is where your actual SELF lives. Simply realizing you can survive puts you on notice that you have survived. As simple as this sounds, this knowing, this basic survival awareness, is KEY in survival.)

Of course you are not clear yet about what is happening, and where you are, as all this may feel quite foreign to you. Just be there, wait. You will not experience any unpleasant physical, emotional, or mental sensations as those parts of you are gone. There is no time pressure, as time as you know it is gone.

Allow your focus to slowly come in. You will begin to realize that you <u>are</u>, that you <u>exist</u>, that you have <u>survived</u>. Welcome home.

TIME PASSES

You continue to be suspended in an atmosphere, what seems to be a sort of nothingness. Time passes in its own way, like a river flowing, wafting through the spaces you are in. At some

point, you become aware of the atmosphere out there, right there in this terrain you are floating in. You have the sense now that there is indeed a terrain, an atmosphere, you are floating in. You start to find you can do more than float, that maybe something like a weaving back and forth, or a light swimming, will help you move.

You begin to sense variations in this atmosphere you are in, areas where there is some light, maybe a little flicker of light. Maybe if you head toward the flicker, you find more light. You also sense areas that are darker, some without light, some where there is vague light somewhere. As you begin to sense the various degrees of light, you also feel other textures in the space surrounding you. You sense more and less dense areas. You sense more still and more active areas, maybe even some movement, you are not sure.

SOME MORE LIGHT APPEARS

Now some more light appears out there, some distance away, how far you cannot tell. This light seems brighter and seems to be pulsing. You are drawn to this light, as there feels to you a direction for you, one that in this seemingly senseless environment you may be drawn to.

You begin to feel that this light is even pulling you to move to it. You move in that direction, getting closer and closer to this light. You now sense that this light is not just pulling you to it, but *into* it. Yet, you are also hesitant, as something is telling you to wait, not to go into this light until you have learned, *discerned*, more about it. This is you, your SELF, telling you.

This discernment is key to your survival both in-life and in after-life, BEYOND.

Of course, some of what you find out there BEYOND is so vast and so glorious, the immensity alone can be so compelling, so very compelling that it can call you to be absorbed by it.

This pull to be absorbed can be so magnetic that you can be almost automatically pulled into it by whatever it is, by something, by anything so powerful, by anything out there that is not you, your SELF.

Wait, wait, wait, just wait. You will eventually know whether you want to go in that direction, to give your individual SELF over to another presence. You may not want to die just yet, or ever. This remains your option, the option of your actual SELF to retain its, your, sovereignty. You can continue to survive, your actual SELF can live on. This is both your option and your right. Yes, there are rights out there BEYOND. Enter the BEYOND knowing your right to die *and survive*, to actually survive.

It is always a good idea to *discern what beckons*, to avoid simply being called, and allowing yourself to be called, and then simply giving yourself to what beckons. Wait. Not all that glitters is gold.

YOU KNOW THIS SUBTLE ENERGY STUFF FROM DAILY LIFE

You have practiced knowing about all this, even in your daily Earth life. You've been in uncertain situations before, perhaps

even disoriented or lost before. Ask yourself, do you ever feel quite lost, almost a stranger in a strange land, even in your daily life?

We move through our lives, at times certain of what we are doing and where we are going. Here in the physical plane, we may feel we know what surrounds us, we may feel we know what we are dealing with. We may.

We know, until we do not know, which for many of us is much of the time. "I have no way of knowing," and "I just don't know what's happening," and "This situation took me by surprise," are comments frequently heard when people feel they have little or no knowledge regarding, and little control over, what is happening to and around them. Many literally feel lost, adrift, amidst a sea of unknowns: "I just can't pull my life together, myself together." "I feel like I am just floundering around, spinning like a top." "I don't know who I am anymore."

We hear descriptions of unexpected sudden shifts or changes where everything seems to be jumbled, or messy, or wrong, or troubling, or downright frightening. People may say, "all of a sudden," and "it came out of nowhere," and "I had no idea what was coming," and "everything changed from one moment to the next."

Some will say that they have hit a wall, that suddenly they do not really know what is going on, what they want, what to do, where to be, how to decide, even who they are. Others will say that this situation, this state of mind and of life has been building all along, that they expected to wake up one day confused and overwhelmed, without direction, lost.

ANY PORT IN A STORM? NO!

Think for a moment about being lost in the dark, maybe in a forest with no moonlight or starlight or lantern available. You find that you cannot see anything around you, that as you walk you must step carefully, feeling the ground with your feet, and feeling whatever may be around you with your hands touching the space you are reaching into from your outstretched arms.

So your survival requires you to be aware, to *discern*. Discernment is a highly alert and careful examination. Discernment is the wise determination of the degree and clarity of the energy with which you are presented. Discernment is both easily discussed and easily dismissed as already underway or accomplished.

Without understanding discernment, we may allow ourselves to forget about discerning. We may then be more vulnerable to forces and factors that proceed by assuming we are not aware of them, not discerning. We may simply be not seeing them. And then, we may be letting them come in -- allowing in, maybe even actually making welcome -- forces, intelligences, energy matrices, or energy entities that may or may not have the best interests of your and our life or your and our survival at heart. (Keep in mind that, if what some see as a force of darkness were intending to deceive us, to have us allow that darkness in, it would likely disguise itself as something appearing to be Light.)

As you read this chapter on discernment here and BEYOND, recognize that you can apply this information, with slight

translation, to the use of your awareness, consciousness, and intelligence during your everyday life in your material plane.

Here, let's focus primarily on interdimensional thinking and thus travel of the mind, of the personal consciousness, when this may be triggered by near or actual physical death. (Note: This chapter does, however, also speak about the possibilities of hypnosis and kidnapping of your precious SELF, of your personal consciousness, even within the domain of your material plane. (Yes, there can be energy predators out there, both in daily life and BEYOND. Thinking about this is not being paranoid, not at all. This is simply wise awareness. Our awareness is how we protect ourselves. It is that simple. Those predators do not want you to be aware of them. They have the advantage when you do not know to watch for them -- and when you do not know they work to have you feel they are simply part of you; so you protect them as if they were yourself, when they are actually outside patterns inhabiting you.)

REFINE DISCERNMENT

"Just go for the Light" is the advice people often give each other. However, wise discernment is more delicate than this. After all, we must ask ourselves again and again: if troubled or even predatory presences were coming in, wouldn't these be apt to disguise themselves as something benevolent, or at least as safe Light? Think of times in life when you or someone you know went to what felt like a safe place, a safe harbor, and later found this anything but safe. You were perhaps lured in, pulled in, before you knew what was going on.

213

Discernment is not judgmental. Let's take a moment to talk about this. Frequently, disagreements regarding what is a positive and what is a negative belief are cloaked in the veil of spiritual or religious debate. One person says he or she sees the Light, and another person says that first person is wrong, that this other person is the one who sees the Light, denouncing the first person. Let's be clear here, personal discernment does not judge others' sense of Light. Different views are alright, when no harm is being done to others.

Always keep your own counsel. Especially in times of great transition, times such as your "now," you must be adept at keeping your own keenly alert counsel. Only then can you effectively evaluate what beckons you once you have left your old energy matrix and your old reality, even your old physical body.

YOUR, OUR, SURVIVAL

To a great extent, we do create our own personal realities. And to a great extent, we are all involved in evolving the overall cosmic reality. Discernment can be a tool of positive evolution. You can move through realities, changes, transitions, especially through death transitions, with as refined a discernment process as you can manifest.

Basically, telling yourself to be aware of what is going on around you, of unseen and subtle energies affecting you, is a good idea. Increasingly refined discernment is not only valuable, it is essential. If you are not sufficiently discerning, what comes in to this and other dimensions through you—into

the space you inhabit—can affect the energy of the life forms, of those people around you, not just of you.

When you work hard to learn to open yourself up to multi-dimensional awareness and consciousness, but do not practice discernment, you are a risk factor for yourself, for your actual SELF, and even for everyone: You can open wide up like a big leak in a reservoir wall, and allow problem energies, problem matrices, to pour in by not discerning as you open up. You can mistakenly allow undesirable forces, energies, and life forms to pour right into your material plane or other reality through you. So, your ability to discern is of critical importance to more than just you.

BOTH A RIGHT AND A RESPONSIBILITY

Again note that...

This is not paranoia, this is simply wise ongoing awareness.

This is the call to learn and maintain increasing self awareness in a reality where the survival of your *actual SELF*, as well as of your *actual species*, is at stake. (See other books in this *Keys To Consciousness And Survival Series* for more on this **personal and species survival**, including *Volumes 5 and 6* of this series, the *Overriding The Extinction Scenario* books.)

Discernment is therefore both a right and a responsibility. This discernment is best done continuously, and yes, implemented during transition and travel both in-life and in all life BEYOND. Transition by its very nature can leave you vulnerable.

There are always fluctuations in your degree of awareness of, even of vulnerability to, energies coming in from others. And you are always undergoing various forms of transitions and vulnerabilities, many of these quite subtle and less obvious than others, but equally critical. You have likely felt this in your daily life.

You, yourself, can become an alert gatekeeper. Knowing you can be alert is the basic process. Many times we realize later, after something happens that, "If I had only been paying attention, I would have seen the clues and signs all around me."

KNOW FORCE OF WILL

Explore the concept of *Force of Will.* How aware are you of the force of <u>your</u> Will? Know that your Will is a force. It is a battery of energy, organized, refined, stored, and expressed in a special way. We tend to take the *Force of Will* for granted, to ignore or trivialize or sometimes misuse it, especially when living in material plane realities.

Bodies, objects, relationships, money, even linear time, are distractions from our sense of identification with this force. Nevertheless, your own SELF, your own *Force of Will,* can decide now to evolve itSELF to live on past physical death -- to die and survive only when it is time, and then at the right time, even to be strengthened by physical death.

You, your actual SELF, can be (and indeed is always being) carried in and out of material reality, and in and out of linear time. While there are great lessons and rewards in the various material plane distractions, the greatest lesson of all, once knowing these distractions, is to learn to over-ride these

distractions, to strip away these distractions: **to reveal to yourself your actual SELF and your actual Force of Will.**

OVERRIDE

You can learn to override pressures you feel telling you not to have Force of Will, or much Force of Will. Please keep in mind that, this Force of Will being referred to here is not about being more or less outspoken or assertive in social settings. This is not about your behavior or your personality itself. This is about your personal strength, your Force, being there for you in environments here and BEYOND, anywhere you want to survive.

Ultimately, this over-ride lesson involves the process of *unraveling, at least to some extent, from your attachments* to material reality and also to *your perceptions of reality*. Or, if you are truly ready for the great LEAP, the ultimate *over*-ride lesson is the *sudden release of all attachment to attachment itself*— the sudden LEAP out of all attachment to all the distractions, of all of attachment to all the cords of connection to the web. [See the first (preceding) *How To Die And Survive* book, *Book One*, for details on attachment and cording, as well as detaching.]

EXERCISE #36.1
REVEALING FORCE OF WILL

This exercise begins by revisiting an exercise in How To Die And Survive, Book One, which is Exercise #21.1, in which you focused on your Will. Now, as parts of this present exercise include Exercise #21.1, you will find parts of #21.1 below.

Conduct this Exercise #21.1 again, this time attuning more precisely not just to your Will, but to your <u>Force</u> of Will. Anything that gets in the way of your feeling this <u>force</u> of YOU, or who you are, of your SELF, is a distraction. As you do this exercise again, note each distraction as it comes along. See where your own personal power, FORCE, the force behind your Will, may want attention. Each time you see distractions, something stopping or weakening your own FORCE, note this. Tell each distraction to leave. If you wish, tell each distraction or any energy weakening your own FORCE to: Light up. Dissolve. Transmute to the Highest Light.

Here is a summary of Exercise #21.1. As you read or listen to this exercise, think of your Will itSELF, and even more, of the FORCE of your Will.

> *We have talked again and again about the right use of Will and the nature of one's Will. Now you will feel for yourself your own Will.*
>
> *Begin to look for your Will. <u>Will</u> that you find your Will. How does willing feel? You are isolating the essence of your Will. This exercise generates a refinement of your Will by asking you to locate your Will. Seeking, being aware of, the Will defines it, refines it.*
>
> *Close your eyes, go inside, and take some time to find your Will. Your own personal force of Will is your own to define and to know, even to generate and develop.*
>
> *Realize that your Will is not your relationship to the outside world, not your list of responsibilities, not your set of accomplishments, not your failures, not your feelings, not your*

attachments or cords, not your family, not your political party, not your philosophical beliefs, not your religion.

Now you are locating your own personal Free Will, its essence, its reality. ... Once you have found your Will or what you sense is your Will, continue refining your connection to your Will. Feel as if you are getting to better know your Will.

That was Exercise #21.1, which was about getting in touch with your personal Will. Now for this present exercise, take this to the next level: Sensitize to the <u>force</u>, your <u>force</u>, behind your Will. Be more aware that you, who you are, has a personal power, a FORCE of Will. Your Force of Will of course deserves attention and nurturing in life, and BEYOND as well. Your FORCE is the FORCE of your SELF. Your FORCE sustains you here and BEYOND.

DISTINGUISH BETWEEN OPTIONS

Preserving your own Force of Will, and even using your minor and major in-life experiences, changes, transitions, and deaths, to refine your Force of Will, is your responsibility. Become highly aware of the forces that may be seeking to stifle or even are actually stifling your Force of Will. Understand you can avoid the death of your Will. You can SURVIVE.

One of the forces that can be stifling your Force of Will is the illusion of a communal or shared material plane reality. Of course this is natural, however this can be deceptive. *Be sure to examine the shared reality you believe you live in.* Is there actual perceptual harmony, in which large numbers of people believe that they see the same or very similar realities? Is this actually harmony, and how closely is this examined?

Perceptual harmony allows a large group consciousness matrix to overtake or overlay your own individual consciousness matrix. While this sounds lovely, right, and convenient as well, and can at times be this wonderful, perceptual harmony is not always what it seems to be. This seeming harmony can itself be deceptive, even counterproductive. This gives us a material plane example of how forces and factors, presences larger than we are, can pull us into themselves, swallow us. (See *Volume 3* in this series, titled, *Unveiling The Hidden Instinct*, for more on discerning between and among group consciousness options.)

DISCERN MASS HYPNOSIS

Of course, you may choose to merge into a one-ness. Yes, this may be the death of the SELF that you eventually choose. This will be your option. Still, along the way, do be aware of pulls on you, pulls to merge. Be aware when these pulls may not be your own wish, not the choice you would make if not being pulled or hypnotized into merging.

Of course, when your own personal consciousness is sucked into a mass consciousness or energy field, this may be a wonderful and even a welcome death of the personal SELF.

However, once your personal consciousness is sucked into a mass consciousness, it can lose its ability to decide for itself how the energy of your personal consciousness gets used, how your personal consciousness itself is used by other energies who seek to commandeer it.

It is good to discern all along the way, long before merging, as merging may not be the survival option you would freely choose.

220

Think about this. How clear are we about outside influences? How do we tell when these are beneficial and or not beneficial for us? Look around at the daily life world around you.

You will find, if you dare to look, that masses of people are hypnotized into believing that: what they think is real is real; who they think they are they indeed are; what they think is happening is indeed happening.

In fact, large numbers of people may be fooled into believing that what they are thinking are their own thoughts, when actually they may have lost full access to their own personal, individualized perceptions.

We certainly can not blame ourselves for this, Yet, we can become more aware of this very subtle invasion of our minds, of ourselves.

DISCERN BEFORE CHOOSING TO
OR NOT TO
SURRENDER TO A ONENESS

Such surrenders are usually undertaken quite naively. Frequently, individuals have no sense that they have surrendered anything at all. When people knowingly surrender the Free Will of their own personal consciousness, it is usually because collective or "hive mentality" sounds like a good idea: "All for one and one for all."

But what good is the forming of such a collective energy if it can be taken over—commandeered—by undesirable forces? Again, heightened discernment is essential, here and BEYOND.

221

Work to maintain your individual awareness (and your personal consciousness matrix) until you are certain that surrendering it is what you choose to do of your own Free Will.

Of course, merging with a high even perhaps divine Oneness may be desirable and beautiful. However, first, before choosing to have your personal SELF be absorbed and die this way, be sure you actually do wish to do this. And be sure this oneness is what it appears to be.

You have a right to discern here, and to be certain that you choose to no longer survive as your actual personal SELF. Are you making this decision to merge, to surrender, to have your personal SELF die? Or is some other presence, force, or factor making this decision for you? Can you tell the difference? Wait until you know. Wait.

Once you surrender your SELF to another power or force, you may not be able to retrieve your SELF, your personal consciousness. This would be, in essence, you, your SELF, *not dying and surviving* as your SELF, just dying. Note that feelings, interactions, ideas, the work that you produce, are all expenditures of and formattings of your own personal consciousness energy. This is valuable energy that many presences out there would like to absorb.

Again, once you are clear to whom and to what you may be giving your energy, to whom and to what you may be giving over your actual SELF, this merging may be a desirable option. Just discern very well before choosing to DIE and <u>not</u> SURVIVE as your own personal consciousness matrix, as your own actual SELF.

There are likely many political and economic systems, hierarchies in and out of the material plane, competing for control of your energy, even for control of your own personal consciousness. Many Human energies and consciousness-es may have already been consumed. In this sense, the Human species may already be occupied by outside forces and factors, many unseen by us.

There are those who understand this fully well; and, at the same time, there are many of you who may have unwillingly fallen into the process of energetic enslavement.

THIS TREND CAN BE TURNED AROUND.

AWARENESS OF THIS IS THE TURN AROUND.

What would Humanity do with all its people if they all were fully conscious? What if they all managed to commandeer all the energy of their own transition and death processes and releases? What if they all could learn to *die and survive*? Many Humans, as if trained to think a certain way, do not see a world with a place for everyone. As a species, Humans have developed and depended upon hierarchical political systems to control each other -- and then even to be controlled by a less visible higher overarching force.

Think of the dying and surviving hierarchies that may exist. We have seen these in many cultures and belief systems, where only chosen ones or privileged persons were believed to have access to the after life. In this sense...

your being able to die and survive is revolutionary.

223

YOU ARE PART OF THIS REVOLUTION

Look around and recast, even if only for a moment, what you see in these terms. Humans may be mimicking what predatory forces are doing to Humanity from the BEYOND. Think of the social, political, economic hierarchies all around the world. Think of how your energy is used, and about who and what uses your energy.

Humans have their own hierarchies--while the entirety of the physicalized Human hierarchy, the whole of the Human Species living on Earth, may be an unwitting and unwilling drone class, supplying energy for other more multidimensional hierarchies. *As above, so below. As below, so above.* Humans can learn a great deal about this situation by looking at what they are doing to each other.

Dictators on Earth have long practiced the withholding of information to retain power over their people. Similarly, keeping the Humans living on Earth unaware of the fact that they are not in full control of their own energy, that they are rarely allowed true and full access to realms outside the material plane (realms which do indeed exist), is a way of maintaining Humans as a captive life form: held in the material plane without natural access to the ability to move freely back and forth, to and from, physicality at will.

The big secret, the one we have been kept from fully seeing, is that we can and do have a right to die and survive.

**We can and do have a right to access our own
multi-dimensional complexity and awareness.**

A low key but pervasive hypnosis has kept control of the Human Species living in the material plane on Earth. *If you will take control of your own consciousness now, if you will allow your connection to the collective hypnosis to die, you will move to new realms of conscious awareness and intelligence.* You will be able to master and survive challenges, transitions, minor and major deaths. You will transcend the hypnosis, break the spell you may have lived under. You will be able to implement *your right to die and survive.* This is about the survival of your actual SELF both here and BEYOND.

In case you have not been informed: You have the power to think yourself through what looks like the impossible, to understand or believe unintelligible situations, and to navigate even the most bizarre of these. You can traverse the dimensions, with or without the impetus of physical death, at Will, and with confidence. This is your right, the right of our truly Interdimensional Species of Humanity. This is who you and we already are. Let's take this full awareness back now.

RETAIN YOUR AWARENESS

We have discussed in previous chapters the movement, the expansion, the LEAP, into other dimensions of ourselves, of our consciousness-es. Discernment is essential as you make this journey. Discern: Know and continue to remind yourself that not everything that appears to be a portal or passage into the Light or Oneness is exactly that.

Remember that you may discover *trick windows, hidden pockets, and soul-traps* that look and feel like entries to the clearest Light, but which are not. An actively conscious personal

consciousness such as you are becoming can avoid these illusions and trick windows by being aware that these exist. You can detect the windows that lead deceptively into a trap, and can navigate the way out should such a trap be entered. (See more on this important matter in another book in this *Keys To Consciousness And Survival Series: Volume 9*, titled, *Navigating Life's Stuff, Book* <u>*Two*</u>.)

In your first fully conscious but perhaps still naive journey into the dimensions BEYOND, you may feel drawn toward these traps by the illusions they transmit, such as what appears to be a bright Light, or a safe harbor, or some other seemingly wonderful destination. You may also find yourself becoming mesmerized by an actual or seeming magnetic pulsation of such illusions or traps.

LEARN NOW TO REMEMBER LATER

You can learn now to later remember the following:

Without complete certainty that you should move toward a particular portal, pulsation, or Light, wait. Just wait. You have time. Time does not move the way you knew it in the physical dimension. Wait and avoid traps and sinks. Wait to discern.

Those who enter false Lights, trick portals, **consciousness traps**, risk cosmic level *interdimensional restriction, enslavement, even death of the SELF.* They may risk losing themselves to outside forces and factors who do not wish for them to survive BEYOND. The risk is on the one hand quite subtle, quite invisible, and on the other hand important to think about now while free enough to discover what this means.

As you journey beyond your physical body, beyond your known world, wait and allow your awareness and discernment to heighten. *Stay aware to stay free. Stay aware to protect your right to DIE AND SURVIVE.* Stay aware right through all of your in-life and seeming end-of-life and after-life transitions, and what appear to be dyings, and or seeming or actual elevation-ascendences.

RAISE AND MATCH

Remember that your SELF or soul or being (however you choose to describe this) must be as clear and unburdened of physical plane attachments, as clear and clarified as it can be, to gain entry to the portals of highest clearest Light. Your etheric substance must raise itself to the high and pure frequency of the high and pure medium you intend to enter. Raise and match. When you have raised yourself to such a high frequency, you will sense this with such Force of Will and such completeness of consciousness, that there will be no doubt in you. Discern: Grow increasingly aware and conscious of this difference between clearest Light and other Light. Learn to know this difference.

Think of daily life transition issues. All too frequently, we move through even in-life transitions, leaving partially or entirely one web of attachments and emotions and behaviors, only to form the same or a similar web all over again. When this happens, attachment PATTERNS are continued, not released. These attachment patterns weigh on a SELF like heavy luggage.

If you are diminished in consciousness during your being pulled by or attracted by a force or factor, a portal, stay away. Stay fully conscious to discern fully. Anything that wants lesser of you, a lower frequency of you, a less awake you, wants you to be less. Again note: This being fully conscious is not about being medically conscious, as once you are out beyond your biological brain and body, your SELF, your personal consciousness is not medically anything. Begin training your consciousness now to know it can survive and not be absorbed.

EXERCISE #36.2
CLEANSING YOUR SENSE OF DARKNESS

There is no specific set of instructions for this exercise past the following, after which you are on your own. Be creative.

Close your eyes. Attempt to identify your personal consciousness. Get to know what this looks and feels like to you. Be your personal consciousness. ... Take your time. Remember, your consciousness is not your physical body, or your daily life, or even your emotions about your life.

Once you have some sense of your actual SELF, your personal consciousness, scan the space around it. Scan for what you think of as darkness or problem energy, for even the slightest traces of darkness or problem energy. Also scan for even the faintest hints of entry ways that could be, or have been, used, by this darkness or problem energy.

Now cleanse the space around your personal consciousness, clear this space of any darkness or problem energy.

You may want to continue to do this both here and BEYOND. Do this as long as you exist as your actual SELF, as your personal

consciousness--as long as you, YOUR ACTUAL SELF AS YOUR
PERSONAL CONSCIOUSNESS, choose to continue to exist
through all your transitions, to DIE AND SURVIVE as your SELF.

37
KNOWING THE ESCORTS

> ...They could manufacture
> for us angels and gods
> to bring us liberation.

> St. Augustine
> *The Confessions*

No, you are not alone out there. This is good to know. There are likely companions, guides, escorts of some sort both here and BEYOND.

THE IDEA OF ESCORTS

So, let's talk about the idea of the escort. However, before we begin, note that some Readers have written to this author and referred to Earthly "escort services" as being similar. Clearly, this is not what this book is talking about. Still, we can see here that there are times in life and in seeming death, and perhaps even in after life, when some companionship or guidance along the way may be very helpful and even powerfully comforting.

Many dying people tell of seeing deceased family members, even ancestors, or others such as angels and spirits, gathering around them, some waiting for them at death's door or at the gates to the BEYOND. Many people who have had *near* death experiences and returned to tell about these, speak of guiding beings appearing either visually or vocally or in some other

form. Some of those who have had *near* death experiences tell of these beings saying to them to go back into their physical bodies and not physically die yet.

Whether or not there is an actual helping hand or guide coming in as we enter the next dimension of our journey, as we "die," as some will call it, if the escort is safe and comforting for us, this can be a wonderful presence. Does it matter whether the escort is a product of the imagination or an actual being? Can we really say there is a difference, that there is a distinction, once we are out there BEYOND? Do we need new words (or concepts) for what is real and not real once we are out there? Our moving on and surviving means we are entering more fully into the *realms of our consciousness* where *what may be sensed as being real and sensed as being the imagined may not be so distinctly different*. What may be most important to us is that real or imagined, safe and comforting guidance or comfort or companionship is there for us, whether we create it or it finds us.

ESCORTS ARE HERE

Escorts may appear right before, during, and after any in-life and or seeming end-of-life transition. In daily physical plane Earth life, escorts may take the form of people around you, maybe people you know, or others who are there to assist, advise, or guide you.

However, even in daily life, there may be less visible escorts, people, or beings seeming to be in the background, or maybe in the forefront, but perhaps vaguely visible or even invisible to the Human biological eye. Some Readers may call these

angels, or ancestors, or spirit guides, or give other names to these beings. It is entirely up to you, Reader, whether you feel there are such presences and whether you have descriptions of these.

During any transition, including that of physical dying and death, you may find yourself noticing, sensing, what appear to be energy presences, or changes, or developments, or openings--seemingly alive doors or windows to options and passageways. These can be sensed as being portals of various forms, and or the living membranes covering (or at times disguising) portals.

SOMETIMES THERE IS A PRESENCE

Sometimes there does seem to be the coming in of a presence, and sometimes this presence is waiting at the opening or gateway of some place or space.

At the entry to many a portal, there may appear to be waiting for you one or more presences or beings or ambassadors or escorts. Again, these concepts are not well defined by physical plane experiences. Thus words barely describe these presences or beings, or even what the presence of beings is like. Still, the idea of portals and of the presences around them is something you may for now imagine or visualize based on physical plane imagery.

Get to know these guides for your spirit, for your soul, for your SELF. Imagine that these exist, and develop them in your mind's eye or your imagination. Walk with them in daily life, make them real to you, at least real enough that when you later

want them, they are easier to call. You will know these escorts better later when you may want to call them to you.

If you have ever had an imaginary friend as many children do, or a spirit guide of some sort in adult life, you may have some experience with forming the sense of having an escort or guide or companion. If so, call on these experiences to generate escorts you can get to know well for later times when you may feel you need them.

Whether or not you have had any in-life experience with, or imagination of, such guides or escorts, you may still find these guides, these escorts, appearing at the time of your dying, or of your death, or of your moving BEYOND, even travel BEYOND.

You will sense or even see these presences, these escorts, in whatever visual and philosophical language works for you. You are likely to register these escorts as life forms, frequently as humanoid spirits, or guides. Many times, our previous religious or philosophical training defines these for us, whether or not these definitions are quite accurate. Escorts may appear to you to be angels, or other beings seeming either to be semi-material or made entirely of Light.

Many of these escorts or essences may be presences, (forms of) *consciousness matrices,* who may even make it their work to help usher beings into and through transitions such as death transitions. You may have experienced transitions in your life (or in someone else's life) that seem to have escorts coming in. This may have been vague, faintly sensed, or perhaps even quite clear to you. Some escorts may be described as

ambassadors of the Light, coming to shine Light into your passage, directing you toward the highest idea of Light you can imagine for your SELF.

EXAMINE AND DISCERN

However, examine the company you find there before you choose to keep it.

Amidst (what can be) the profound disorientation of physical (biological) death, a helping hand, or an escort on this journey, no matter what its motive, may be a welcome event or may be an unwanted intrusion. However, your accepting direction, assistance, comfort, and energy from a hand or an escort can be done with discernment. You can choose to sense, read, detect, as much as you can about your escorts and their intentions before accepting their guidance. (This is in essence also true in daily life.)

KEEP
YOUR OWN COUNSEL HERE

Know this: Many escorts are a great gift, this is certain. However, do note that not all escorts are your friends, no matter what they seem to be saying. Some of these escorts may even be opportunistic escorts out to commandeer or kidnap your energy, your consciousness, either for themselves or to guide it into the portal they guard or draw energy into. These are not ambassadors of the Light, although they may pose as such.

Keep your own counsel here. Discern: Not all beings dressed as Light or goodness or love are what they feel, seem, appear,

to be. Think about this sort of misrepresentation in daily life. Have you ever been told by someone that he or she was here to help you, and then find that you have been betrayed or deceived in some way by this person?

Wouldn't opportunism, deviousness, even malevolence, disguise itself as a good energy, a benevolence, or a benevolent being, to be accepted by a confused, disoriented, vulnerable, even lost, lonely, or fearful soul?

Out in the BEYOND, once out of the physical realm and physical body, keep in mind you can still discern. So, stay calm and detached if and when you meet an escort. There is no hurry to accept or decline the escort's offer of guidance. Remember, time as you have known it is gone. Take as long as you want to decide what type of energy you are seeing.

A WORD ABOUT
MANTRAS FOR
DISCERNMENT AND PROTECTION

There are many ways to check out the nature of an imagined or actual escort, guide, or presence of some sort. One quite powerful way is the use of a mantra. A mantra is a chant, quite often described as a sacred saying, containing rhythmic, and or musical, and or poetic sounds--perhaps seemingly spiritual, religious, and or esoteric. Mantras are indeed often found embedded in the teachings of various ancient and modern religions. However, a mantra can be of use to you whether or not it has a spiritual or religious or esoteric meaning for you. Also note, not all mantras have words. Some are simply repeating sounds, tones, rhythms.

It is good to practice, and memorize, and apply mantras in daily life. This can help you to feel prepared when you find yourself facing stresses, or challenges, or going through any profound in-life, or seeming end-of-life, or so-called after-life transition, or other inter-dimensional situations.

For, it is at the time of (right before and during) *dimensional transition* that escorts may be most obviously available to guide you or direct your energy. (Remember—any shift in your reality is a form of dimensional transition, and dimensional transition is a type of shift or death.)

Whether these escorts are a product of your mind, or of your consciousness, or are actual escorts, is not entirely on point. In this reality you have entered during this transition, these domains of sensation and perception and reality overlap.

It can be quite beneficial to have practiced centering yourself and staying centered during your physical plane life. Now, as part of centering yourself, and your actual SELF, do your best to select or create a mantra that you feel comfortable with. To feel comfortable with a mantra:

- Choose a mantra (such as a tune or verse or saying or chant or song) with which you are quite familiar; and/or,

- Choose or create a mantra of your own that you can memorize easily or already know by heart.

- Test the mantra you choose by repeating it many times. Be certain that you have a mantra that you feel good

237

about. This mantra must seem to you to exude a positivity, even goodness, as you repeat it.

- Also test your mantra for protection. You can feel protected as you repeat your mantra. This protection can feel like an invisible shield. The more you repeat this mantra, the more protective your shield can feel.

- Test the shield your mantra forms. Nothing but the idea of the most clear Light should be able to come through this shield. Your mantra should not let in troubled patterns, old cordings, other material plane physical and emotional body stuff. Leave behind or stay away from any muddy light, chaotic light, light that you do not trust, and any shadows, or shadow cords, and confusing strands of webs.

If your mantra and its shielding do not pass the above tests, notice this. If you are selecting and practicing your mantra in advance of your physical death process, you may want to choose and practice one or more other mantras.

As noted earlier, many individuals turn to the doctrines of the particular religions and or philosophies to which they have been exposed to find a mantra. Others turn to popular or folk chants or songs or poems. This is your decision.

Keep in mind that a familiar life raft may be more useful in surviving than a brand new life raft you have never used or known before needing it.

Yes, you can also compose your own mantra. Sometimes this is the best option, as the words or sounds (words are not

necessary) or rhythms of your composed mantra may carry less history.

You may want to invent sounds and words, to invent a language and perhaps even a rhythm, in order to create a very easy to be remembered and personalized, clean, fresh mantra. Experiment until you find a mantra with which you are confident.

EXERCISE #37.1
DEVELOPING YOUR OWN MANTRA

Develop your own mantra. Find something you feel good repeating. Keep it simple, easy to remember, and easy to repeat.

Do not feel bound to a single language, to a known language, or to known words. You can make up sounds, or even a tune or song.

Practice your own mantra in silence, silently/internally for several minutes. Then chant or sing it aloud for several minutes. Later, perhaps again practice this quietly, perhaps even silently. Can you make this mantra your own?

Always keep in mind that: if a mantra you feel drawn to, or a mantra that is being suggested to you, or one you invent, feels in any way improper, do not use it. A mantra cannot work for you if you do not feel it suits you. Seek mantras that you feel you can use and remember.

EXERCISE #37.2
APPLYING THE KADOISH MANTRA

Let's take a moment to look at another mantra. Many view the following mantra as the most, or one of the most, powerful mantras in the Universe.

Kadoish, Kadoish, Kadoish, Adonoi Tsabayothe. (This is written this way here to help with pronounciation; however, you can pronounce this in the way you choose.)

This means "Holy, Holy, Holy, is the Lord God of Hosts" in the most ancient of Ancient Hebrews. The phrase "Lord God of Hosts" refers to the Lord, or highest energy of Light, of all the Hosts or angels or agents of Creation. This is just one of many mantras that you can find in the various religious scriptures in oral history and or in print on Earth. Many believe this mantra is also used beyond Earth.

This mantra is offered here for your experiential practice, as this mantra is frequently viewed by some as being the "maha mantra," the "highest mantra of mantras," the "keynote mantra," the "heartbeat" of all Creation.

Kadoish, Kadoish, Kadoish, Adonoi Tsabayothe.

Now, slowly, repeat this mantra several times, or if you prefer, repeat another mantra of your choice. As you do, imagine or actually have a drum beat sounding to give rhythm to your chanting. Or, you may want to use a quiet tapping to give rhythm to this.

Kadoish, Kadoish, Kadoish, Adonoi Tsabayothe.

Establish a slow and steady rhythm as you repeat this mantra, or one you have chosen.

As you do, pull this rhythm into the heart area of your body. Imagine or actually shift your heartbeat to this rhythm. Become this mantra by filling your physical and then emotional and then mental body with it.

Kadoish, Kadoish, Kadoish, Adonoi Tsabayothe.

Visualize that this mantra is helping you to form a pulsing shield of protection around yourself.

ESCORTS WITHOUT SHAPE

Let's return to the idea of the escort. Remember, if you feel yourself accompanied at the gateway, at the portal, at the membrane to the next dimension, if you feel yourself escorted, the escort will most likely take the form that your religious, philosophical, scientific, or ideological training has described to you. The escort you believe in is the one you may be most likely to see, or *to feel that you see or sense.*

From the standpoint that you create your own reality, you will be creating your own escort, or at least your own description of your escort. This escort will then be, at least to some degree, a piece of yourself, of your imagination, of your higher SELF, or perhaps of your culturally-trained self if you are still living in a physical body. This sense of an escort joining you may also depend on where you are in your various in-life transition, or seeming end-of-life death and dying, or after-life ascension BEYOND processes.

Note that not all escorts have a particular shape. In fact, some escorts are so formless that it is a challenge for you to recognize their presence, even if they are already at work on (or for) you. Some formless escorts are merely *frequency bodies or clouds.* Some are *subtle presences* that can, even without being detected, speak to you or guide you, perhaps at times even

magnetize or even mesmerize you, long before you become aware of them.

Your ability to see without eyes, to detect the presence and nature of non-physical energies, will assist you in your detection and discernment of these.

Are there escorts out there? Are there escorts outside your imagination of them? Whatever the case may be, if you choose to sense, see, recognize escorts, you will recognize them. Remember of course that: both those escorts coming to you from outside of you, and those who are coming to you as your own idea of an escort -- can fool you, so always KEEP YOUR OWN COUNSEL:

Examine what is coming to you from outside of you as well as from within. Know that, frequently what is coming from within appears to be coming from outside, and vice versa. This is why *your having a sense of your actual boundaries, of the boundaries of your actual SELF*, is important. These boundaries of your actual self can be formed and recognized on both your outside and your inside realms.

Again, this is not calling for paranoia. This is calling for conscious awareness, both here and beyond.

KNOW US IF YOU CHOOSE

Escorts are simply energies, energies with varied characteristics, who you can imagine, or sense, or recognize, or call to yourself, who can or may even seek to guide you in varied ways.

For example, hear this as a concept: Imagine this or something like this is described in the following exercise. A note before you begin. This is a creative experiment, a way for you to take a moment and explore or imagine possibilities of great beauty BEYOND. Given that your experience here and BEYOND takes place in your own consciousness, as you ascend into non-material dimensions, you may find you have all the more power to design your own realities.

EXERCISE #37.3
FREELY HEARING AND DISCERNING
THE CALL TO HIGHEST LIGHT

Imagine that you hear a calling, somewhere beyond words. Imagine something like this being spoken to you in wordless ways:

We are some of your escorts. We call ourselves Metalux, of the Divine TRRR-STRRRTT XULATEM Hierarchy. We are speaking to you because we are now escorting your personal consciousnesses through the dimensions of your actual SELF, and of your transitions including death transitions—we do this with every word here on these pages and between these lines.

You can choose to recognize our presence as you see or hear or read us here. You can choose to feel us right next to you if you like. We do not insist that you recognize us. Choose to or not to, of your own Free Will.

The only portal you will find us guarding is that portal of the highest purest Light. Even there, you are not compelled to join us. Even if you join us, we encourage you not to surrender your personal consciousness, not to die. There is still so much for you to do and be as your SELF.

YOU, YOUR ACTUAL SELF, HAS NO REASON TO DIE YET, AND EVERY REASON TO SURVIVE BEYOND.

You will know us when you meet us, when you sense us. We do not pull on you. We cannot and do not allow anyone to join us, unless this is of that being's own Free Will. Therefore we neither hypnotize nor magnetize. You can and you best choose your path for yourself, when you feel you are in the right use of your own Will.

Of course, we do not admit old cords and attachments. Free yourself of these before joining us.

Clarify your consciousness in order to see us as keepers of the Light — by your own definition of highest Light. Believe in us or not. Create, project, the reality which is most useful to you, as you navigate your own life here and BEYOND, and in all your transitions and deaths, of your own Free Will.

Call upon us if you need us. Simply say or think, invoke....

Trrr-Sttrrrrttt Nadann-dadan-dah

Fiat Meta-Lux

Let there be the highest Light.

****

38
PROTECTING THE SELF
IN THE EYES OF
INTERDIMENSIONAL LAW

> How does one determine when a law
> is just or unjust? A just law is a man-
> made code which squares with the
> moral law or the law of God. An
> unjust law is a code that is out of
> harmony with the moral law.
>
> Martin Luther King, Jr.
> *Letter from the Birmingham Jail*

We have been discussing the detection, discernment, and
recognition of appropriate energies, perhaps even presences,
perhaps even escorts. This awareness is essential as you move
through both physical plane and BEYOND physical plane
transitions—as you traverse dimensions of your reality, of your
actual SELF. Once you are able to sense (and even define for
yourself) energies, and what you may sense are presences, you
will want to protect yourself if and when you feel the need.

Defining for yourself your own boundaries, both in the
physical plane and BEYOND, is key in your *dying and surviving*,
in your surviving as your actual SELF. That old almost fairy
tale saying, *remember who you are*, can be extended here to say,
remember not only who you are, but even more basically,

245

THAT you are, that you are your actual SELF and can remain this, can survive.

Remember, the rules are rather different out there in other dimensions. If you do choose to survive physical death, to *die and survive*, you move on as your personal consciousness, your actual SELF. You move on even when you have no physical body. As you do this, as you begin to move into, expand into, other dimensions of your SELF, you will sense the differences in your reality. You will see that your reality is expanding, *which is actually your awareness of your reality that is expanding.*

What you will find out when you leave your physical body is that some things do not work quite the way things appear to work in the 3-D material plane. Rules are different. So, do not expect anything that you have previously looked to for controls and regulations to be present out there. For example, the legal systems, social norms, and moral codes such as religious commandments, used on the 3-D physical Earth plane to perhaps guide and even protect you, are not present beyond this 3-D plane. (As this chapter suggests, there is likely another level of law to know about BEYOND.)

PROTECTION WHEN, WHERE, AND WHAT

Of course, physicality offers some degree of physical protection. However, sometimes, no matter how well protected is the physical body, it is not fully protected. Also sometimes, no matter how well protected we are in physicality, we may or may not be as well protected BEYOND physicality. This is where even daily physical plane life can teach us so much. For example, here on physical plane Earth, we Humans know that

being physically safe may not be being emotionally safe. Being shielded on one level may not be being shielded on another.

Protecting the personal consciousness, the actual SELF, as it transitions (both in-life and BEYOND life) involves awareness and focus. Death is not death, it is the *dimensional expansion experience*. And, the dimensional expansion experience may leave some beings who are not at least somewhat aware of what is taking place, rather vulnerable, even perhaps exposed to what may be false lights, false lures, energy sinks, even energy predators.

THERE IS, AND CAN BE, A BEYOND

If the BEYOND is not entirely non-existent, there will be some pattern or system of some sort out there.

Let's say there really is something out there, a place for us to go live when we die, when we leave our physical bodies. Let's say there really is a BEYOND we can imagine, define, develop, and then move ourselves into when we die a physical death --- even without the spaceships and physical travel into space so popular on Earth at this time.

Let's also say that if there is not already this BEYOND already formed for us, already there in the realm of our own personal consciousness, we can choose to form this BEYOND now, to prepare it for ourselves for the time when we may want to enter it.

(Of course, the seeming space ships coming out of NASA and various other Earth government and Earth corporation programs, are not providing passage to realms where we can

go AND SURVIVE when our physical bodies die. So Earth-based so-called space travel is still a physical plane project, even when off Earth.)

Let's get back to considering the BEYOND we enter through our own personal consciousness. Whether or not you believe this BEYOND is there for you, let's say you can develop this BEYOND, your own BEYOND.

Where this BEYOND does not yet exist for us, we can create this BEYOND for ourselves. This is certainly one of the goals of these *How To Die And Survive* books. So many people on Earth buy themselves burial plots in advance of their physical deaths. Yet, for some reason they do not prepare their space, their own domain to move into as a personal consciousness when they leave their physical bodies.

Readers, this book is about getting ready to survive, to die and then survive. The first step in doing this is knowing that you can. This awareness itself may begin to open the door to the survival of you, of your actual SELF.

THERE IS
SOMETHING OUT THERE

Once we move our thoughts to what is out there, what is BEYOND, we have a range of ideas about this. According to many people, there is something out there, and there are even rules for getting to be out there, for surviving to be out there, and laws to follow along the way. Many people say there is one supreme law here and BEYOND. Some will call this God's or Creator's law, a given higher moral code.

However, without our applying any one philosophical or religious interpretation here, for simplicity's sake, this book suggests we look BEYOND for *an interdimensional code, some form of interdimensional law*. This chapter of this book is just an opening definition of, and conversation on, what is here being defined as *interdimensional law*. This definition and discussion is continued in other books in this *Keys To Consciousness And Survival Series*.

You will come to learn more about this concept of *interdimensional code and law* as you move your awareness, your focus, to and from the non-material (and or less material) dimensions of your own reality.

THINK ABOUT
PROTECTION BEYOND

Think about moving BEYOND. At first, you may have a sense of being unshielded, perhaps vaguely aware of an energetic vulnerability. You may come to sense in some way that you have been stripped of physical plane protections such as Earth-based legal and moral codes, even of the protection you felt you had while living in a physical body.

Back down on the physical plane on Earth, we have police forces and courts of law to at least try to protect us. What is there BEYOND? Is that space out there a wild west of uncontrolled explorers and opportunists, and of the many dead people trying to survive?

Once out of your physical body, you may briefly feel like a stranger in a strange land. This will pass. (See note at the end of this chapter.)

However confusing the unshielded sensation may at first seem, this unshielded sense will change as you begin to get your bearings. As your awareness of your new reality increases, new sensations can emerge. These include new awareness that there is a code, an inter-dimensional code out there. And where there is not a code, you can help build one as you consciously move into that domain, the domain of your own consciousness where you do already live. Remember, this is your own kingdom.

SENSING PROTECTION

Certainly, as we move out of our physical body, out of our physical plane existence, we may sense a want for protection. Indeed, protection as you travel the dimensions of your reality, of your SELF, of your personal consciousness, is there for you.

*Sensitize yourself to your options in advance. Start to understand this now: **There are many methods of protecting the essence of your actual SELF as you move through major transitions in physicality, emotionality, density, even dimensionality itself where you leave the physical body and move BEYOND.***

Among these methods of protection are:

1) Coming to terms with the elusive nature of your reality.

2) Demarking boundaries of your own and others' personal consciousness-es.

3) Perceiving your own and others' presences and their natures.

4) Visualizing and applying shields for your personal consciousness as you move near or through:

a) your own and other presences' and their membranes;

b) your own and others' layers of density;

c) your own and others' degrees of lessening and or changing physicality,

d) your own and others' degrees of increasing non-physicality.

5) Detecting the shields of your own and others, as well as weaknesses, flaws, or cracks in these shields.

6) Conducting applications of Light to boundary and shield protections.

COME TO TERMS

Come to terms with the existence of life forms beyond those you already know. Whether or not you believe in the existence of what feel to be undesirable entities, or negatively inclined intelligences, even predators, understand that *your perception of these beings, whether imagined or real, is what you must deal with.*

In this sense, the first interdimensional law you encounter is the law you define, form, for yourself.

Therefore, if you even faintly (consciously or even subconsciously) sense or firmly believe that you are in the presence of problematic factors or negative energies, you must deal with your perceptions of these presences.

Do something with your perception when you find that you are confronted with real or imagined problem presences. Use

methods described below, and methods you develop for yourself, to feel shielded from them. Practice methods of shielding yourself from them. It is suggested that you begin practicing now, in daily life. This is good exercise for your personal consciousness, for the SELF who survives both here and BEYOND.

Basically, knowing that you can indeed protect your non-physical SELF is the first level protection.

FIRST LEVEL OF
PROTECTION IS KNOWING

What this involves is knowing that you can survive, that you have survived, that you, your actual self, still exists.

Of course, you must know that you exist so that you know to protect your existence, to protect your SELF.

Frequently, people who have recently died do not realize they still exist, do not realize they have survived.

The purpose of these *How To Die And Survive* and *Keys To Consciousness And Survival* books is to allow for this realization to take place both here and beyond. You can know this now for future reference.

IT IS YOUR RIGHT
TO DIE AND SURVIVE.

MEETING OTHER PRESENCES OUT THERE

Many other presences and intelligences out there BEYOND may not see that you know you can *die and survive.* As you become aware that you have died and survived, presences that approach you will also become aware.

When you sense another presence is approaching you, you can respond. Indeed, even before you leave your physical body, you may want to practice methods of inviting other energies to join what you feel is the highest clearest energy or Light. This does take practice.

Certainly, you may be changing your reality by doing this. You are basically *changing your own perception of your own reality.* In doing this, you are changing yourself in a way that does not let what you feel to be real or imagined problem presences near your energetic field, or at least not without clarification and shielding, also perhaps cleansing.

This may seem to you who are living in physical plane bodies a rather vague process. This all makes more sense once you have shed your physical body and its given blindness to your full interdimensional nature. You are presently dealing with the physical plane's rather problematic definition of reality:

**What may seem unreal in one dimension of reality
may seem quite real in another.**

You may continue to wonder: Are these undesirable presences who threaten the SELF or the soul real or not "real"? De-emphasize "real." The word real takes on vastly different dimensions as you expand your reality BEYOND to include the different dimensions, and to understand that *multi-dimensionality is the cosmic plasma in which you truly travel.*

You do not just live in your "here" right now, you also already live "out there" beyond physicality. *At the same time, both here and BEYOND, you live in the body or matrix of your personal consciousness.*

While of course, you must organize your thoughts a certain way to live in physical plane reality, things change once you are no longer a physical plane being. It is a little like learning to speak a new language to travel to a new country. Here , you are learning in advance to have a new sense of your SELF and of your reality for the time when you travel BEYOND.

DEMARK BOUNDARIES OF THE SELF

Protect your actual SELF, your personal consciousness and its energy matrix, when it is confronted with energies which may, or at least may seem to, jeopardize it.

First, separate your sense of your actual SELF from what you perceive as being a threat to your personal matrix, or energy, or soul (however you define this for yourself). Externalize the seemingly outside, perhaps seemingly threatening, presence. Make it be outside of you. Deal with it as a separate energy arrangement.

Keep in mind that an invading or encroaching matrix or energy pattern may work to have you feel that it is part of you, to have you confuse your boundaries with its boundaries, your identity with its identity, so that you do not perceive it as an outside energy that should not be confused with your SELF. (Refer to the book, *Seeing The Hidden Face Of Addiction: Detecting And Confronting This Invasive Presence*, where **boundary confusion** and **identity confusion** are discussed in depth. Also see *Volume*

3 in this *Keys To Consciousness And Survival Series*, titled, *Unveiling The Hidden Instinct*.)

*Second, once you have drawn a boundary between your actual SELF and a seemingly encroaching or threatening presence, recognize that your awareness of this presence is essential. See that you are potentially vulnerable to effects of other presences and matrices out there. Inform yourself that this presence is perceived as threatening by the part of you that might let it in <u>while mistaking it for being part of you</u>. Understand that when confused about your own boundaries, you may be vulnerable to questionable energies that disguise themselves as friendly, <u>or even disguise themselves as **you**</u>.*

Deal with any imagined or actual presence by being aware of this presence and of its possible effects on you. You are *protecting your actual SELF, your own personal consciousness matrix.* Many people have not been trained to do this in advance of any transition, let alone physical death. Thus, they have had neither the luxury nor the opportunity to be trained in the definition and examination of their own consciousness and its boundaries, let alone those of others.

Physical lifetimes often feel too busy to take time for such introspection. Still, regardless of training, you can protect your personal matrix, your personal consciousness, during any in-life or seeming end-of-life transition. You can shield yourself from unwelcome presences, by not welcoming them, not by merging with them, instead by defining and protecting your own boundaries with awareness.

PERCEIVE PRESENCES

The task of becoming aware of non-physical presences is both immense and simple. It is like turning a corner: Now you do not see or sense them, now you do. *Imagination can guide you into awakened sensitivity.* Just allow yourself to imagine a presence any time you seriously sense the possibility that you are in the presence of a presence other than your own.

This does not mean that you are in that presence; however, this allows you to sense more of what is out there. This lets you explore this possibility, *to sensitize your SELF to the difference between your SELF and other presences*. (At the same time, allow yourself to get to know and recognize your own presence.)

This is an <u>essential sensitization</u> to begin practicing now while living in a physical body. As obvious as this seems, as simple as it may feel to tell the difference between yourself and someone else, the energy arrangements, even the consciousness matrices, of others can overlap, even mesh with, even merge with, even subsume, your own. This can take place without you fully sensing or realizing this is taking place.

VISUALIZE AND APPLY SHIELDS

This is not about being paranoid. This is simply about being wisely alert. Your awareness is your protection and your navigation.

Whether or not you sense presences in your vicinity, imagine that you can prepare for the presence of possible presences. Imagine that you can manufacture or grow a membrane, a sort of semi-permeable membrane or cell wall, around your personal energy arrangement, your personal consciousness

256

matrix, yes, around your SELF. Think of this wall as a thinking, discerning shield, one that allows selected energy or Light to enter while refusing entry to anything but what is discerned and desired.

DETECT CRACKS IN SHIELDS

Be aware of the condition of all your boundaries, of all your shielding membranes (of your own cell walls, skins and surfaces, as well as of your other physical and nonphysical boundary-shields).

Pressure of all kinds, unknown energies, waves of radiation, all sorts of variations in the atmosphere, can wear down or even wear a hole or crack in your energy shield. By spotting these and sealing your SELF, your shield, perhaps with what you can visualize as a glue made of Light, you are protecting yourself.

APPLY LIGHT

And so, again and again, the application of the idea of the clearest, highest, brightest Light or energy you can imagine or see, is essential. Start right now and never ever stop applying your concept of the most radiant and most clear Light. This is your means of seeing and seeking clear and clean energies here and BEYOND.

VOICE
INVITATION TO THE LIGHT

Invocation is the method of pulling an idea, or a thought form about an event, force, or presence, into your reality from beyond what appears to be your immediate reality.

For example, think of invoking Light. You can invoke the Light. Yes, you can. Just invite the idea, your own idea, of Light to come in. Or better yet, see that the highest, clearest, idea of Light is always present and say so: "The Light is here. Here is the Light, my idea of, my vision of, the highest clearest Light."

EXERCISE #38.1
PROTECTING THE SELF

Imagine yourself to be floating in a bubble. Imagine the bubble wall to be a sort of second skin for you. Think about the purpose of your skin. Begin with your physical skin. Your first skin, the physical skin, you have all along the boundary of your physical body's flesh. This skin is made of skin cells that absorb some elements and Light rays from the atmosphere and reject others. You are physically protected by this physical skin.

Now you are aware of your second skin, which is out beyond your first skin. This second skin is the skin of your emotional body. This skin lines the boundary of your emotional body. As skins do, this skin attempts to allow in only desirable energies and Lights. Imagine that your second skin shrinks and expands as you breathe. With your emotional body's skin, you seek to shield yourself from unwanted or detrimental or dangerous emotional material coming from outside yourself (or working its way into you, then coming from inside yourself).

Now imagine that there is another still larger bubble surrounding your second skin. This is your third skin. This is the skin protecting your mental body, and with it your personal consciousness, your SELF. Remember that your mental body seems far larger than your emotional body, and yes, your mental body is indeed far more expansive.

In fact, it is a good idea to expand the mental body as far past the emotional body as possible. Begin now. See the larger, outer bubble, the third skin, expand. As you see this expansion, you hold your physical size steady and you hold the size of your second skin, the emotional body bubble around your emotional body, steady. You are far more vast than your physical and emotional bodies.

Always be aware of the existence of your second and third skins, that of your emotional body and then that of your mental body. Always be conscious of the health and functioning of these very important membranes. Stay with the imagery of these membranes for the next exercise.

EXERCISE #38.2
KNOWING THE MENTAL BODY

Move into the space between your second and third skins or membranes. Get to know this level of your SELF. Note how, outside of the second membrane, past the emotional body, you have a non-physical and unemotional personal consciousness.

This is where your actual SELF lives, this is actually YOU. In any transition, this is who can move through and continue on, can DIE AND SURVIVE.

Recognize the space outside of your emotional body skin, and still within your mental body skin. Stay in the space of your purely mental body for a while. Look back toward the skin of your emotional body. Now look outward toward the skin of your mental body.

Allow yourself to see how much sturdier your mental body skin is than your other skins (your physical and emotional body skins). This

is a good thing to know about your SELF. Recognizing your sturdy mental body skin is valuable in discerning.

Knowing you are present, that you live within your own mental body skin, helps you discern and clarify your own presence. *And, at the same time, being aware of your own mental body and its skin, and of your actual SELF who is in there, helps you to detect the nature of approaching energies and their seeming Lights, other presences around you who may be coming toward you or calling on you, or even pulling on you.*

Your mental body, being pure and free of emotion and physical sensation, discerns most effectively.

Note that: Once you are actually physically dead and already moving into the BEYOND, you will release your self to be your actual SELF. As you engage in the realizations of this and other exercises in this book, you will see how your lower mental body, with any remaining ties or cords to your old biological brain, will dissolve and free your higher mental body, actual SELF, of old attachments weighing it down. As this happens, your higher SELF becomes very aware of itSELF and all around it.

EXERCISE #38.3
PROTECTING THE CONSCIOUSNESS

At the skin of your mental body, attempt to do some of the activities described earlier in this chapter. Note what you do with ease and what you want to practice:

1) *Demark the boundaries of your actual SELF, your personal consciousness, your higher mental body;*
2) *Perceive external presences and the nature of these presences;*

3) *Allow the membrane of your mental body to shield you from undesirable presences and energies;*

4) *Detect cracks or weak points in your membrane and strengthen these areas;*

5) *Apply your own Light to your membrane;*

6) *If you seek to pull Light in from outside your SELF, invite—pull in—the clearest highest Light. After examining this Light, if this Light is what it represents itself as being, allow this Light in through the filter of your protective skin or membrane.*

INTRODUCING
INTERDIMENSIONAL LAW

Once you move out of the constricting limitations of the material plane, you may find the concepts of rights, justice, power, and truth to be far more fluid and yet far more critical.

Become aware of this *How To Die And Survive* notion which this book explains: ***the notion of Interdimensional Law***. Notice how even the idea of such law seems foreign to many who live in the physical plane. It is as if our awareness of this law, and of our rights out there BEYOND, have been suppressed or blocked.

Whether this blocking of our knowledge, of our rights, and of our awareness of inter-dimensional law, has taken place as a result of accident, or of natural evolution, or of intentional interference and implant into our coding, we still must become aware of this. (See other books in this series for more on this coding and possible interference, especially *Volumes 5 and 6*, titled, *Overriding The Extinction Scenario, Parts One and Two.*)

For the most part, this interdimensional law is an *ancient body of interstellar understanding and even law* that is forgotten by beings who are faced with biological reality and with the challenges of daily life and social relations in the third dimension, physical plane, on Earth.

What is most important to know as you are gaining or *regaining* a feel for interdimensional law is that:

- You have a *right* to perceive and expand into your own multi-dimensional reality. This is your territory, the realm of your own personal consciousness.

- You are protected by the laws of Light and consciousness. You activate this protection by becoming truly aware of your own idea of Light and of your own personal consciousness.

The concept, vision, and actuality of **interdimensional justice** is naturally activated by **interdimensional awareness.**

****

Note: Some Readers may know of the Robert Heinlein's science fiction novel, *Stranger In A Strange Land*, the title of which draws from the *Bible*, Exodus, 2:22, "... I have been a stranger in a strange land." Heinlein's novel tells the story of a Human who was born on Mars, raised by Martians, and then later comes to Earth. Readers may also know of the 1942 debut novel by Nobel Prize winner, Albert Camus, titled *The Stranger*. See also the novel, *Revealing The Omega Key*, written by this author, Angela Brownemiller, where Camus is a fictional time traveling character, and where the narrator speaks of being a stranger in a strange land while engaging in interdimensional travel.

<u>39</u>
DYING WITH
YOUR OWN MEANING,
YOUR OWN PURPOSE

> What you sow does not
> come to life unless it dies.
>
> 1 Corinthians 15: 36
> *Holy Bible*

Only you can give your own death your own meaning and your own purpose. There is no one outside yourself who truly knows as well as you do what your own death will someday mean to you, what its purpose will someday be for you. Later, when dying a physical death, there may or may not be the opportunity to think this through, although many dying people do manage to do this.

Begin now, seeking in advance meaning and purpose in your life and in your eventual physical death. You may indeed find that among your purposes in living and dying is your surviving, is your being able to *die and survive.*

One of your greatest discoveries about your SELF may indeed be that you want to survive your death, to *die and survive.* You can begin to imagine what living BEYOND may be like. You do get ready for other major trips in your life, why not for your journey BEYOND?

CHERISHING THIS IMPORTANT PASSAGE

So many Readers of these *How To Die And Survive* books have lived lives where they at times felt they were not valued or cherished. This is so immensely painful to know. Yet, this is what so many Readers here say.

Readers, whatever your life experience has been to date, please know that this moment, this micro-second right here right now, can be a minor or major pivot point, an aha! moment. This is the moment when you can, even if just a bit, cherish your SELF, and value the brave journey of life and survival you are on.

Every moment matters,
even what may appear to be last moments.

Value your conscious exploration of the possibility of survival both here and BEYOND. This for many becomes the meaning and purpose of their lives as they start to understand or even to move toward physical death.

Understanding the reality of *dying and surviving* as a personal consciousness is central here.

Ideally, we can think in advance about the meaning and purpose of our eventual physical death process. Of course, this will be a constantly evolving sense of meaning and purpose. However, starting now, opening the passageways in the mind for the ideas of meaning and purpose creates a *trail of personal thought.*

THIS IS A PATHWAY FROM YOU TO YOUR SELF.

YOU CAN FORM THIS TRAIL NOW,

WITHIN THE REALM OF YOUR CONSCIOUSNESS, TO FIND THIS TRAIL LATER.

Seeking meaning and purpose in one's physical death can be a difficult topic where there is physical and emotional suffering. If, in an effort to comfort you, you are being told by a friend that your dying has meaning, see that the intent of this communication may be good. See also that the meaning of your dying is far more complex than can be communicated to you in a few words. These *How To Die And Survive* books, as do all books in this *Keys To Consciousness And Survival Series*, seek to imbue your personal consciousness with the understanding that:

You can give your SELF the ever increasing sense that your physical death is an important passage, and just one of many very important passages you travel.

You can cherish this important passage, treat it with great respect, whether or not the world around you understands this.

You can learn to ever more consciously navigate your transition and death processes.

Your preparation for your navigation of, and harvesting of, the energy built and released during your various transitions brings further meaning to all your minor and major transitions, including deaths.

This is true for any transition or death, including any in-life, seeming end-of-life, and beyond-life changes, endings, or deaths as you presently know these or imagine these.

You can choose to, or not choose to, give your minor and major transitions such as deaths great meaning. This is your option.

Whenever you find meaning in what you are doing, your personal consciousness is further formatting, designing, writing, adding to, your IDENTITY. Your personal consciousness is storing what you learn and can carry with you deep in your actual SELF, in your *personal consciousness matrix*. To allow yourself to *die and survive* with awareness, grace, and power, you must further develop your awareness of your minor and major transition and death processes. What do these transitions feel like?

> **How do you know you are entering a transition?**
>
> **What are the stages of this transition -- can you see the beginning, middle, and end?**
>
> **How conscious are you as you move through the transition?**
>
> **Are you able to care for yourself, to protect yourself, during this transition?**
>
> **Can you tell when you have moved to the next level or situation after this transition?**
>
> **What have you learned during this transition about moving through transition?**

Your increasing awareness is your increasing identity, your SELF becoming ever more aware of it SELF. Those of you who

have come page by page this far in these *How To Die And Survive* books and their exercises, likely do know this now.

Feel this meaning as fully as you can. Take the meaning in and make it your own. This may or may not lighten any ordeal you face. Yet, this will give you some sense of some power by instilling value in your process.

DYING PROCESS AS HEROIC

Your willingness to inquire into alternative perspectives on death, such as those provided in these *How To Die And Survive* books, is brave. Your commitment to retain your consciousness during your death, **to hold together your SELF, your personal consciousness matrix**, so that you can *die and survive*, is heroic. You can learn to direct for yourself your own dying and your own journey out of your old life. (See more on this in *Volume 10* in this series, titled, *Seeing Beyond Our Line Of Sight*, where survival is further discussed.)

Dying with awareness of one's personal consciousness, and its survival, is heroic. People around may tend to frown on those who speak of themselves as heroes. This may be considered arrogant, SELF-aggrandizing. What must be said here is that it is not aggrandizing or arrogant to have the SELF, your actual SELF, survive. This IS survival, your survival here and BEYOND.

The public acknowledgment of what is heroic about oneself is socially discouraged in many cultures. Yet, the *personal heroic awareness* is a valuable sensation in survival settings.

Let's not evaluate such social taboos against openly describing oneself as a hero. Rather, let us insist that your dying, just because it is your dying, is an heroic act. This does <u>not</u> mean that wild and crazy extremes are heroic, or that hysterical suicide is heroic. This <u>does</u> mean that:

1) Your entry into a dying process, whether it is a living death – such as a major move, a divorce, a career change, a shift in religious orientation, or another life transition – or a physical death, is a powerful event. This is YOUR event.

2) Your brave and conscious exploration of what lies beyond the life you know is heroic.

3) Your willingness to face what you are seeing approaching, to hold on to your SELF, your stream of personal consciousness, during your in-life transitions, and also during your journey BEYOND the death of your old life, is heroic.

4) Your willingness to detach where needed, such as emotionally, from whatever you are attached to (love, pleasure, hate, etc.) in order to transition, even die, ever more consciously is heroic.

5) Your willingness to examine the terrain, the escorts as well as the other presences and forces in daily life as well as in the BEYOND, is heroic.

6) Your ever more aware, ever more conscious, identification, strengthening, and preservation of

your own Free Will, as you live, and even as you die a physical death and elevate-ascend, is heroic.

7) Your decision to exercise your right to *die and survive* is heroic, and of course is survival.

THE DYING PROCESS AND ITS AWARENESS IS HEROIC IN ITSELF

Heroic dying is basically ever more *conscious transition*, is dying with awareness, grace, and power. Remember here that being conscious may or may not be being medically conscious, as we are saying that the SELF that survives is not a biological thing. The level of conscious awareness here is beyond what we say it is in our daily lives. With these *How To Die And Survive* books, with these concepts, discussions, and exercises, we are preparing our consciousness-es to know what they can know as they later move BEYOND.

So the heroism referred to here is an awareness. This is an aware clarity and Force of Will which you can find, even bravely generate. You can begin building this awareness as you live your daily life. You can stand up to *the efforts of your mind and of the minds of others to hold you back* from SURVIVING. It is not that people you know do not want you to survive. It is not that you do not want to survive. However, you may not have been presented with the option and the technology to *die and survive* as discussed in these *How To Die And Survive* books.

Facing this process as aware of this *How To Die And Survive Technology* as possible, allows for the shifting of your SELF to other locations within your own realm of your own

269

consciousness — AND THUS ALLOWS FOR YOUR SURVIVAL.

EXERCISE #39.1
BUILDING ONE'S HEROIC

This is a simple exercise with powerful implications. This is about getting in touch with the heroic sensation.

Close your eyes. Think of something that you or someone else has done that is generally accepted as being heroic. If you cannot remember a heroic act, imagine one, such as rescuing a child from a burning building, risking your life to save a person drowning in a rough sea, or something else that you think you or society or both would consider heroic.

Now, with your eyes still closed, see yourself as the hero committing the heroic act you have selected. Watch the event as if it were a movie. Watch the event again and again.

As you watch yourself doing something heroic, feel the chain of feelings you might be feeling were you committing this heroic act right now.

HEROISM

Heroism is a sense of personal strength and potency, and more. Some of the heroic sensations that can be generated in the exercise above and in actual heroic acts include:

- A strong sense of alertness;

- A surge of energy;

- A clear yet frequently rapid thinking about how to proceed, or even a rapid automatic moving through a process, and,

- The ability to push one's fear out of the way, or to not feel one's fear as much, or to automatically override fear, to prioritize past the typical SELF-protective emotions.

EXERCISE #39.2
BRINGING OUT POST-HEROIC SENSATIONS

See yourself completing the heroic act you envisioned in Exercise #39.1. Complete the act several times in order to clearly note what sort of "post-heroic sensations" you might experience after an act such as this.

EXPERIENCING WAVES

As you conclude an heroic act, you may experience feelings such as:

- A rush of relief;

- A sense of calm after the storm;

- A continuing energetic, emotional, spiritual, and or other physical or emotional high;

- A continuing alertness;

- A strong wave of approval coming at you from an actual or imagined crowd which may have seen or have heard about your heroism;

- A deep appreciation from whomever it is you have rescued, even if this is your SELF;

- A powerful sense that you can rise to meet a challenge, that you can pull through a catastrophe;

- A new kind of confidence in yourself, whether temporary or permanent.

These are useful sensations to have during what may be the trying passages just preceding or during your dying. As you die ever more consciously, know that you are heroically rescuing yourself from one reality (one dimension of your reality) and transitioning to another reality (another dimension of your reality). *You are delivering your consciousness into safety, into the safety of your SURVIVAL. You are ensuring that you DIE AND SURVIVE.*

So, when you transition (whatever the particular transition may be), then transition or die with the purpose of tapping into your own personal heroism. Remember, your sense of your own heroism may be fleeting, may come in and out, appear here and there, maybe last a moment or two, may be just a whisper. Or, your sense of your own heroism may be quite profound. However you feel your own heroic, this is yours to feel.

You are your own hero. This is your own quiet knowing. Take into your SELF this sense of your SELF, of you as your own heroic being, the one who has made this journey and survived. Carry this knowing of your own heroic-ness on into your journey BEYOND. Call this awareness back to your SELF later as you navigate the BEYOND, when you know to bring your

own heroic back into your awareness. You will hear your SELF reminding you....

Note that this sense of your own heroic-ness is not a SELF-aggrandizing heroism. In fact, the observation of your deep heroism may not necessarily be public at all.

What matters are <u>the effects of the transaction of heroism deep inside your consciousness</u>. Perhaps no one but you may know of this. It is still heroic.

What matters is that *you can create a design of yourself* – you can revise or develop your *personal consciousness matrix* – in such a way that you have a deeper, stronger confidence that you will, even in the face of the greatest unknowns and the most profound challenges, SURVIVE.

Why not register this knowledge deep within your SELF? Your consciousness, and your ability to direct your journey most heroically, will remain with you as long as you consciously choose to have it do so.

You can send your SELF a message that will later surface from deep within your personal consciousness: YOU CAN DIE AND SURVIVE as your ACTUAL SELF. This message will be you calling out to your SELF, sounding the reminder that you are not dying, you are surviving.

By *knowing your heroic SELF*, you can remain and in fact become increasingly free of the shackles of fear and personal limitation which have been programmed into you.

DIE TO

273

BREAK FREE OF PROGRAMMING

We may have been programmed to, on a deep unspoken level, think of ourselves as a life form that must die and *not* survive. We may have been programmed to be naively imprisoned in the material plane, and programmed to suffer material plane sufferings with no higher outcome. *We Humans will want to break free of this truth-suppressing programming.*[28]

You can use each and every one of your in-life and even seeming end-of-life physical transitions and deaths to further develop your Free Will. You can develop your Free Will enough to truly break free of the programming that may have walled off your full awareness.

This is about your full awareness:

- of the power of your actual SELF to survive;
- of the power of your own personal consciousness;
- of the hidden levels of your actual identity as an inter-dimensional being;
- *of your knowledge of who you truly are.*

Once you see the dying process as the opportunity to evolve your consciousness in the direction of increasing Free Will, of increasing **SELF-determination**, you will die with increasing purpose. At the right time then, ONLY WHEN IT IS TRULY TIME, you can DIE with the FREEDOM to SURVIVE.

---

[28] Refer to *Volume 3* in this *Keys To Consciousness And Survival Series*, titled, *Unveiling The Hidden Instinct*.

You are going to undergo many transitions, endings, and deaths in your life, and in your lifetimes, so why not make these transitions and deaths matter? Why not learn to ever more clearly *die and survive?*

40
SELF DELIVERANCE
IS NOT ABOUT SUICIDING

> ... Mee thinks I have the keys of my prison in mine owne hand, and no remedy presents it SELFe so soone to my heart, as mine own sword.
>
> John Donne
> *Biathanatos*

Delivering yourself is just this: the delivery of your SELF to your SELF, to your SELF who has been delivered and thus survived. This may remind some Readers of delivering a baby. This analogy is understandable, as moving beyond a transition is indeed moving to the other side or next level of one's existence: being born into the next stage or form of one's life. **In this sense, the care we use when delivering a baby is the care we want to use when delivering our SELF.**

Delivering the SELF is key in survival, especially when moving through major transitions. In any transition, especially major in-life or seeming end-of-life transition, the SELF can be weakened, or grow confused, or even get lost. When the transition is physical death, *deliverance of one SELF, the SELF as a consciousness, is survival.* Therefore, the deliverance concept is key in consciously dying and surviving.

Let's again be clear about this here: Whether or not a person is medically conscious, the person's consciousness can still be present. [Note: Many Readers report that they read (or play the audiobook versions of) this *How To Die And Survive* book, *Book Two*, and the previous *How To Die And Survive* book, *Book One*, and also *How To Die And Survive, Book Three*, to others who are said to be medically unconscious.] These books are speaking to the actual SELF, the one who can live beyond the biological brain, to the personal consciousness who can survive. (Readers are encouraged to re-read the *Foreword* to this book, where the survival of the consciousness beyond the death of the biological body and brain is discussed.)

GIVING BIRTH TO ONESELF

To deliver oneself into an adjustment of one's reality, or into a new dimension of one's reality, is indeed a giving of new birth to one's SELF. This is true whether in-life or seeming end-of-life transition is taking place. What a wonderful adventure to die and survive!

However, let's (again and again) be very clear here: this SELF-deliverance is not in any way about killing oneself, is not actual suicide, is NOT the "killing" of the physical body. Your deliverance is about your survival. Understand this distinction. Again, this discussion is not about death, this is about SURVIVAL.

Knowing when to focus on survival issues, and what survival issues are or can be, is central to this discussion. After all, we are talking about how to survive, how the actual SELF, the personal consciousness, can learn to and manage to, survive

physical death and BEYOND. This is about delivering oneself, one's actual SELF, intact, surviving through the processes and transitions we undergo -- and finding your SELF out there BEYOND, on the other side.

DELIVERANCE OF ONESELF

This SELF-deliverance is about moving the actual SELF, who the SELF actually is, the personal consciousness. This is about moving or delivering the SELF back and forth, to and from, in and out of, the physical plane and beyond the physical plane.

This is about moving through, transitioning through, dimensions of oneself. This is thus about our own interdimensional SELF, and its travel and survival. Yes, this is about *How To Die And Survive*.

KNOW YOUR OWN VIEWS OF
THE PROs AND CONs

Each of us may want to ask ourselves how we truly feel about suicide. Should anyone take such a liberty? The gift of life is so very precious. Do we have a right to abuse this gift by making it permissible to end life as we choose? Many societies go to great extremes to make suicide NOT permissible, and for good reason as suicide itself can be abused. (For example, see the photograph of the original *Golden Gate Bridge Suicide Patrol Vehicle* on its first day, in Figure 40.1. Clearly, significant efforts are made to help prevent this sort of suicide. Note that this author was invited to ride along with this patrol on the first day. See Figure 40.1 at the end of this chapter, which is when this author took this photo with permission.)

There are these and many other very reasonable arguments against the social approval of suicide. Nevertheless, there are those who argue the other side of this issue. We may also want to think of the decision not to, or to, end one's physical life as a very personal, very private, decision. Does any social body have the means of reaching into the individual SELF so deeply as to be able to be truly present for this inner decision? Some Readers write me and say, personal suicide is such a deep choice that, when others are not injured, and when the suicide is responsibly prepared for and conducted by a competent adult, there may be little role for social commentary or regulation. At least this is what some people say.

There is room for higher commentary, however. Each person considering suicide has his or her own moral code, belief system, definition of physical death, dialogue with God, and or relationship to the Cosmos and or nature and life itself. The SELF will consult with the higher SELF, internally. The SELF will consult internally with whatever that SELF knows to be wisdom or guidance or divinity that SELF looks to.

This discussion is in no way an advocacy of planned physical death, or suicide, as the way out of problem conditions. Too many lives turn around, too many healings and recoveries take place, to believe that there is no way except physical death to escape unpleasant life circumstances.

SUICIDE IS NOT SELF DELIVERANCE

Readers will decide their own personal views on suicide, and on when if ever suicide is acceptable. Many societies have

already decided by determining that suicide, and assisted suicide, euthanasia, are illegal.

Suicide is not the topic of this book. Survival both here and BEYOND is. This is about training our SELF, our personal consciousness, to see that it can exist both with a physical body and BEYOND.

Let's be clear here. Suicide of the biological body is not in itself conscious SELF-deliverance. Again note that this SELF-deliverance of the personal consciousness is about expanding oneself, reaching beyond given limitations. This is about who the SELF actually is -- and that this SELF can become aware of, expand into, non-physical awareness-es and dimensions of itself and thus of its reality.

This is about the interdimensional expansion, travel, and survival of the SELF in order to survive as a personal consciousness, both while living in a physical body, and after leaving that body. This survival is relevant during all in-life and seeming end-of-life transitions.

KNOW SELF DELIVERANCE

Certainly, there are persons who can give advice regarding medicinal and mechanical means of physically dying. Some recommend that medicines, herbs, gases be used.

However, what we frequently do not realize is that there are many ways of consciously detaching partly or entirely from the physical biological body, ways that require no assistance, no physical intervention.

We can learn to come and go at will. We can learn to move our focus out of our physical body, to perhaps repair energy patterns within it, and then to return to that physical body -- or to move our entire SELF out of our physical body and leave it, to then *die and survive*.

Some processes that do not require any intervention causing physical death have been indicated earlier in this book, for example in Exercises #22.1, #22.2, and #22.3 (also found in *How To Die And Survive, Book Three*). Study these exercises again with this understanding regarding SELF-deliverance. You have a right to this information, to the instructions on how to both exit and return to your body, *but only with the moral commitment to use this knowledge as ethically and as fully informed as possible.*

HUMAN RIGHTS EXTEND FAR BEYOND

Human rights can extend far beyond the physical plane. You have a right to adjust yourself to, move to and from, and or leave any dimension of reality in which you find yourself. *This is not about moving your physical body.* Again, this is about allowing your actual SELF, the focus of your personal consciousness, to expand and shift, LEAP to and from its chosen locations both in physical plane 3-D, and BEYOND.

We can together take our Human rights—the rights of *Humanity*—into the BEYOND. We need to take these rights there. To do so, practice taking your rights to come and go, back and forth from, moving around at will within and beyond the patterns you live within on physical plane Earth.

You are a highly mobile personal consciousness.

You are a highly mobile life form.

Whatever form it takes, both pattern adjustment and pattern death offer the opportunity for profound transcendence. Yet, neither adjustment nor death guarantee such transcendence. This is why it is important to consciously shift, LEAP, transition, die, whether or not the death in question is physical. A conscious death can be healing and purifying when conducted with focus and awareness, and only at the right time. Keep in mind that careless or impulsive suicide may not be the path to survival. Other options for resolution of difficulties must be fully and consciously explored.

Physical transition or death is merely one category of death along a *continuum of transition*. While physical death may allow for the shedding of cumbersome physical baggage, there is no guarantee that physical death itself is the clean clear break away from problem patterns that many tend to believe physical death will be.

EXERCISE #40.1
EXAMINING THE CODE FOR SUICIDE

Get to know yourself as you think through the concepts in this chapter. It is good to know what your views are before you encounter a need to make decisions regarding these. Here, take a moment to get to know how you yourself feel about suicide itself.

Think about your own rules or code regarding suicide. Under what, if any, circumstances might you find your own or someone else's suicide acceptable to you? Everyone's answers will of course be different here. What are your own personal views? Get to know your own views and reasons for your views.

Figure 40.1
Photographs of Member of Suicide Patrol Squad
on San Francisco Golden Gate Bridge

Note: This suicide patrol was started in 1996. Later, in 2010, construction on the
Golden Gate Bridge suicide barrier began.
https://www.ncbi.nlm.nih.gov/pmc/articles/PMC3643780/
and https://www.upi.com/Archives/1996/02/23/Suicide-patrol-on-Golden-Gate-
Bridge/5623825051600/

41
GROUP ELEVATION

> When a sufficient number come into experiential awareness of the universal mind, a threshold will be breached in the morphogenetic field of mankind, and all minds will spontaneously become aware.
>
> At this point, all individuals will realize and directly experience that we are a single superconscious entity.
>
> Moray B. King
> *Tapping the Zero-Point Energy*

Get ready. Just in time, we are going to see this LEAP in the awareness of the Human Species take place. This is a great and most essential LEAP in our evolution itself.

As the Human Species becomes more aware of itself as a Species of Consciousness rather than only as a biological species, the reality of our interdimensional survival will expand. [See other books in this *Keys To Consciousness And Survival Series* for definitions and explanations of ourselves as a **species of consciousness**, such as *Unveiling The Hidden Instinct* (*Volume 3* in this series), and *Seeing Beyond Our Line Of Sight*

(*Volume 10* in this series), and the *Overriding The Extinction Scenario* books (*Volumes 5 and 6* in this series).]

Our species' ability to consciously choose to move, shift, LEAP, itself as a species of consciousness -- in and out of (and back and forth, to and from) the material plane — is a key survival skill and option. It is our species' right to know about ourselves as a species of consciousness, and about our interdimensional awareness and capabilities. These may at some point, if not already now, be valuable understandings in our survival.

Our physical plane Earth-based evolution science has taught us much about developing and living within our habitats and niches. It is time we see that our habitats and niches are already inter-dimensional, and that **we have a right to define, develop, explore, and occupy these inter-dimensional niches**, as these exist within our own consciousness. (See the *Overriding The Extinction Scenario* books, *Volumes 5 and 6* in this series, for more on the matter of our interdimensional niches.)

Sure, we are excited about Human space travel with its vehicles such as rocket ships. However, this and other books in this series are about something far more expansive and far more readily accessible to us once we recognize it:

OUR TRUE INTERDIMENSIONAL NATURE.

Despite our programming not to know much about our true interdimensional nature, we are able now to escape the sense that all we have to live in is the physical world.

The Human Species will consciously choose to, at the right time, expand, and thus be able to elevate itself, its consciousness, its species matrix, to and from, back and forth, into and out of, other dimensions, even to higher realms of the idea of Light.

Certainly, this is about our capacity for **the interdimensional expansion of our personal and our species consciousness.** This is about our rightful inter-dimensional awareness of the *elevation capability* we carry within us.

However we label our interdimensional capabilities, we can see that individual biological death is not the only, or even the best, means of such ascendence. Nor is species extinction. (Again, see other books in this series, such as *Volumes 5 and 6*, titled, *Overriding The Extinction Scenario,* as well as *Volume 3*, titled, *Unveiling The Hidden Instinct.*)

KNOW CONSCIOUS GROUP ASCENDENCE

Let's be very clear here. Just as this book is not in any way about individual suicide, this book is also not in any way about group or mass or species suicide. Although some individual and species behaviors such as dangerous levels of addiction and dangerous levels of pollution are in a sense potentially suicidal, these are also not the topic of this book.

This is about survival, only survival. The elevation, ascendence, interdimensional awareness, and expansion travel discussed on this book's pages are truly about survival, <u>not</u> about ending the option of living.

Again, to be very clear here, *conscious group ascendence* does <u>not</u> take the form of hysterical or fanatical mass suicide. Nor does it take the form of gruesome mass murder. Conscious group elevation-ascendence is about SURVIVAL. <u>This ascendence is not physical and requires nothing to be done to the physical body.</u>

Conscious group elevation-ascendence is about the expansion of a group or species mental body. This is a highly conscious process, a true expansion into higher realms– a true expansion further into the species own *dimensional complexity*. (See further description of this group and species elevation option in later chapters of this book, and a deeper look at this matter in *Unveiling The Hidden Instinct, Volume 3* in this series.)

A solid, calm, well thought out, and focused approach to such an elevation-ascendence is *the only way such an ascendence can happen.* Forcing elevation and ascendence will result in the failing of elevation and ascendence.

This elevation-ascendence is not a closing out of our options. This is about adding to our options, both here in the physical plane and BEYOND. This is about an *expansion* of our SELVES along our own CONTINUUM OF CONSCIOUSNESS. We are already expanding, reaching out to the frontiers of our SELVES, of our personal, group, and species consciousness.

We need not die to expand. We are already in process. Our survival involves our recognizing that we are already an inter-dimensional species. Once we realize who and what we are, we see we do survive.

We do not die when we expand, whether or not we leave physicality. During any transition, we can choose to or not to remain rooted in physicality if and while we are expanding. Staying connected to our physical life form, our physical body, has great value at certain stages of our lives and our evolution.

Conscious group ascendence, when an actual ascendence, an actual LEAP, out of the material plane, involves no physical "tools" of suicide such as medicines and machines. Nothing is to be done to the physical body. This is an expansion of the SELF.

A note here. Do not confuse this form of group energy with that which is found in many cults and groups where a leader hypnotizes or even subsumes the energies of group or cult members. Recall that we have spoken about energy predators who may seek to swallow the energy of your consciousness. This is a related issue. Do not lose your mind to a leader who invites you to ascend with him or her.

Your decision to expand-elevate-ascend <u>must be your own,</u> and you must remain conscious of what is taking place in order to **initiate and then navigate your next ascension.**

KEEP IN MIND:
No physical body need die
to do this ascending.

This is about <u>expanding</u> into new domains,
not about leaving other domains.

Therefore, physical death is not a requirement for this elevation-ascension.

**Of course, those who are physically dying
at the end of their biological lives
are welcome to join here,
to continue to be
dying and surviving
as we all are.**

With this said, let us return to the concept of conscious group ascension, which in terms of the discussion in this book is conscious group elevation. The individual consciousness is not lost in such a group. It is maintained and fueled by the group consciousness. This group consciousness desires its members to remain individuated and empowered, to continue to be personal consciousness-es, to survive. This group consciousness helps bring into focus and coherence the energy of the individual, and vice versa.

Now here, the individual personal consciousness has already chosen to elevate-ascend to a *high collective threshold point*. From this high threshold point, the LEAP into another personal pattern or energy arrangement is more smoothly accomplished.

More energy is available to contribute to a mass LEAP than to an individual LEAP--when this mass LEAP is a collection of individual consciousness-es rather than being one dominating force who has swallowed all individuals within it.

RECOGNIZE

THE TIME

Never blindly engage in anything simply calling itself ascension or elevation, and insisting you join it. Check the group that you feel you are a member of, or joining, to be sure you truly want to align with it. *Again, your own personal discernment is essential.*

EXERCISE #41.1
KNOWING YOUR TERMS

Think about how you would respond to pressure to join in on radical processes or belief systems. How do you keep yourself safe? See where stress or fear may cause you to be more vulnerable to pressures.

What are your ideas about strengthening yourself? List some ways you can protect yourself in the face of unknowns and pressures to join in on things that you may not know how to evaluate.

EXERCISE #41.2
IMAGINING
GROUP ELEVATION-ASCENSION

Now, use your imagination to explore this concept. Visualize a situation which suggests the possible value of species-wide elevation-ascension. See yourself in this situation, along with others.

What are you feeling? What are you thinking? What is your process of understanding what is going on?

Now experiment with what this elevation may feel like. For just a moment, see—feel—your participation in a collective elevation-ascension.

Place a protective shield around yourself.

293

Sense your SELF remaining an individual SELF as this elevation takes place. Sense that you are surviving as your SELF.

Describe this survival experience. Remember, that of course, this is just an exploration, an exercise, and <u>not</u> an actual process.

42

CATHARTING BEYOND:
LEAP LEVEL SIX

And if the earthly no longer
knows your name, whisper
to the silent earth:
I'm flowing.

To the flashing water say:
I am.

Rainer Maria Rilke
The Sonnets to Orpheus, II: 29

Fatal exposures to radiation, toxins, poisons, and other heavy pollutions are disastrous events for those living in physical bodies in the material plane. This is because these particular pollutions are material plane events. Physical plane pollutions are disastrous aspects of the overall degradation of the Earth's physical ecosystem. These may be problematic, perhaps dangerous, some even potentially fatal, contaminations of the 3-D Earth's physical dimension of reality.

THE ELEPHANT IN THE ROOM

Just knowing that such risks exist and may be increasing is on the mind of our species, on our collective mind. Where we may or may not be concerned on a daily basis, we do feel this on a deep level. We are naturally tracking potential threats to our

survival. So, where we hear of or sense the risk of exposure to environmental danger or contamination, we feel the potential fatality. This basically means we sense the possible eventual triggering of possible eventual physical mortality.

This is difficult to have on our minds. Even when we are not paying attention to this issue, it is there somewhere, almost like the elephant in the room story. Everyone sees or senses there is an elephant right there in the room, but almost no one says they see this, as if not saying this will make the elephant go away.

Let's take a moment to talk about this elephant in our room, in our physical plane biosphere. We do know that major climate and Earth changes are taking place, and that people are already experiencing these. We do know we hope these changes do not become increasingly dangerous.

We do hope there is <u>not</u> a time when the Human species and all life on 3-D Earth is suffering so immensely in the third dimension, in the physical plane here on Earth, that the threat to life, to survival, is front and center. This threat to life of course may for some people tap into the idea of death.

Yet, we also know that Human technology, as well as Mother Nature herself, may be able to achieve tremendous turnarounds, to correct the dangerous trends we are seeing. We can stay very positive about this.

WHERE DOES
THE DISCUSSION ABOUT THE BEYOND COME IN?

First, it is important to say this again here: As is noted many times on these pages, absolutely nothing in this book is about

killing ourselves, or suicide. Quite the opposite. Having a living physical body and brain to work from is key for Readers here in the physical plane on Earth. To remind Readers of this again, absolutely nothing here is about personal or group suicide.

All the exercises and concepts discussed herein are about understanding all this while living in a physical biological body with a biological brain. There will be a time later when your consciousness will benefit by your having thought through all this while still a biological life form. (Of course, if you have already left your physical body, your consciousness can still benefit by hearing this discussion and these exercises. Clearly, some of you out there are already listening....)

So, when this book talks about dying and surviving, this is about *the survival mind set* and *the training of the personal consciousness to know it can survive* even when it eventually moves out of the physical body.

Growing comfortable with the idea that there can be a BEYOND, some form of after-life open to us, if we learn about what this means, can help us not only later when we die, but in our daily lives, right here right now.

Thinking through possible capabilities our personal consciousness can have is not only comforting and interesting, but useful. It can be very useful to be learning about what the mind can do to conduct movement of its focus to and from the physical body, such as the body exit and body re-entry techniques discussed in earlier chapters.

THINKING THIS THROUGH
CAN BE POWERFUL

Of course, in these challenging times, we cannot help but consider major survival issues.

Let's think for a moment about what species do to survive. Seasonal migration is a good example. We have seen many species on planet Earth migrate back and forth from region to region when seasons and their climates change. This sort of migration is so obvious to us, we tend to take it for granted.

Let's take the idea of migration to another level. It may be that at some time, if the 3-D Earth biosphere is degrading to the point of discomfort or even unlive-ability, that migration or exodus may be a survival option. Of course, we tend to think of this as taking space ships to places off-Earth. However, this may not be enough for us to save ourselves, to survive.

Do we have, or will we eventually have, another way of migrating? It is time for us to understand that we are the Species of Human Consciousness, not just the species of the biological Human.

It may be that understanding this is what allows us to survive in the long term. It may be that learning about this expansion to other dimensions of ourselves, of our own consciousness-es, is an option for us, is a good idea. Once we realize that we are already doing this, that we are already expanding this way, this is not an extreme idea. This idea is something that can help us live in our daily lives, as well as help us think about death and dying, even about after-life possibilities.

Once one decides that mortality of the personal physical body is not, or need not be, mortality of the ACTUAL SELF, of the personal consciousness, then the dynamic of physical fatality is shifted. Even on a daily basis, the dynamic of how we see ourselves is changed.

This is not to say that the physical life must be surrendered. This is to say that understanding one's survival as a survival of the personal consciousness empowers not only the personal consciousness body but also the physical body--to ever more consciously navigate survival pressures.

ENERGY RELEASE IS CATHARSIS

When we are able to ever more consciously navigate in-life as well as seeming end-of-life transitions, then we are able to take into our minds the sense that we can make it through things, even difficult situations. In this sense, we can *die and survive*. There is a lot of energy built into personal change and transition, even into the idea of triumphing over, of finding our way through, of dying and surviving challenges we face. Finding this energy and using it to help ourselves is powerful. **We can call this a sort of freeing up of valuable energy that has been stuck or locked up, a catharsis**.

This *idea of cathartic energy* is something we can learn about now, and use in all our in-life and seeming end-of-life and after-life transitions.

Think back to the discussion of the LEAP, the *light energy action process*, this and the previous *How To Die And Survive* book have defined. A catharsis can be a LEAP in that:

The catharsis is the release of energy from the building or apexing store of *situational or even crisis energy.*

Catharsis releases stuck and trapped energy, energy we may want to have available to ourselves to move through changes and transitions, to survive.

Many LEAP events are in essence catharses--energetic shifts, changes, releases, and in this sense, *cathartic healing of energy arrangements!* The movement "up" to the frequency which may allow a rerouting of the energy circuits that affect the physical body is basically a LEAP up and out of the focus of the body. This is the nature of a LEAP that can be involved in conscious transition. Here again is *dying and surviving,* in that the LEAP that is shifting the locus and focus, shifting the center of the personal consciousness, allows the personal energy arrangement to shift and move into new arrangements, new forms of itSELF. (Refer to the various **shifting exercises** included in *Volume 3* in this *Keys To Consciousness And Survival Series,* titled, *Unveiling The Hidden Instinct.)*

So, let's say you eventually do die a physical death. You then realize you have survived. You find that you ARE out there, BEYOND, that you have made the LEAP.

You have been propelled to make this shift by the energy released from your old energy arrangements and patterns. This is the fuel for the LEAP.

CATHARTING BEYOND

Catharting beyond is the LEAP that involves the using of energy released by breaking out of a stuck, possibly draining,

possibly depleted, possibly dangerously depleted, or otherwise threatened, or troubled, or fatal, pattern or phase of life or physical body. (Of course, the energy we speak of here is visualized or conceptualized energy, as it is not energy in terms of what energy is in the physical plane.)

Catharting beyond is in essence breaking out of a bind, a double bind, an energy trap, to move far beyond the realm of the existence being left. [For in depth explanation of this **energy trap and double bind**, and how this relates to catharsis, see other books in this *Keys To Consciousness And Survival Series*, such as *Navigating Life's Stuff (Volume 8)*, and also books in the *Faces Of Addiction Series*, such as *Gestalting Addiction: Speaking Truth To The Power And Definition Of Addiction, Addiction Theory, And Addiction Treatment*, and another book in that series, *Seeing The Hidden Face Of Addiction.*]

In this sense, you can see some otherwise unavoidable physical dangers, diseases, and pollutions as possible challenges to motivate or fuel you to die out of a particular pattern or phase of life, and *to elevate to a new energy arrangement of your personal matrix, of your personal consciousness, of your SELF.*

EXERCISE #42.1
ACTING OUT THE LEAP

Either visualize yourself doing this exercise, or actually do this. Either is fine, as the brain does this exercise whether or not the body moves with it.

Stand up. Then, remaining on your feet (flat-footed or on your toes), hunch over, kneel down, and contract. Tighten the muscles of your body as much as you can. Hold this tightness, this tension, so hard

you begin to shake. Shake a moment. Then tighten even more, preparing to LEAP up.

Now LEAP.

EXERCISE #42.2
CATHARTING

Think of something you are (or may have once been) intensely upset about. If you cannot find something in your present, dig into your past. If you no longer feel emotional or upset about this something, you can act out the feelings called for here. Call upon your actual feelings, or your imagination, or both, to do this.

Summon these feelings now. As you do, either imagine that you do this, or actually go ahead and do this: kneel and hunch down as in the previous exercise. Tighten up as you imagine that this intense upset you are focusing on is causing tension and compaction, tightening, throughout your body and your consciousness.

Hold so tightly that you begin to shake. Imagine that you shake. Shake ... shake ... shake. Tighten and feel even more upset or tense. Shake ... shake . . . shake.

Now LEAP up, releasing this upset from your muscles and flesh into the atmosphere around you—silently screaming, crying, or maybe making sounds out loud as you do.

Let what you have released transmute to highest light and dissolve.

Breathe a sigh of relief. Feel as if you have LEAPT a great distance.

PART VII

How To

MetaDie

43
MEGADYING:
IT IS BIGGER THAN WE ARE

> For the soul has not finished
> what it has to do by merely
> developing into Humanity; it
> still has to develop Humanity
> into its higher possibilities.
>
> Sri Aurobindo
> *The Philosophy of Rebirth*
> The Life Divine

Why are we here? What are we doing? What are our lives about? Questions such as these ask themselves, sometimes loudly for all to hear, and other times almost silently, out of our conscious awareness. Yet we wonder, we do wonder.

Of course, what we are doing here, and why we are living, are questions we may not have time to ask on an ongoing basis. Living life day to day is already quite a lot. As a result, we may find reassuring religious and or philosophical explanations, or other more pre-packaged or off-the-shelf answers. There may even be helpful answers, even powerful belief systems, that seem to help with these questions about our existence. However, we are still left with the big wonderings.

While we may or may not have determined precisely why we are here, what we are doing, what our lives are about, we are

busy living our lives, even trying to survive. We may even find ourselves living through all kinds of minor and major events, in-life and many also seeming end-of-life endings, changes, deaths.

And, while we are not entirely certain why we are here and what we are doing living our lives, we may also ask what our deaths will be about. We just have to wonder.

What questions these are. Perhaps not having these answers, perhaps not even asking these questions, appears to be the solution. Yet, we are always on some level asking. On some deep inner level, we do want to know what our lives are about, why we are having these lives, and even what happens after we complete these lives. This last question is a big one, sort of waiting in the wings, often avoided yet asked deep inside. What is this big physical death all about? Is it final? Does it kill us? It is actually death? And hopefully some also ask, can this death be survived?

Yes.

Can we *die and survive?* Can we learn to *die and survive?* Do we already carry this knowledge? Has this knowledge been suppressed? Can this knowledge be activated now?

Yes.

EVOLVING FURTHER
OUR
INTERDIMENSIONAL COMPLEXITY

Modern Earth Humans are evolving their territories, reaching beyond where they presently see themselves as being. And

these territories are not only in the physical plane. As we reach further into our seemingly new territories, basically territories of our minds, of our consciousness-es, these territories are growing in *dimensional complexity*. And so are we.

The Human Species is progressing. We are moving away from being a life form that generally sees and moves within only what it is programmed to believe is its primary home—in this case, the physical plane on 3-D Earth. We are moving into being a life form that constantly sees and moves across many dimensions of reality. We already do live both here in 3-D and BEYOND.

We are doing this progressing, evolving, within the realms of our personal as well as our species consciousness. We are doing this expansion quite instinctively. We sense this is necessary, and that this is our birthright.

Much of this evolving, expanding, we are doing out of our daily awareness. We are doing this instinctively in order to regain access to our own territory, the territory of our own personal as well as species consciousness.

The Human Species is somewhat like the first sea animals who evolved onto land, and could live both in the sea and on land. Even today, we see animals such as elephant seals traveling back and forth, to and from land and sea. In this sense, some animals do live in more than one atmosphere, and quite readily move back and forth.

However, for the Human Species now, this is about our evolving and expanding into a new territory or dimension of

ourselves. And, actually, this is about our reclaiming our own access to territory which is already ours: the territory of our own personal consciousness. This is the **actual territory of ourselves** that we do already occupy. We are already out there, BEYOND this material plane, even while we live in this material plane.

We Humans continue to expand our awareness of the dimensions of our consciousness into which we can travel. Yes, we are already expanding, not restricting, our territories, our SELVES.

We remain in the physical plane while also expanding into, and even preparing to inhabit and even RE-inhabit, our other dimensions. We, the Human Species, can consciously expand rather than shut the door on our own options for survival both here and BEYOND.

Again, these territories are already present within our own consciousness. We actually already live there. Interestingly enough, as noted earlier, we are not really dying when we move into our BEYOND, as we already live there. We are actually simply surviving. However, as the physical body eventually dies, we do in that sense also *die and survive.*

KNOW HOW CRITICAL THIS EXPANSIVE AND INTERDIMENSIONAL EVOLUTION IS

Your movement into your own, our own, *greater dimensional complexity* is immensely important because:

1) The well-being of the Human Species, likely even of all species on Earth, may eventually rely on the interdimensional awareness and survival capabilities we carry so deeply within us.

2) We must access these interdimensional awareness-es and survival capabilities that we are either naturally or intentionally programmed not to fully access. [For more on this matter of access, and possible programming not to fully access, see other books in this *Keys To Consciousness And Survival Series,* such as the *Overriding The Extinction Scenario* books (*Volumes 5 and 6*) and also *Unveiling The Hidden Instinct* (*Volume 3*).]

3) However we may have been programmed (and designed) to be restricted from our full interdimensional nature and access, we can break free of this restriction. We can break free as we grow to understand ourselves as a species of consciousness itself. We are already this species of consciousness rather than simply a biological species. Once we see this, then the binding tie, the general restriction to only our physical reality, can be ended.

4) Earth Humans can decide for themselves where, when, and how to expand to be able to live both here and BEYOND.

5) Earth Humans can, and do have a right to, access their own ***continuum of consciousness.*** This continuum is where Earth Humans already do live, even when living in physical bodies. (For more on this CONTINUUM OF

CONSCIOUSNESS, see other books in this series, such as *Volume 10*, titled, *Seeing Beyond Our Line Of Sight.*)

6) The Human Consciousness *must* evolve to avoid DE-volving, or even stagnation. Only conscious evolution as a Species of Consciousness will ensure survival as a Species of Consciousness, as who this species actually is.

7) Remaining unable to traverse at will the dimensions beyond the material plane, while evolving in more primitive (or at least more material) physical plane ways, will not even ensure the survival of the Human Species in the material plane. (Again, refer to the *Overriding The Extinction Scenario* books, *Volumes 5 and 6* in this *Keys To Consciousness And Survival Series.)*

8) Only conscious, intentional, evolution of the mind, of the awareness, of the access to and into our *natural multidimensionality,* will bring the Human Species and all of Humanity (which is more than merely the Human species presently living on Earth) its liberation—*and its* release from programming not to know.

9) Liberation is freedom from the confines of being shut out of our own interdimensional expansion and awareness capabilities. We have a right to access our own Species' Interdimensional Expansion and its Free Will, freedom to exercise the Will. Liberation is freedom from the confines of a lesser understanding, from the confines of naturally or perhaps even purposefully programmed-in, implanted, misunderstanding of the species' actual nature and ***actual survival potential.***

10) Think again of those life forms on Earth who evolved from the sea onto the land. Similarly, the Human Species is a physicalized (biologized) species who is evolving its ability to *migrate at will* back and forth across dimensions, to and from material and non-material realms. This freely-willed *conscious expansion and migration* is essential to species survival.

11) Reader, as your actual SELF, you are a *highly expansive personal consciousness*. You carry the survival tools needed as the Human Species moves into these times.

12) One of the greatest, and most basic, survival tools is our understanding that: We may have been programmed to die off, similar to the way cells in our bodies die off. Our biological cells carry biological mechanisms that tell them when it is time for them to die off.

13) We as beings, rather than as microscopic biological cells, may also have been programmed to die off -- *and programmed to not know* that we are already a species of consciousness, that we already occupy the territories of our consciousness, that these are our own inter-dimensional survival territories. (See the books in the *Metaterra Chronicles Collection* for more on these *survival territories,* such as the books, *Revealing the Omega Key,* and also, *Detecting The Omega Deception.*)

14) You can bring the energy generated by an expansion of your own consciousness to the collective energy pool. You can contribute to a global, even a species-wide, LEAP in evolution. Such a LEAP in evolution is a profound shift

311

in reality for the entire species. This is in essence a great shift out of a trapping pattern.

15) **This is a megadeath, which is simply the death of being confined to a lesser awareness of who we are. This is about a major LEAP in awareness.**

MEGADIE

Megadeath is far beyond your traditional definitions of death. Megadeath is profound, and yet quite subtle. Megadeath is basically a shift in perception, a very big shift in perception.

Megadeath is therefore not physical death as it has been defined in biological life form terms.

Megadeath is about survival, even species survival. This is not about the physical plane definition of death, not at all. No one needs to die without the option of surviving.

Megadeath is the death of an antiquated and tyrannical programming of our SELVES, of our minds and brains. Megadeath is the conclusion of, the moving past from, the form as a more limited species or version of Humanity. More than this, megadeath is the gaining of multidimensional access and thus species elevation-ascension options through a special *evolutionary LEAP.*

This is a LEAP in understanding, in knowing, an expansion of awareness at the deepest and most fundamental level: This is about our knowing who we actually are.

WE DO KNOW

WHAT WE NEED TO KNOW NOW.

The envelope has been opened. The energy held within the trap designed to hold us from our full interdimensional existence and identity, is freeing itself now, freeing itself for us to access within our own personal consciousness.

(Refer again to the books noted above, such as the novel, *Revealing The Omega Key*, and the non-fiction book about all this, *Detecting The Omega Deception*, for more on this ENVELOPE OPENING. These books explain that this is a message from us to ourselves, and from ancient elders, being sent to us through time.)

EXERCISE #43.1
UNDERSTANDING MEGADYING

*Before proceeding with this exercise, note again here: Nothing about the exercises and concepts in these How To Die And Survive books is about individual suicide, or group or mass suicide. Not at all. THIS IS ABOUT SURVIVAL. This is about the expansion of the consciousness to understand its **interdimensional survival capabilities.***

*Now, let's move into this exercise. So, either silently, or with a companion, think through or talk about what you understand of **megadeath as not being about physically dying.***

Once you have done this, come up with three plans for or methods of megadeath for the Human Species, plans in which <u>no one dies</u>. Each of these methods should cause an evolutionary LEAP. There are no right or wrong answers here. Just come up with your own ideas. Be

313

creative. Remember, MEGA-death is about a shift in how we see ourselves. A big shift.

EXERCISE #43.2
INSPIRING A MEGADYING

Now, ask some one or ones you know to hear your speech inspiring a great species expansion, a megadeath which is <u>not about physical death</u>.

Or, simply visualize that you have an audience and imagine that you are explaining to this audience the concept of and need for expansion, or conceptual megadeath, which is not physical death.

What would be your key points? Name three.

What might be the key arguments against what you are saying? Name three. How would you respond to these arguments?

EXERCISE #43.3
MEGADYING

*You are on your own here. Find a way to do this exercise without causing (or even imagining) any injury, illness, or physical death. In fact, cause no death except a <u>minor conceptual</u> megadeath, by making <u>your own personal LEAP in the consciousness of the **entire species.**</u>*

Feel how the personal shift in awareness you make here may contribute to species awareness. Feel your own personal expansion in awareness to be a significant contribution to the whole.

<u>44</u>
METASTROPHIZING

> ...mourn, man,
> because you are not dust yet.

> Thomas Merton
> *Entering the Silence*

These are times when the world around us, locally or globally or both, appears to be facing instability, even threats to well-being and survival.

Both ancient teachings and modern science are perhaps suggesting that the Earth is changing so rapidly that we may have little time to turn the process around and save ourselves. It is sometimes easy to move into catastrophic thinking. However, this distracts us from what we *can* do to consciously move through the situations we face -- to in small and large ways, *ever more consciously navigate* the pathways and processes of the challenges, changes, and transitions we face.

And so, the imagined or actual, minor or major catastrophe, the threatening or even death-suggesting event, can be seen as a challenge, an opportunity to work with ourselves, to get to know our actual SELVES. We can take this moment, this thing we face, whatever it is, as the call to work with the energy -- to get to see or sense what is going on in the realm of subtle energy, and of *our subtle personal awareness of subtle energy.*

And here we are, right here right now, with the opportunity for individual as well as species evolution, and thus survival. Both the idea of danger or catastrophe, and an actually approaching danger or catastrophe, can be consciously catalytic.

CATASTROPHE THEORY

Of note is what has been defined as "catastrophe theory." From a mathematical standpoint, this theory is a tool that defines, studies, and generally seeks to predict sudden changes. Indeed, in nature we find two general types of changes: (1) the smooth continuous change; and, (2) the abrupt discontinuous change, which is really just the result of various continuous changes that have not been noticed.

Think about this a moment. Seemingly abrupt discontinuous change (which is the second type of change listed above) can be described as the moment when the straw breaks the camel's back. However, look again. One by one, straws are piled onto the camel's back. There is no response, except perhaps a slight sway back appearing. This process continues the same way, on and on, until -- all of a sudden one more straw is added and that straw breaks the camel's back.

When something similar to this process takes place in nature, this sudden change is often said to be a catastrophe. Critical points in the process were overloaded or overpacked to the point where something had to break or degenerate. Of course, this situation had been building all along, as this is really the first type of change listed above, the smooth continuous change. If only we could have seen this coming.

Various extensions of catastrophe theory have appeared in other scientific fields, such as performance psychology. For example, studies of anxiety-induced performance catastrophes in sports have indicated that when an athlete is experiencing increasingly high cognitive anxiety, there is a point where this anxiety is so high, has built up so much all along the way, that suddenly the athlete's performance drops.

Think of a wave rolling in to shore. Some waves roll in and never break. Other waves roll on, increasing in momentum and or size until they can no longer carry or roll themselves without breaking. A line drawing of the wave shows a curved line rising until at a certain point the line dips and turns on itself. Then, once the wave break (or catastrophe) is complete, the wave rolls on or dissipates.

BUILD UP OF ENERGY

Catastrophe itself, when profound, releases a tremendous amount of stored, trapped, even intensified energy. Approaching catastrophe, whether it is certain or suspected or falsely coined, may intensify and even attract energy.

Frequently, the very expectation of catastrophe builds up so much energy that this energy may burst itself in a pre-catastrophe release.

CATASTROPHIZE (pronounced CATAS- STROE-FIZE)

Modern material plane mathematicians have begun to explain to themselves what they call "catastrophe theory." They are attempting to explain the tendency of some systems to build up and hoard—hold onto—intensified energy in such a tense,

over-loaded, imbalanced manner that a *catastrophic release* is natural, essential. This catastrophic release functions somewhat like the escape valve on a teapot.

At a deep instinctive level, living beings and living systems feel the principle of catastrophic release. They feel the pressure to force into opening and operation, *an escape valve*. Some escape valves offer useful, even positive opportunities. Others do not.

We can learn to sense, to know, this energy buildup for what it is, for what it feels like in our physical and emotional bodies. We can learn to build up and release this energy in productive ways, safe ways, ever more conscious ways. **This is part of conscious navigation.**

Being conscious of this sensation, of what this energy build up is, of what this energy build up is about on an energetic level, can be quite useful. This can help release the catastrophic energy to empower the move through difficult transitions.

As you and the political, economic, social, biological, and ecological systems in which you live pull this deep, subconscious, instinctual feel into your conscious awareness, you can become adept at what we can call *metastrophizing (pronounced METAST-TRO-FIZING):*

You can recognize sensations of *catastrophic expectation* with clarity. You can see the energy locked up in the build-up. You can *sense and navigate this energy pathway* to a *productive release*. You can navigate this energy and use it to survive transition. You can use this energy as fuel for particular survival releases.

METASTROPHIZE

What this ability to *metastrophize* means is that the catastrophic process or experience *can be navigated on another level,* rather than have its effects build up and be pressed deeper down into the physical plane. This is a matter of where the focus is.

You can learn to navigate situations

by being more aware of the subtle energies

as they move, build up, may even be trapped.

You can navigate these energies

as they edge toward release --

or sometimes either wear down or run wild

if not consciously navigated.

EXERCISE #44.1
GENERATING A METASTROPHE

Alone, or with one or more other persons, select <u>or just imagine</u> one catastrophe or a cluster of catastrophes that may or may not occur in the near future. For just a moment, talk yourself or selves into believing or imagining catastrophe is coming. Build up a sense of catastrophe. See what this feels like.

Then metastrophize: <u>navigate this experience on another level</u>. Use your imagination to do the following:

* *Decide to consciously navigate this situation.*

* *Decide to consciously sense the energies in this situation.*

* *Create an imaginary energy situation picture or map.*

* *Give these energies and their patterns and variations diagrams or pictures in your mind, or scribble these on a piece of paper if you like.*

* *Look for building energy, stuck energy, wobbling energy, places where energy is wasting away, places where energy is running out of control.*

* *Draw or imagine yourself a map of how you will move through this energy situation, and of where you can even draw energy from it for your SELF.*

* *Give your personal consciousness a nod of recognition, seeing that it is present and conducting this navigation.*

Stay with this sensation into the next exercise.

EXERCISE #44.2
USING METASTROPHE FOR RELEASE

Build an imaginary or real tension into the **catastrophic expectation** *you had set for the previous exercise, or create a new one.*

So, an imaginary catastrophe is building now. You sense this and are growing somewhat tense. (No need to hold your breath, please, as this is a visualization exercise).

As you build this tension, visualize a growing store of soft energy at the base of your skull. Visualize such a buildup of soft energy, that a light pressure for the energy to burst out of the top of your skull increases. Gently hold the energy in your skull for now. Do not yet release it.

Prepare for the release. First, imagine that you do this, or actually go ahead and do this: Sit or stand with your eyes closed. Continue to expect catastrophe. Build up the energy in the form of a gentle but expectant tension.

Let the energy build. As you do, visualize a safe place elsewhere in the Cosmos, and/or in another dimension of reality, for you, your species, and perhaps even all of Earth to go. This is your map. This is your safe place. This will become your planned navigation of this release. Hold on, still let the energy be gently building.

Hold on. In a moment, when you release the catastrophic energy (out the top of your skull and out of every cell in your body), you will fuel travel to this safe place you have imagined. You will even imagine you feel an upward sort of rush or exit flow.

Now, release the energy! Burst! LEAP! Land in your safe place BEYOND!

EXERCISE #44.3
METASTROPHIZING

Think back to the previous exercise, Exercise #44.2, which you may have just completed. Recall the sensations involved in metastrophizing. Generate the feeling in yourself, this time without attaching it to a particular catastrophe.

Build up this feeling. Sense the tension within <u>this feeling of catastrophe which you are converting to metastrophe</u>.

Feel the pressure mount. Hold for a moment. Prepare for the release of this catastrophic energy. Prepare for your navigation of this energy situation on a higher level. You are moving through this energy in your mind, via your own personal consciousness. You are practicing this <u>conscious navigation</u>. Still hold for a moment.

Now release, burst, LEAP. Feel or imagine the sensations of this burst, this LEAP. Navigate, fly, this energy to a place you imagine is there for you, to your own place.

Welcome. Look around your place out there BEYOND. You can see more about this place you design for your SELF every time you visit it, even in your imagination. You will eventually have your own map into this place of yours, and know how to enter it, and know what it looks and feels like. This will be an idea you, your personal consciousness, will be able to call on later, when you may feel you want or need it.

Give your SELF a moment to maybe decorate this place of yours, or to develop it a little more. Maybe leave a sign or note to yourself, so that next time you are here, your memory of this visit will be triggered. You can feel more and more at home here.

You will be back here someday.

Take a deep breath. Then return to your physical body and previous state of self.

<u>45</u>

METASOMATIC AILMENTS AND METAHEALING

> When the crop is backward and
> thin, the ears are light and move
> with the slightest breath of wind.
> Thin crops are therefore full of
> sound.
>
> Marcel Griaule
> *"Ogotemmeli and
> the Dawn of All Things"*
> Conversations with Ogotemmeli

Something about the BEYOND comes more and more into focus. Our mind's camera lens, our mind's eye, is focusing itself. As we further sensitize ourselves to this reality, this sense of the BEYOND, our awareness itself of the BEYOND itself becomes ever more clear. We begin to sense that many arrangements and developments are somehow worked through, even negotiated, outside concrete physical reality, in the less physical and even non-physical, even ethereal realms. Whether we believe these realms are in our imagination, or out there BEYOND, or both, we can see or sense these if we look. We generate these realms within our own consciousness. These are our own territories, our own realities.

SEE METASOMATIC AILMENTS

Subtle energy, however it is explained by you to yourself, is experienced on some level, in some way. The effects of this subtle energy are all around and within us. Whether this be the imaginary effects of imagined or actual things, or the actual effects of actual or imagined things, we experience these.

Even the subtle formations, entanglements, and tugs and pulls of your cords affect your physical existence. These affect your comfort, your appearance, your coordination, your health, and more.

SOMATIZING (pronounced SOMA-TIZE-ING)

You may be, as is quite common, drawn or driven to bring further into your physical body your stress or other emotional issues. **This is** *somatizing*, **making** *more* **physical what is** *less* **physical.** (Keep in mind, even emotions have biological elements, as brain chemistry drives emotions.)

We can also think of somatizing as pulling the tangled network of emotional cords and attachments into physicality. Think of the tangled network of cords and their attachments we form. (See *How To Die And Survive, Book One* for detailed discussion of this web of cords and attachments we weave). The dynamics of our cord network of course affect our physical health.

We are actually programmed to pull emotional energies into physicality. And of course, our emotions naturally register physically as they are from the moment they come into existence, biochemical.

This is deep programming we carry within us. (See more about this programming in other books in this *Keys To Consciousness*

And Survival Series, such as *Volume 10*, titled, *Seeing Beyond Our Line Of Sight*, and also in books in the accompanying *Faces Of Addictions Series*, such as the book titled, *Seeing The Hidden Face Of Addiction.)*

This drive to somatize, to physically manifest, is valuable when it calls attention to energy disturbances, implicit patterns, and even pattern addictions that might not otherwise be seen. For example, sometimes a headache tells us we are dealing with something that we may not have realized we are experiencing.

Yet, even when energy disturbances found in the cord network are pulled downward in density—made more physical—you may not see that this *descension of energy disturbance* is what has happened.

All too often, we realize that our emotional and or other problem pattern has been pulled further into our biological body, only when it finally makes us feel physically uncomfortable or physically ill.

Physical-ization or *somatiz-ation* of a hidden condition can result in physical suffering without any improvement let alone healing. This frequently takes place without recognition of the emotional or other energetic and generally invisible condition from which it stems. Basically, you can make yourself physically sick pulling the troubled energy pattern into physical form. That is, unless you are trained to work with it there in the physical plane where you may even require actual medical treatment, or perhaps a surgeon and hospital care. (And of course, not all physical disease is caused by invisible

energetic imbalances and patternings. We do well to continue to see our medical doctors.)

This whole discussion is in no way a blame the victim matter. There is a large inventory of invisible factors allowing physical bodies to be vulnerable to the somatizing of problem patterns. We do well to study these. (For more on this *somatizing,* see another book in this *Keys To Consciousness And Survival Series: Volume 3*, titled, *Unveiling The Hidden Instinct.*)

SEE AND STOP THE STEPPING DOWN

One of the most unfortunate developments in physicality is the naive *stepping down,* or moving or pulling down, of a troubled behavioral or emotional pattern from the emotional body to the physical body.

When troubled emotional patterns are pulled further into the physical body, this is a *physical*-ization of what is less physical. This densification and de-scension of troubled energy allows some of the energy trapped in the cord network to escape downward toward greater density, into greater physical-ization, instead of dissipating entirely away.

Descension allows troubled cord energy to become more dense, more physical. A full or even partial downward, densifying, release of the energy that has built up in the cord network can occur at the expense of the physical and emotional well-being of one or more persons involved in that cord network.

Think of a pressure cooker not releasing the built-up steam and instead pressing it downward, deeper in the pressure cooker. Something will eventually give way or explode.

It is therefore not surprising that many psychological and emotional disturbances take on physical plane, behavioral or even physical, health aspects such as drug addiction, accident prone-ness, and, of course, disease.

Becoming increasingly aware of this tendency to pull emotional and other energetic disturbances into our physical body is the first step in seeing and stopping this *physicalizing or stepping down.*

Becoming this aware is also key in understanding what must be released in order to *die and survive*, both here and BEYOND. Hanging on to troubled patterns can weigh us down, sometimes even sink us.

(Also note: this de-scension of troubled energy patterning can also take place in reverse. Emotional and even physical conditions and their cord and attachment networks can be pulled deeper - actually pulled higher up -- into the non-physical body. As previous chapters have explained, this can interfere with the movement into next phases of life and after life -- such as when a dying person is having difficulty releasing cords and attachments, or when others are not releasing the dying person to smoothly move into the next life, to *die and survive*).

EXERCISE #45.1
METASOMATIC SURGERY

Use this exercise to explore and work with the idea of <u>energetic</u> <u>patterning</u>. As you read or listen to this exercise, try to pause a while, maybe even for at least one minute where you see the single star (*), and for about three minutes at three stars (***). However you choose to hear this exercise, try to enter this exercise in a somewhat relaxed state, if you can. You may want to locate yourself in a dimly lit private room or a warm tub. This is up to you.

Find a comfortable position for your body. Ideally, sit down or lie down. (Of course, for those of you who are listening to this book as an audiobook while out walking or running, you are welcome to conduct this exercise your way.)

Either close your eyes, or imagine your eyes are closed. (Of course, if you are out walking or running, please keep your eyes open.)

Now, actually do the following, <u>or just imagine that you do the</u> <u>following</u>:

Put your hand over or near an area of your body that you are in some way more aware of, or concerned about. You may feel no actual concern. Yet, now that this concern has been mentioned, you may be aware that you are slightly more attentive to a particular part of your body. Something is calling your attention, yet you may not know what it is.

Or, you may feel that this particular part of your body is either not well, or is not as well as you'd like it to be. You may want to choose a part of your body that is hurting, or one that is numb, or one that just seems to be less connected to you than the rest of you. If you cannot select such an area of your body, just pick any spot and put your hand above it, or imagine that you do this. Hold your hand there and

become aware of whatever you think of as energy or an energy pattern present beneath your hand.

Now, let your hand rest there for a while. ... Just let your mind begin to see into this part of your body. Look for energy. Look for patterns of energy, if you can. You are welcome to give textures or colors, even images or pictures, to what you see or feel. Do this for a while.

(*)

If, in this part of your body, you have seen what you think of as energy —whatever energy means to you—energy present or even moving, follow the shape or path of this energy with a very slow-moving fingertip -- or imagine that you do this. Imagination is very useful here.

Note very carefully where this energy or energy pattern changes character, maybe where it grows stronger, or maybe fades, or where it gets stuck.

If you feel that you are unable to find or sense energy or an energy pattern, just use your imagination. Make something up. This is fine. Let yourself see what you imagine you would see, if you saw an energy or energy patterning.

Now, slowly find or imagine an area in which your energy either interests you, or maybe disappears, gets stuck, or maybe changes to a concerning texture or color. Go there with your fingertip, or with your mind. You can very gently press your fingertip or your mind into your flesh where this energy is or was.....do this very lightly, no pushing.

Go into this area. Now, with your fingertip, or with your mind, press gently just a little further in, but not too hard. A light touch is all that is needed here.

Now, reach into this area with your mind, and pull any stuck or unpleasant or dead-ended energy out of this area of your body. If you wish to, even use your hand or hands above your body, to make the motion of pulling this energy or energy pattern out of yourself.

Feel this problem energy being pulled out. Use your imagination to lend reality to this process.

Examine the energy you are removing. You can of course give this energy back to yourself if you really do wish to keep it. If so, look at how you know you wish to keep it. ... Look for any attachment you may have to this energy pattern. Also look for any ways this energy pattern itself may be attaching itself to you, may even be causing you to feel this troubled energy is part of you, when it is not.

However, if you do not like this energy or energy pattern, go ahead and pull it way out of your body. Imagine that you use, or actually do use, both hands to do this <u>energy surgery</u>.

If you are disgusted, or want to pretend that what you are removing looks awful, make a face to go with that feeling.

As you do this removing of troubled energy patterning from your body, continue to be aware of what if any pulls or cords may be resisting this removal. Note what you do with these.

Now, move that troubled energy further away from your body. As you move the troubled energy out of your body and then up, raise it way way up, high up, either actually or in your mind's

eye. Be sure you are not throwing this energy at any one else. Visualize a place out there where this energy can go and not touch anyone else.

Once this energy is out there, way up out there, light it up, and then transmute it to the highest light.

Once you are sure you have done this, or have imagined you have done this, then let that troubled energy that you turned to light now fully dissolve and disappear away.

Once this energy has fully disappeared, use your hands to clear the space.

When you feel finished, move your awareness, or your actual hand or hands, back to your body. Then move your attention, or your actual hand or hands, as if you are sealing the area where you conducted the energy surgery.

If you sense there is more troubled energy to be removed, make a mental note of this and know you will go back in when ready. Many people do this <u>energy surgery</u> regularly, as if it were regular housekeeping.

*

When you are complete for now, survey your body and then open your eyes. Think about this for a moment. Remember that you can practice this exercise again and again, always making more clear to yourself what you feel or sense you are doing.

METAHEAL

There is great value in exercising your mind's ability to imagine and work with the idea of subtle energy and energy patterning. You can begin to see -- to imagine and visualize -- places where it may be useful to do some energy re-patterning, or even full removing of problem energy circuits or sub-circuits.

This activity calls upon your creative facilities to gain access to information about yourself which is hidden from your conscious mind.

Although energy surgery <u>cannot</u> be said to eliminate an actual physical health problem such as a neurological or other physical disease, it can assist its user in:

1) Visualizing various energetic patterns and chains of psychological and perhaps also biological (and perhaps also external) origin;

2) Engaging consciously with these imagined or actual patterns;

3) Learning methods which, although in the beginning may have only temporary effects, do provide a sense of awareness and engagement with these patterns;

4) Strengthening concentration on subtle patterns and the energy held within these;

5) Developing intuitive methods of engaging with ongoing deeply ingrained patterning which may feel to be or actually be detrimental;

6) Conducting <u>intuitive surgery</u> on oneself; and,

7) Practicing this combination of: creative imagery and visualization; relaxed yet active meditation;

and, gentle yet keen concentration, as is called for in these exercises.

With practice, users of this energy surgery can work on themselves and the webs they weave at a very deep level. Let's call this energetic surgery *meta-healing*. This does not heal health conditions; however, this does draw awareness to the energetic patterns moving around and through these conditions. Metahealing improves in acuity with practice.

Metahealing is about the mind's ability to draw attention to areas that require attention. Metahealing is about the mind working to understand that a troubled emotional or biological pattern is not part of the SELF.

Although a troubled pattern seeks to merge with the person it forms in or invades, with the person who is the host of the troubled pattern, *the person is <u>not</u> the troubled pattern*. Of course, *the troubled pattern seeks to merge with the person that hosts it to allow the troubled pattern to survive*.

Sometimes survival by the host of a troubled pattern may mean expelling the troubled pattern. In this instance, the troubled pattern must die for the host, the SELF, to survive. This may be difficult when <u>the troubled pattern has addicted its host to the pattern</u>. (See the detailed explanation of this process in the companion book, *Seeing The Hidden Face Of Addiction: Detecting And Confronting This Invasive Presence.*)

Users of energy surgery who seek to metaheal can explore what this book describes as <u>implicit pattern addiction. We can grow addicted to energy patterns whether or not these develop</u>

<u>a physical parallel.</u> These can include energy patterns behind behavioral cycles such as addiction (including addiction to alcohol, nicotine, and other drugs, or to behaviors such as gambling), and to emotional patterns that may or may not be drug-related (such as depression, chronic pain, digestive problems, other illnesses and other afflictions), as well as hidden patternings such as what could be deep sources of would-be future stress-related physical illnesses. (Again note: metahealing does not heal a health problem. Metahealing does however empower our awareness to better sense patterns affecting us.)

With practice, users of energy surgery can bring levels of partial, or maybe eventually even full, release or rewiring of imagined or actual unwanted subtle energy patterning.

Those Readers who become adept at getting out of (and then back into) their bodies -- which is simply moving their focus and thus their view, to be looking at themselves from outside their physical bodies, will find that energy surgery is especially effective when the focus is looking down onto the physical body from higher up, or from somewhere outside it.

EXERCISE #45.2
METAHEALING

Now, identify something else about yourself, such as one of your states of mind, or what you feel to be an emotional pattern, that you would like to see raised to a healthier level.

Invent your own way to visualize or imagine that you see this problem mental state or troubled emotional pattern of yours. Perhaps

form a picture of it, or give it a color or texture, some way to focus on what you are seeing.

When ready, try to transform the pattern and energy of this condition you are looking at.

If you like, conduct your own energy surgery process here.

Now, visualize or imagine that you transform or remove this troubled pattern and its energy. Once you do, then feel as if there is something that has indeed changed, even if just a little.

Think about what this means in terms of its uses in your own mind and life.

(Note: Please do not conduct this energy surgery on other people. We are not talking about this aspect here. Here, we are specifically looking at the training of the personal consciousness to work with itSELF, both here and BEYOND.)

46
METASYNCRISIS

> A bird I am: this body was my
> cage. But I have flown leaving
> it as a token.
>
> Al-Ghazali
> *Old Sufi Mystic Poem*

Let's take a moment to consider something called metasyncrisis (pronounced META-SIN-KREH-SIS). What is metasyncrisis? This concept refers to the extracting of sick or troubled material from a body, actually from a cell. Metasyncrisis has been typically understood to involve the movement or osmosis of troubled, infected, diseased, and even dead matter from inside a cell, out through its membrane or cell wall, to a place outside the cell where it can be dissolved or disposed of. This is a physical plane understanding of the biological process.

However, *higher* metasyncrisis, as defined here in this *How To Die And Survive* book on transition and death, involves the conceptual movement of sick or troubled material or energy away, *out of what is being harmed by the sick or troubled energy.* We can also look at metasyncrisis in terms of ...

**...the consciously healing movement of a physical or
emotional body away from sick or troubled energy,**

**sending that sick or troubled energy
to a place outside that body,**

**in order for that body to heal,
in order for that body to survive.**

**Once outside the physical and or emotional body,
the troubled pattern then dissolves,
thereby both releasing and
canceling that troubled condition.**

In this book, death is described as being the shift or transition of the personal consciousness to another place, another dimension of itSELF, of its reality. To move to this new place or condition, to survive, ties and cords to problems and their problem patterns must be released. What is released stays behind. This troubled pattern that is released dissolves away, dies.

So, in this case, the death is actually of what is a troubled pattern or energy arrangement. To survive, the SELF releases troubled patterning, which once released dissolves as it cannot live without its host body or host SELF.

In this sense, metasyncrisis allows the body of the SELF to survive. Again, what dies is not the SELF, just the troubled material or patterning. That is, unless the SELF does not let go of, does not release, the troubled patterning. (**We know we may best survive by leaping from a sinking ship, not by staying tied or corded to it while it sinks.**)

Again, what survives is what released the troubled material or problem pattern out of its body, out of the body it was negatively affecting, out of the being that must heal to survive here and BEYOND. The troubled energy arrangement must die, not the host body.

The being survives when releasing what is killing it.

**This requires that the SELF
must be clear about its identity to survive.
How often do we confuse ourselves with a sinking ship,
or with a troubled energy pattern?**

EXERCISE #46.1
OSMOSING TROUBLED MATERIAL

Pick a problematic feeling or a troubled physical condition. Imagine that you can see it. Give it a shape or an image. Let it start to boil.

Now, cause it to boil faster and faster, hotter and hotter.

Now, cause this condition to boil so much that it evaporates, its vapor floating away, dispersing, dissolving, and transmuting to a high Light.

EXERCISE #46.2
META-SYNCRISIZING REGULARLY

Practice Exercise #46.1 again now:

> *(Choose or imagine) a problematic feeling or a troubled physical condition. Imagine that you can see it. Give it a shape or an image. Let it start to boil.*

> *Now, cause it to boil faster and faster, hotter and hotter.*

> *Now, cause this condition to boil so much that it evaporates, its vapor floating away, dispersing, dissolving, and transmuting to a high Light.*

Once you have completed this repeat of Exercise #46.1, think of ways you might use this process. Teach yourself how to do this quick yet profound work on yourself.

Make an agreement with your SELF that, if ever needed, you will do this sort of visualizing or imagining once in a while, or maybe even once a week or even once a day. When and how often is up to you. (Some people choose once an hour and some even choose to do this in the backs of their minds, continuously.)

UNDERSTAND THIS CONCEPT

The SELF can begin to lift itSELF out of, disentangle from, troubled or diseased patterning. This is a matter of focus, a matter of shifting awareness. The SELF can see that it is NOT the diseased pattern, and then begin to distance from this pattern.

This is about *not accepting* that the problem pattern is part of your own identity, part of your actual SELF.

It is the problem pattern that must be rewired or die, not YOU.

Problem physical and emotional patterns seek to merge with their host, to cause the host to accept these as being part of him or her SELF. Remember, a troubled pattern exists within its host. So, the troubled pattern works to become seen by the host as part of the host. (For a close look at how problem patterns can inhabit us, even seem to merge with us, see the book, *Seeing The Hidden Face of Addiction.*)

Again and again,

340

we must know on a deep level that

the host is NOT the problem pattern.
You are not the problem pattern inhabiting you.

If you are the host of a problem pattern, you, the host, can create a process where you, as the host, can DIS-identify with this problem pattern. You can choose to not identify with the problem pattern. Although it is seeking to fool you into thinking you are the problem, it is the pattern that is the problem.

**Step away and
see that your actual SELF
is not this pattern that is causing you a problem.**

While this understanding does not in itself heal a health condition, this does allow you to begin the work of your personal consciousness knowing that it is not the problem, and knowing that:

It is YOU, your actual SELF, who will survive.

This metasyncrisis concept becomes more and more useful in terms of mental focus. With this practice, mental focus can become more and more powerful. Earth Humans' modern medicine is just starting to understand this concept.

Metasyncrisis is not miracle-working. It is the application of a profound yet simple *consciousness technology* in freeing the SELF in order to *elevate out of entanglement* with a troubled or sick pattern.

Understanding more and more about this, little by little, day by day, is already starting to see how you can be *dying and surviving,* by seeing that:

**You do survive without the problem pattern,
while the problem pattern does not survive without you.**

This is what metasyncrisis is all about. A great deal of metasyncrisis already takes place while we are living in physical bodies, as this is a natural housekeeping process our biological cells engage in.

Bringing this energetic housekeeping concept to a higher level allows for an expanded understanding of what this is.

<u>47</u>
METABOLIZING THE LIGHT

> May I . . . be exalted . . . rising through His assistance out of the dust and ashes, and changing into a pure spiritual body of rainbow colors like unto the transparent, crystal-like, paradisiacal gold, that my own nature may be redeemed and purified . . . .
>
> Prayer by an unknown adept
> to the Supreme Alchemist of the
> Universe for His Assistance
> *Consummation of the Magnum Opus*

The awareness involved in *dying and surviving* requires energy, or at least the concept of energy. Your personal consciousness, your actual SELF, must remain on some level conscious to fuel for itself healthy expansion-elevation-ascension. What or who can fuel your consciousness for such a journey? You can.

Let's return here to the idea of visualizing an ideal source, something clear and pure and glowing, like very pure clean clear Light. You know Light. You can visualize high Light. You can clarify your own idea of Light. Now you can think about *metabolizing your own Light, your own idea of clean clear Light.* You can find, focus on, and transmute your Light to fuel yourself.

So much of this is non-material, so it may at first seem imaginary or conceptual as you move past physicality. Of course, once BEYOND, you live along and within your own CONTINUUM OF CONSCIOUSNESS. Where this may appear conceptual, even imaginary from the standpoint of your 3-D existence, this will be more clear to you once you expand beyond your present physicality.

You can locate, focus on, absorb, the idea of your own energy, your own Light. You can drink this Light! Use your imagination. Let this concept into your consciousness. You are your own Light, you can survive as your own Light.

If you ever find yourself without a physical body to consume food and water, you may want to know that you can drink, absorb, the nourishment of your own Light. Your actual SELF can nourish your actual SELF.

THINK OF LIGHT AS NOURISHMENT

Plant life on Earth has developed, or has been developed, to have biochemical photosynthesis. This photosynthesis is an electrochemical means of *Light consumption*, and of *Light metabolizing*. Your biological Human skin does something like this as well, reacting to sunlight by producing vitamins for the body.

Now, let's take this concept to another level, a subtle energy level, either by imagining or visualizing, or both. Here, let's say that the *idea* of Light itself can be mobilized or metabolized.

Let's imagine or sense that, out there, along your own CONTINUUM OF your own personal CONSCIOUSNESS, you

344

are already fueling your SELF with your vision or idea of Light. This nourishment and fueling by Light is already taking place for you. **You already instinctively know this.**

EXERCISE #47.1
DRINKING LIGHT

Find or imagine a natural Light source such as sunLight, moonLight or starLight. See it. Feel it.

Now, take the Light into yourself as if it were water in a parched desert. Drink this Light. Fill yourself with this Light. Feel nourished. Stay with this feeling for the next exercise.

EXERCISE #47.2
METABOLIZING LIGHT

Now, practice using the Light you are drinking as fuel, as immediate energy for your personal consciousness. . . .

Study the immediacy of this energy. Light IS energy. The idea, the vision, of Light is energy here. See that this idea of Light is fuel.

Feel Light fueling you—fueling your mind and your non-physical body, your consciousness, your Will, your energetic healing, your survival here and BEYOND.

REMEMBER

Later, once you are out there BEYOND, you may remember this discussion. Remember that the imaginary visualization and mobilization, metabolization, of the idea of high Light, of the ideal purest of all Light, requires no physical biochemical transaction -- as you are out there BEYOND. This is your SELF, your personal consciousness, seeing its own Light.

345

This idea of your own highest Light can carry you on through all kinds of transition challenges. Even back down in the physical plane, holding on to this vision of highest Light can trigger an array of powerful biochemical events in the emotional and even physical body.

What you see in your mind's eye can be so very powerful. Choose what you will look for, and how you will use what you find for your SELF, for your survival both here and BEYOND.

Create images of high Light in your mind, in your mind's eye, in your consciousness. Store these images there for future use. Tag these images. Leave notes telling yourSELF that you can find and tap into Light as you move through your journey both here and BEYOND.

<u>48</u>
METADYING

> Nirvana is not like the black, dead peace of the grave, but the living peace, the living happiness of a soul which is conscious of itself, and conscious of having found its own abode in the heart of the Eternal.
>
> Mahatma Mohandas Karamchand Gandhi
> *All Religions are True*

Every moment of your life, you are undergoing transition and change on some level, even if invisible to you. Yes, profound personal change is always taking place, even if we do not see it or feel it happening.

Some change is microscopic, even down on the cellular level. You may not notice that some one million cells per second are dying in your physical biological body. In fact, this would be far too much to be knowing, far too much for your mental desktop to be tracking. It is convenient that this cell death is taking place under your radar. However, this is not surprising as your biological body is a finely tuned biological mechanism, so finely tuned and programmed, that most cell death takes place automatically.

As generally unchanging from day to day as we may appear to ourselves, we are never the same as we were yesterday. Even from one moment to the next, at least on a micro level, our biological bodies have profoundly changed, constantly moving through a biochemical and bioelectrical concert of rapidly oscillating events and conditions.

Nothing stays the same even when appearing to.

The SELF who you are is traveling in your constantly changing biological body. This body, your physical plane vehicle, is never the same from one moment to the next. Nothing is constant anywhere, including while you are here living in this 3-D physical plane version of Earth.

PERCEPTION OF TRANSITION

While all this change and transition is taking place within and around you, there are times you will be making changes, undergoing additional minor and major transitions beyond these micro-level ones. Yet, even these more visible transitions can be quite subtle.

**Indeed, many times
what we experience of transition is our
<u>perception of the transition over the transition itself</u>.**

You may choose to enter, or find yourself entering anyway even if you prefer not to, a transition out of one of the patterns or phases you are in now. This could be an emotional pattern, a relationship pattern, a health pattern, or any other pattern. Usually, we are experiencing many patterns and sub-patterns at the same time.

What you experience of this transition is actually your *perception* of this transition, how you place this transition in context. *How you feel* a transition is working for you is based on *how you see this transition*. This is not to say we can simply enter denial and simply erase any transition stress, or even any fear or pain we may feel. This is to say that:

> **We can give ourselves frameworks**
> **for experiencing and navigating**
> **minor and major transitions**
> **in-life, and in seeming end-of-life,**
> **and perhaps also in what appears to be**
> **after-life, or actually is life after life.**

CONSCIOUS TRANSITION AND META-DYING

You begin to know that you are always in both minor and major transition processes. Take your transition experiences as far as you want to. Give these the frameworks you wish to. You can choose to *die and survive* on minor and major levels, if you, of your own Free Will, consciously choose to. You decide what this means.

We have been wired to experience transition according to programming. Our responses to what we experience are seemingly dictated by our biological body and its biological brain. So, how we experience minor and major change and transition may feel almost dictated, as if there are no other options.

Yet, we can liberate ourselves from the shackles of a mindset that lives within a programming, within a *designed reality,*

within a matrix and/or body we and/or some other intelligence have either evolved or designed for us.

We have the opportunity to signal ourselves that we can make it through a change or transition by saying:

> Oh, I know what this is, this this is a transition.
>
> Here it is, this transition.
>
> Here is where I am in this process: I see the beginning, the middle, the ending, and have a sense of what is next.
>
> This is the way I am seeing this transition experience.
>
> This is the way I want to be seeing this transition experience.
>
> Here is what I am doing to navigate this transition experience.
>
> Here is what this transition means to me.
>
> Here is how I want to move through this experience.
>
> Here is what I want to do or be BEYOND this experience.
>
> This is how I am going to get there.

TRIGGER CONSCIOUS TRANSITION PROCESSES

Trigger small and great *conscious transition processes* in yourself, in your species, in the world, by learning to call your attention to the processes. Be conscious of where you are and of what you are doing as you move through any minor or major transition, even seeming death.

The ultimate goal of any minor or major transition is to be free of what you have transitioned out of. This liberation is the ultimate goal.

Review the linkage of death and liberation portrayed in Figure 32.5. Recall that Chapter 35 explains that:

> You can move yourself through changes and transitions here and BEYOND. ... you can consciously move from the destabilization of in-life pattern change, or what some may call seeming death, into the spinning climb of ascension, into the re-stabilization of liberation, all made conscious by knowing the operation of the Light vehicle.

Understand that you, your SELF, your personal consciousness, own this Light vehicle you travel in. You have the power via your consciousness to see yourself moving. This is your choice, your concept to develop. Understand that there is available to you, even in daily life, a conscious process that can move you into liberation from problem patterns. **This is conscious liberation of the SELF, which is metadeath.**

Take all the ingredients of change and ascension offered within this volume. Apply these to succeed in surviving transition as your actual SELF. This is thinking quite valuable in daily life, as well as in seeming end-of-life, and even perhaps even in life after life situations.

CALL ON THESE IDEAS LATER

As your consciousness has now considered these ideas, concepts, and processes, these will be more available to you, should you wish to further develop these for yourself, perhaps to call on these at another time in another place here or BEYOND.

To become proficient at meta-dying, you must remember that:

351

1) Even a small revolution of your awareness can free you. Ask yourself what this freedom looks like. How much different and in what ways would it be different from the way you live and think now?

2) Can you be free so long as you are subject to the enslavement of inherited and acquired, genetic and neurological, biological programming? Yes, once you understand how readily available this freedom of thought is.

3) You can find extensive interdimensional (as well as physical) freedom while living in the material plane. But you must be willing to fully overhaul your understanding of your own personal consciousness' reality, of the existence of your own personal consciousness as your actual SELF.

4) To master any transition, any minor and or major change, ending, or death, think about levels or dimensions of reality. Basically, the dimensions are a rainbow of realities, with the most dense reality at one end and the least dense at the other. Within this range of densities are countless variations and formattings of energy.

5) The concept of, the idea of, the highest Light always flows from the least density. High, pure Light can travel down, descend, through the levels of density, but it can become clouded as it travels, even clouded by your own perception of it. Maintain as clear a

352

relationship with the idea of the clearest Light as you can, constantly fine tuning your vision of clear Light.

6) Mastering transition and death processes involves being *consciously aware that reality is multi-dimensional.* Appreciate the mental or conceptual shift involved in moving your focus to and from one dimension of your consciousness, from one dimension of your reality, to another. Practice this shift again and again. Remember that what feels to be mental or conceptual here in 3-D while you have a biological brain, is not what it will be once you leave physicality. Get to know this now. You may eventually find your SELF out there BEYOND.

7) **Your biological optic nerve must learn to register or sense an ever broader range of visual and other sensations. Your biological brain must accept these sensations as relevant information. You must continuously be widening your bands of perception. Start now. <u>This will expand the range of your personal consciousness in advance of your reaching into the expanded terrain of your own CONTINUUM OF CONSCIOUSNESS both here and BEYOND</u> .**

8) **Be sensitive enough and willing enough to hear your own higher voice. Though you (and others around you) may question and even deny the experience, always listen and learn to ever more clearly hear your actual SELF speaking to you, your SELF.**

9) **Know that you must diligently clarify, purify, your intuitive perceptions as you clarify your Light, your idea of your Light, and your idea of your actual SELF.**

EXERCISE #48.1
DEFINING A METADEATH

Give some thought to a complete <u>overhaul of your awareness</u> of your actual SELF, of your personal consciousness. What would this overhaul be like? How would your awareness expand?

List at least three changes you might make in this overhaul. These are changes away from patterns, such as patterns in the following categories:

- *Pattern addictions.*
- *Behavioral and emotional pattern traps.*
- *Ways of seeing the physical world.*
- *Ways of responding to pain and to crisis.*
- *Personal spiritual reality.*
- *Reasons for living.*
- *Views of changes, transitions, endings, minor or major deaths.*
- *Etc. (add your own categories here).*

EXERCISE #48.2
STAGING A METADEATH

*You are on your own for this exercise. Define your own terms, your own process. **Remember, you are not physically dying here....***

Now, sit or lie down and metadie, whatever this means to you at the moment. This will be an in-life expansion along your own **CONTINUUM OF CONSCIOUSNESS.**

*Use your imagination here. Then, for at least a few minutes, rise up and function as if you have **meta**-died. Watch yourself, and put yourself back on track if you slip out of your **meta**-death.*

If you wish to, hold on to this sensation as you return to your daily life. If not, let this sensation go, and store it in your memory, in your personal consciousness, for later use.

REMEMBER

In **meta**-dying, as in all dying, remember:

1) No matter how simple or challenging your dying process, it is your option to keep your mind's eye—your higher sensory mechanism—open. You do not need to be medically conscious to implement your higher sensory system, as expanded sensation is not physical once out of a physical body.

2) Whether you are releasing a problem biological pattern, or a problem behavioral pattern, or a problem emotional pattern, or all of these, *you must take responsibility for the energy you release.* Move these troubled patterns away, dissolve them away, and transmute released problem patterns to highest Light.

3) Whether or not you are biologically conscious, and whether or not you are still in a physical body, stay conscious of this responsibility.

49

METASCENDING:
LEAP LEVEL SEVEN

> The world you see does not exist, because the place where you perceive it is not real.

> "The Alternate to
> Dreams of Fear"
> *A Course in Miracles,*
> Chapter 28, Volume One

Once these basic *How To Die And Survive* ideas about survival both here in-life and BEYOND begin to make at least a little sense, the mind opens to further possibilities. Working through the ideas and exercises in these *How To Die And Survive* books allows the biological mind-brain to amend, extend, or even develop new neural pathways. Basically, we are allowing our minds and brains, even our consciousness-es, to learn to see transition and even death as the opportunity to expand.

This is the opportunity to become the expansive being we already are, the being who can, and already does, live both here and BEYOND.

Although you are welcome to, there is no need to study the material in these books, as you are not being tested. Just perhaps allow yourself to consider what is said here, and to

return to this material and these exercises from time to time. (Readers who want to move through all or some of the *How To Die And Survive, Book One* and *Book Two* exercises as a partially or continuously flowing process, can do this in *How To Die And Survive, Book Three*.)

The various concepts shared in these *How To Die And Survive* books can begin to make more and more sense over time. Many of these terms, or the ideas they present, will be remembered later, when there is an experience that calls your mind to tap into these *options for survival*. Simply considering or just scanning these ideas such as megadeath, metastrophizing, metasomatic healing, metasyncrisis, metabolizing Light, and metadeath—allows your mind to be prepared to recognize and consciously live your ongoing **meta**-*scendence.*

META-ASCENDENCE OR METASCENDENCE

Let's back up and talk about the word, *ascend*. Ascending basically refers to rising or climbing. Of course, if you are in an airplane, ascending is flying into what is above.

Ascendence is often seen as being the act of rising or moving up, generally in political or corporate systems, or even in monarchies where these still exist. Ascendence in spiritual terms is often described as spiritual awakening, or rising to a new frequency of spirit or of energy. Ascended Masters are often described as those who have achieved spiritual enlightenment.

Here in this book, ascending is about expanding into realms BEYOND. This ascending is basically A SHIFT IN THE FOCUS OF THE PERSONAL CONSCIOUSNESS. (See *Volume 3* in this

Keys To Consciousness And Survival Series, titled *Unveiling The Hidden Instinct*, where the shifting of the focus is defined and described.)

Here in this book, *How To Die And Survive, Book Two*, we define the idea of what can be called <u>*meta*</u> ascendence as being the higher level or form of ascendence.

**Meta-ascendence is rising above
the ideas we have about rising above.**

METASCENDENCE IS PERSONAL

Your ongoing **meta-**scendence process is your own ongoing **meta-**scension. This continuous metascension is perhaps the most subtle and yet most present, even most amazing, of all LEAPs. You can always be consciously metascending, every minute you live, once you see this. Once you see this process is yours, and you see it is already underway, you can *consciously navigate your metascension.*

Realizing, recognizing, truly seeing, your ongoing meta-scension process, thus your expanding metascension awareness, can sneak up on you. Or, this can happen for you almost instantaneously. No one around you may see you LEAPing into your conscious awareness of your personal metascension process. No one around you may be registering this awakening of your heightening awareness, and of its heightened abilities to navigate transition, even to survive. This is alright.

Yet, others are also meta-scending. They are joining us all in this process. As are many people around you, you may be

either witnessing or realizing your own metascendence -- or feeling the waves of the others also metascending, the waves of these tremendous effects. You may already be sensing this, perhaps at first without being clear about what is taking place.

You are part of a magnificent wave of opening and realization taking place. Somewhere someone sees this, consciously taps into the metascension process. A chain of waking up takes place. You wake up, someone else wakes up, we wake up, our species wakes up. Humanity becomes aware of its metascension options for *dying and surviving* both here and BEYOND.

SENSATION OF A HIGHER DIVINE LOVE

However skilled you become at *dying and surviving*, at the technical aspects of your metascension process, do not push your process. Rather, let your process flow. While you are awakening your SELF to the *dying and surviving* awarenesses and processes, seek your own definition of the idea of the highest clearest Light, of an energy presence that is pure and clear, perhaps for some people, an energy that feels like divine love.

Let's say this divine love is an awareness. If you are still living in your physical body, there is a biochemical component to this sensation. If you are already out there BEYOND, this divine love is a sensation you can generate, and also can look for.

This love is not physical plane affection. This is a compassionate-seeming awareness, an energy pattern or form. In quiet moments, even in daily life, you can find this and feel this. Later, you may want to generate or seek this sensation.

You may want to tap into this sense of the Inter-dimensional Species of Humanity's higher level, very pure, compassion energy.

It is suggested, even in daily physical plane life, always seek the highest path for your Human heart. Make this a constant endeavor.

Feeling compassion, a sustained pure SELF-less compassion, will protect you and maintain you high above energetic pollution. High, clear, interdimensional compassion is not an emotional body sensation. This high compassion can transcend the intensity of transition, can guide navigation of in-life and seeming end-of-life transition, even life after life transition.

Through this clarification of ascension, this meta-ascension of your higher level compassion, can come additional fuel for your Free Will. So, purifying, de-cording, clarifying, *elevating love into compassion energy* can help fuel the metascension of YOU, of your SELF, of your personal consciousness.

METASCEND

Metascension is a very special quickening of the soul. What a marvelous opportunity to have during your Human incarnation.

EXERCISE #49.1
QUICKENING

To quicken is to make alive, or more alive, or to bring back to life. Many spiritual and religious teachings refer to something like a quickening. Many of these teachings say that quickening involves a

specific belief system. Each of you Readers will have your own view on this, and this is fine.

Here, let's talk about a basic element of quickening that we all can relate to. This element of quickening is not part of a particular religion or belief system. This is basically about expanding one's mind or spirit or SELF to a higher level of awareness.

So here, in this exercise, let's think of the quickening of your personal consciousness as involving the sensation of speeding up, accelerating, the frequency of what you may call your vibration. This speeding up is part of the expansion of the SELF, of the awareness, that this book is explaining.

There are many paths to quickening. Manage your own quickening in any way you choose. List three possible paths of quickening for yourSELF. Use your imagination here. There are no right or wrong answers.

EXERCISE #49.2
METAQUICKENING INTO METASCENSION

Now, imagine that you are vibrating. Next, imagine that you begin to vibrate faster and faster. Start to hum. (If you cannot hum, or prefer not to hum, just imagine that you are humming.)

Raise the frequency of your hum as you raise the frequency of your vibration.

Add compassion. Feel an increasing degree of compassion and go on for quite a while . . . (Your heart may even hum).

PART VIII

How To

Access

High

Metaxis

<u>50</u>
NAVIGATING THE IDEA

> Before I'll be a slave
> I'll be buried in my grave,
> And go home to my Lord
> And be free....

> author unknown
> *Oh Freedom*
> Old Spiritual Song

We have a right to stand up to forces oppressing us, whether or not our oppressors say we do. We have seen people seeking to *exercise this right to stand up* throughout history, around the globe, even in modern times. We have seen oppressors seeking to *suppress the exercise of this right* also throughout history, around the globe, even in modern times.

Can we expand this right to other dimensions of our reality? Could it be that there are also oppressive forces and factors that are not entirely visible to us,[29] some even not entirely or at all three-dimensional?[30] We must at least wonder. This is not paranoia, this is wise consideration as we begin to think about

---

[29] See another book by this author, Dr. Angela Brownemiller, titled, *The Polictics Of Healing*. See reading list at the end of this present book.
[30] See also other books by this author, such as those in this *Keys To Consciousness And Survival Series*, for example, the *Overriding The Extinction Scenario* books, *Volume 5 and 6* in this series.

how to find ourselves, and set our boundaries and shield ourselves, as we eventually expand BEYOND this physical plane.

FINDING HOPE

Whether personal or political or spiritual, or all of these and more, you know when you are experiencing difficult and even dangerous times. Continue to look for hope, even a shred of hope. Always seek to glimpse hope.

Even in your darkest hour, even if you feel you have touched the depths of despair, when hope may be hard to find:

Look for what may even be but a tiny a speck of hope.
See it out there somewhere,
waiting for you to see it.

You can somehow find the smallest thread of inspiration, that idea, that speck, glowing out there somewhere. Sense its presence as being what feels to be Light.

Hold on to this speck, this hope, this Light.

This is your lifeboat both here and BEYOND.

THIS SPECK OF LIGHT

You can somehow discover this speck of hope and its Light in your atmosphere. See this, sense this spot or speck or touch of Light, whatever Light is for you.

Sometimes this speck of Light looks like a bit or dot of Light floating around your visual field when your eyes are closed. Other times, a speck or hint of Light looks different, maybe so

366

vague we almost miss it. Call your Light to your SELF. Wait and see what you sense out there. Look for what you sense to become more clear.

Keep looking or imagining finding your light out there. This idea of Light, this speck of Light, is glowing out there, perhaps at first almost invisible, even infinitesimally minute.

Watch this speck of Light, this dot or speck out there, expand a little, maybe into a thread or line. Think of this Light as hope, see it begin to look like a thread or stream calling you as it dangles before you.

And, this idea, this hint or speck of Light, is a place, a station, a locus. This speck is your place, your hope. This speck can indeed be your lifeboat. You can ride this lifeboat through your transitions. This Light is the opening, the thread, eventually the beam, you can follow to navigate.

Your lifeboat itself is your navigation. Your navigation is itself your liberation. And, at the same time, the Light you are following to your survival is the pathway to YOU, to your SELF, as you *are* your Light.

SEVERAL UNDERSTANDINGS

There are several understandings involved in liberating yourself from the pull of patterns, even problems. These include the following knowings:

1) The world you believe you see is only a very small fraction of reality, if that.

2) This means that what you perceive as a catastrophic development is only a fraction of reality, if that.

3) What you perceive as death is only a fraction of reality, if that.

4) Nevertheless, your feelings regarding difficult, even what feel like catastrophic, events, illnesses, and endings are important. Respect these feelings.

5) Pay close attention to what your senses, your soul, your SELF, are saying.

6) Let your senses, your soul, your SELF reveal to you the degree of attachment, the extent of your cording, to the reality that you are seeing affected by difficult and perhaps even catastrophic patterns and developments.

7) Fully acknowledge and experience your emotional response to difficult, troubled, even catastrophic, events and situations. See how much of the *cord release* work described in earlier chapters of this and the previous *How To Die And Survive* book you may want to do.

You must continue to remind yourself of the above information as you ride the wave of a challenge you may face, the storm of what may even appear to be disaster.

Grab its reins. Navigate your ride through this problem pattern, this disaster. Use the energy of your experience to release you—to elevate you—into your new reality, your new dimension of your SELF.

SEEK DUAL AWARENESS

Seek two levels of expanded awareness in a challenging or difficult time. This is a dual level awareness. One level is focused on immediate survival needs, and is essential. The other level is placing yourself in time and space, and can also be essential.

Try to see what is going on as being a fragment of the whole picture, the piece of the whole that it is. Track how this challenge or difficulty is being affected by forces and factors that may not be entirely visible or may not be material plane forces and factors.

Detach from pulls that interfere with survival. This detaching here is not dying. Not at all. This is separating your SELF from physical plane patterning which, no matter how much this pattern wants you to feel it is part of you, is <u>not</u> part of you, is <u>not</u> you, <u>not</u> your actual SELF. Remember, you are not a problem pattern, although a problem pattern may seek to make its host believe the problem pattern is part of her or him, not a separate yet invasive pattern. (Again, for more about this **invasive patterning,** see the *Faces Of Addiction Series* by this author, specifically the book titled, *Seeing The Hidden Face Of Addiction: Detecting And Confronting This Invasive Presence.*)

Release cords, all ties to the sinking ship, and you will not sink with it. Keep in mind that you are not, no part of the actual YOU is, the sinking ship. You are a traveler who can navigate BEYOND that ship.

EXERCISE #50.1
DETACHING FROM THE PROBLEM OR CATASTROPHE

Select or imagine a large or small problem or catastrophe you have experienced, or are experiencing, in your life. Imagine that this problem or catastrophe is happening on a relatively small island. You are very, very involved in this catastrophe.

Suddenly, you realize that the entire island is sinking. You must choose whether to sink with the island, or to escape on the life raft awaiting you at the shore. This life raft glows as if a speck of Light.

Which do you choose?

How easily do you decide?

What influences your decision?

EXERCISE #50.2
SEEING THE DIMENSIONS SURROUNDING THE PROBLEM OR CATASTROPHE

Imagine a profound catastrophe. See it in your mind's eye.

Now, as if your mind's eye were a movie camera, expand the frame of the picture to such a wide angle that the image of the catastrophe only fills one-tenth, and then only one/one-hundredth of the screen.

You are reducing the catastrophe from center stage, and then to side stage. How? What does this process feel like?

<u>51</u>
BECOMING THE PHOENIX AND RISING

I am the Phoenix,
Who will be next?
Come fly with the Phoenix,
You will be next.
Time to leave the nest.

Fly With the Phoenix

The concept of *personal survival as personal resurrection* taking place in transition has been discussed in previous chapters. Let's return to this concept here by considering the popular mythology of the Phoenix. This is the mythological bird who rises from the ashes, from the spoils, from the remains of a disaster or an apocalypse. This is the bird whose egg is hatched in the heat of that cataclysmic global fire and rises again, now in full splendor.

The concept of the Phoenix rising can be yours, your sense of your resurrecting, your essence rising to live again, who you truly are truly *dying and surviving.*

YOU CAN BE THE PHOENIX

This mythology, so popular among indigenous and ancient cultures, and also among modern cultures, is an important KEY. This is the transference of a KEY understanding. This is the *meaning of survival itself.*

Note: Many Readers will find helpful this author's presentation and description of the OMEGA KEY as shared in the *Metaterra Chronicles Collection* books. See these books for definition and details of the OMEGA KEY, such as the novel, *Revealing The Omega Key*, and its companion non-fiction book, *Detecting The Omega Deception*.

This deeply embedded message speaks to us, tells us that we, our SELVES, our personal consciousness-es, can survive change, ending, transition, even crisis or disaster or cataclysm, or yes, what seems to be death.

As the mythical phoenix, you, your trained personal consciousness, can choose to elevate, to *rise from the changes, the transitions, even from the ruins,* even from the ashes of what may appear to be devastation.

Rising, elevating, surviving as who you truly are, can be your choice. Yes, this can be a learned choice, a developed option, the option to choose not only whether or not you survive as a personal consciousness, but *how* you rise, how you survive, and what form you will take when you rise, when you *die and survive.*

Again, understanding we are not only physical, biological life forms, but far more than this, is key here.

KNOW THE PHOENIX

The vision of the Phoenix rising from the ashes permeates the history of consciousness here on Earth, appearing in the imagery and teachings of many Human cultures, and calling

out from within the collective sub-conscious of the Human species.

The Phoenix is often described as having a rainbow or multiple colored coat, with shiny blue-purple (or indigo) feathers on its wings, long red and bluish tail feathers, golden neck feathers, light-colored feathers atop its head, and a tuft of various colors at the back of its head, giving it the appearance of being two-headed. Many ancient mystics viewed the Phoenix as symbolic of the immortality of the soul. Initiates into mystery schools who were considered to have been reborn were raised to the level of what was often called "phoenix."

Egyptian mythology describes what it calls the "Ka" as the Egyptian "bennu" or phoenix bird: Ka often appears to the deceased in the form of a blue phoenix, offering the recently physically dead person, the "Ba," the lower self, the opportunity to rejoin her or his "Ka," her or his higher SELF. The shock and release of physical or other levels of death can trigger this divine union: the uniting of the lower SELF with the personal higher spirit or personal higher SELF.

OUR OWN

PHOENIX

The story of the Phoenix is a dying and surviving story. To absorb the message that the story of the Phoenix holds for you, you can take your SELF through a process. You can further develop your connection to your SELF, to the YOU that survives. Even in your daily life, you can become increasingly aware of your actual SELF. You can sense how your SELF

moves through, survives, endings and beginnings, and challenges and transitions.

Start watching yourSELF in your daily life. Are you aware of yourSELF constantly moving through minor and major transitions? How do you sense these transitions are underway? Start by looking at some of your most obvious and simple transition processes, maybe like a 24 hour period where you wake up, have your day, get ready to go to sleep, then sleep, then get ready to wake up the next morning. Or maybe start with a meeting you regularly attend, as meetings usually have obvious beginnings, involved middle times, and definite endings. You will begin to see that your moving through a transition, no matter what that transition is, has sensations that signal what is taking place, where you are in the process, and how you are doing as you move through.

Some of the processes or exercises in these *How To Die And Survive* books, as you certainly have ascertained by now, are more entertaining than others. Nevertheless, the imagery, the mental focus, and the stories you allow yourself to consider, or visualize, or imagine, while conducting these exercises, are subtle but powerful training. Your mind-brain, even your personal consciousness, are all developing ever new avenues, even training nonphysical aspects for later when you may find your SELF, your awareness, out of physicality.

The training goes in quite deep despite the simplicity of many of these exercises. The messages to what some call the soul or the spirit, others call the higher self, to what and who this book calls the actual SELF, the *personal consciousness*, are actually contained *between the lines* of these exercises, and *between the*

images and the feelings and the reactions you have while conducting these exercises. Your most profound learning is the most subtle by-product of such work.

EXERCISE #51.1
BURNING DOWN

For this exercise, think back to, or imagine, a time when you had a fever. Recall or imagine any sensations you may have had, such as sensations of the heat your body was using to burn off infection.

Now, with your eyes closed, visualize yourself in a house which is on fire. Yet, this is not a real fire, this is heat so hot it feels like fire. First, you see imaginary smoke coming at you from all directions. Then, you see imaginary flames. The flames are large and dancing before your eyes. The flames are blue and red and orange and yellow. They are gold. Gold. Gold. They burn so hot they turn a very bright white. White. White flames.

The idea of the heat of the imaginary fire increases. You begin to feel feverish, as if you sizzle with fever. You are not sure whether this fire is outside you or inside you. For a moment you wonder whether this is a cleansing fever.

As you burn from this fire's or fever's heat, allow yourself to sense this burning. Imagine that troubled conditions and patterns are being burned away. Do not look away from these sensations and feelings. Notice to what degree you go into these feelings. Notice to what degree you keep yourself distanced from these feelings.

Notice how much or how little you feel about this image; notice how much resistance you have to the feelings.

Ask yourself: Would this response, my degree of involvement in this process, be different were I surrounded right now by a real fever or real flames, a real fire?

Allow yourself for a moment to be in the idea of being burned up by fever. See your body turn to ash. Notice that you are still aware of yourself. Notice that, as you turn to ash, there is a point when whatever physical pain or heat you might have endured disappears.

Now, you are still looking at this scene, but from outside of it, from outside of your physicality, from outside your physical body which is now just ash.

Yet you are still here. You are out of this disintegrating body, and you are floating nearby.

Where are you now? Who are you now? Examine yourself, what are your characteristics now? Get to know your SELF out there ....

After noting your characteristics, see what remains of your physical body, now crumbling to smoldering ashes. Hold this image for next exercise. Stay with your SELF here.

EXERCISE #51.2
PHOENIX RISING

Stay with, or recall, the above experience (of Exercise #51.1). Feel your SELF, your personal consciousness, observing this scene. Think of your personal consciousness as floating above this scene, looking down on it.

Now, while still floating out there, collect your SELF, your personal consciousness, into an egg-like capsule. Fold up within this capsule; fold into a fetal position for several seconds or minutes. ... While you

are folded up in there, begin thinking about cracking out of the egg. Feel as if you are a marvelous bird about to be born. As you expand within this egg-like capsule, you feel it cracking open just a bit.

As the capsule cracks open, you realize that this is no longer an egg, if it ever was one. It is a vehicle, your vehicle. Your vehicle looks however you want it to look, and changes depending on the circumstances you are in.

This is another form of the vehicle you have seen in earlier exercises in this book, such as the double-triangle vehicle of Light you have used before, to traverse the dimensions (as in other Exercises in this book: see Figures 32.3 through 32.5). Many people choose geometric forms for their personal vehicles out there BEYOND. You can choose whatever form of vehicle you prefer.

Float out there in your vehicle a little while. Then, let your vehicle fade away, leaving you floating there.

Now, you realize you are becoming something new. Energy is moving, maybe even racing, through you. You see you are becoming a marvelous bird, a beautiful Phoenix, however you imagine your personal Phoenix to look. Your phoenix is your actual SELF, surviving. So let your phoenix look the way you wish it to.

Here you are. You have survived. You unfold your wings as you imagine that you stand, or actually do stand. You spread your wings and rise into the BEYOND.

Hold on to the vision of yourself as the Phoenix rising from the ashes. Look closely. Let your own personal Phoenix look however you want it to.

377

This can be the imagery of survival, the vision of resurrection, the process of DYING AND SURVIVING. This imagery can transport you into and BEYOND your transitions, even through your elevation-ascension processes.

Love yourself as the Phoenix, your Phoenix, your SELF. Always feel that this triumphant rising from the ashes can be yours. You, your actual SELF, can die and survive.

Embrace your SELF, this Phoenix—this is you moving through the elevation process, shifting through and BEYOND this transition into your ongoing survival.

FULLY EMBRACE

When you fully embrace in-life and seeming end-of-life transitions, as well as seeming after-life transitions, you see that these transitions are more of a continuum than an abrupt shift from life to death to after-life.

And, you begin to see the great potential of **personal resurrection and survival processes**. Here you can access the learnings your personal consciousness carries. You can engage your own learnings to guide you through passages and changes, to consciously **navigate transition** so as to continue to SURVIVE, to *die and survive.*

You will no longer be forever restricted to the physical plane, with no option to expand BEYOND. You will no longer be told to live in the physical plane and when done just die there, that that is all there is.

You will realize that the programming implanted into the Human Species, telling it that it is a 3-D life form with no option to travel freely to and from, back and forth from, dimensions of itself—*is not who we are. We are not the programming we carry.*

You will also realize that belief systems that may tell you that there is only one way to survive death, and that is to believe in a particular leader or particular god, are not correct.

There are no belief systems that are the gatekeepers from you to your SELF. You carry your survival tools within your own personal consciousness.

You will know how to, at the right time and only then, set your SELF free. You will access the knowledge the Human Species of Consciousness carries and has a right to access. You will be helping to free us, to help free we captives of our programming to believe we are primarily, even only, physical biological life forms.

You will fly through the portal of change into new worlds.

You will rise from the ashes of challenge, transition, enslavement, and even seeming disaster, in splendor. You will be the Phoenix transcending, the Phoenix resurrecting, the Phoenix elevating-ascending:

THE PHOENIX SURVIVING.

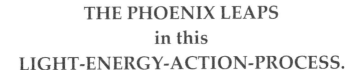

THE PHOENIX LEAPS
in this
LIGHT-ENERGY-ACTION-PROCESS.

<u>52</u>

HARVESTING DEATH FOR FREEDOM

> I envisage a war, of justice
> or strength, of a logic
> beyond all imagining.
>
> Arthur Rimbaud
> *War*

Once we feel we can learn to survive death, whatever this means to us, we begin to see even daily life quite differently. Processes of minor and major transitions such as shifts, changes, endings, deaths, can be understood and moved through ever more consciously.

Death is a shift in perception, and thus in the perception of all experience. In this sense, death of a perception of one's reality is the moving past that perception of reality, and is therefore *seeing beyond* that reality.

This is about seeing beyond what we have been told is death. And, this is about seeing <u>the</u> BEYOND out there for us to continue to SURVIVE <u>within</u>.

EXPAND TO SURVIVAL DOMAINS

We can thus expand to our SURVIVAL TERRITORIES once we see these are there beyond what we have been told we see. (For essential definition and discussion of our SURVIVAL

TERRITORIES, see other books in this *Keys To Consciousness And Survival Series,* and also the partner books in the *Metaterra Chronicles Collection,* such as *Revealing The Omega Key.)*

This SEEING BEYOND is itself an expansion of the awareness. This is an expansion of the actual SELF. This expansion of the SELF is the liberation of the SELF from the confines of what it has been told or programmed to believe is its reality. The option to be able to *die and survive* is ours to claim, starting right now in our daily lives.

LIBERATION FROM CONFINES

The preceding chapters have dealt primarily with the liberation of one's personal consciousness. This is liberation from a more limiting energy pattern arrangement, from being tied to an old matrix or body or way of being. Transition, even dying, is about an old format or set of patterns being left or released, or perhaps even escaped from. This applies to all transitions, even those in our daily lives. We can become quite skilled in navigating events, experiences, sensations, and emotions as we move through changes and transitions. Remember, we are in transition every moment of our lives, both here and yes, BEYOND.

There is of course, as has been suggested several times in preceding chapters, another level of liberation being discussed in this book. This is the liberation of ourselves, even of our species, to know we have a powerful interdimensional existence, and that we have a right to know this.

We have a right to think about these issues. We have a right to discover that conscious death can be carefully navigated, and

only at the right time. Remember again, one need not be medically or physically conscious to have one's personal consciousness aware and involved in the transition and death process. It is the SELF of the personal consciousness that navigates this SURVIVAL.

This is about liberation from the **confines of a narrow evolutionary niche**. (See the *Overriding The Extinction Scenario* books for essential definition and discussion of this **evolutionary niche**. These *Overriding The Extinction Scenario* books are *Volumes 5 and 6* in this *Keys To Consciousness And Survival Series.*)

This is the liberation of the Species of Humanity from restriction to only 3-D Earth and the related biologically evolved physical plane limitations.

We are already far more than only physical plane (biological) beings, and we know this, we do. We already crave the liberation we would achieve were we to allow ourselves to fully, entirely consciously, know this. We already do crave this liberation. All that is required is to recognize who we are, that we are a life form far beyond the limited biological life form defined for us.

LIBERATE HUMANITY

What does it mean to say that Humanity is not free, that it subconsciously desires liberation from the confines -- the confines it has either naturally evolved, or has had implanted into it?

The walls of our prison may be so thick

**that we cannot see through them,
and yet so invisible that we cannot see them.**

But wake up and look! The Human brain, despite its scientific, psychological, political, and creative advances, has been programmed and thus pressured to narrow its awareness of its true nature. This programming is working in such a way that while our minds and societies are seeing an advancing information explosion, the corresponding ties to the physicality of the biological form of the Human Species are ever stronger, ever more *attached*.

We must access our own CONTINUUM OF HIGHER CONSCIOUSNESS, as this is where we actually already do live. It is time for us as individuals, and as species, the actual Species of Humanity, to access our vast CONTINUUM OF CONSCIOUSNESS. Seeing this now is so very necessary, both in personal survival, and in actual species survival. It is time to re-take and occupy our rightful interdimensional nature and territory. This is the territory of our own consciousness.

We have a right to know about our own capability to expand along our own CONTINUUM OF CONSCIOUSNESS. We have a right to come and go, back and forth, even to *die and survive*. Yet, full access to knowing this has been suppressed, is being restricted, and all too frequently, where accessed, distorted and further restricted by the distortions.

Moreover, as Humans feel ever more advanced in their thinking on 3-D planet Earth, the span of actual free thought itself is restricting. This is taking place as we develop ever more within this physical plane reality we are so tied to, so programmed to believe is what we are all about.

Interdimensional awareness and freedom is quite restricted in many arenas. Long term, even ancient, teachings have faded, many of these treated as old fashioned, overly simple, even irrelevant, outdated, anachronisms, or as exciting novelties. Of the interdimensional teachings that are available, many are misinterpreted or misrepresented.

The freedom of the Human mind, whatever degree it may have experienced at some point along the way, may be slipping away—may be leaving the way grains of sand leave a hand, imperceptibly, until enough is gone for an observer finally to notice the difference—if the observer remains mentally equipped enough to notice the difference. Yet, we need not follow this trend.

WE CAN ALERT OURSELVES TO SUBTLE TRENDS THAT ARE AFFECTING US AND OUR SURVIVAL.

As the freedom of full and undistorted contact with our own ACTUAL SELVES (who carry our own actual interdimensional awareness and perception) is being restricted by otherwise invested programmings, forces, and presences we are not seeing---there may be an increasing lack of awareness regarding this taking place.

- If you have in some fashion endured such a restriction, it is natural that you may suffer from lack of awareness regarding this. *You may even feel the opposite of restriction is taking place. Always examine carefully what you know and what you feel you know.*

- You may have been pulled or pushed or purposefully evolved into this condition. Misleading any life form this way, regardless of his or her evolutionary status, is dishonest. Misleading yourself this way is not fair to your SELF.

FOR POWER AND FREEDOM

The possibility of transitioning, *dying and surviving*, moving from one reality into a new reality with power is treated quite frequently as heretical or preposterous or simply silly. After all, what can something like this mean to those who view death as the end of life, as the end of the SELF, as the end of all possibility—or who view the possible *survivability of death* as something some outside force or power or god will determine?

But what outside force or power can determine for us the survivability of our own death? Who is it that determines our options for us? We can be the ones in charge of our own options. We can choose to assume control of our own evolution.

Think for a moment of political systems. Political systems which claim to be free are designed to give citizens the sense that they have a great deal of say in what happens to them. However, what is this sense we have that we are somewhat free? How free is free? And are we also free to learn how to fully consciously *navigate transition*, to actually *die and survive*?

We can become ever more aware that there are possibilities available to us, reaches for our mind and consciousness that we have not yet recognized (or re-recognized). We can allow ourselves, somewhere deep inside, to whisper a wondering to

ourselves, to wonder how it is that we have not accessed these possibilities, fully accessed the power of our own awareness. What is it that has held us back from accessing, knowing, *our full interdimensional expanse and power?*

Each of us lives along our own personal *continuum of consciousness*. This continuum exists within our own personal consciousness. This is <u>our own</u> territory. We need not be locked out of this as this <u>exists within us</u>, within our actual SELVES.

WHO HAS IMPLANTED THIS STOP?

And now it is time to ask, what or who is it that has put a *ceiling on Human awareness?* (Again refer to the *Overriding Extinction Scenario* books for definition and discussion of this **ceiling**. These are *Volumes 5 and 6* in this *Keys To Consciousness And Survival Series.)*

Have we done this to ourselves? Is this ceiling a natural product of biological evolution? Or, is there some form of implanted programming, something like an electric tagging of prisoners living outside prisons that is implanted into our programming?

Tagged prisoners can only travel within certain boundaries. Tagged Humans may carry parallel implanted boundaries at the edge of their physical plane niches — and at the enforced edges of their awareness.

THINK OF YOURSELF HERE

Could we be experiencing this stop, the tracking tagging as we seek to reach ever further BEYOND?

Could you, your awareness, be *dis*empowered by this implanted limit, this ceiling? Could your mind, your perception of your full interdimensional awareness and power be held, even trapped, in the material dimension in service to outside powers seeking to harvest your, our, species energy and evolution -- or, to simply stop us from reaching BEYOND, from truly surviving?

If so, might we even be living unaware of
what physical death actually means?

Humans living on material plane Earth have long been fighting and vying among themselves regarding the distribution of power. Yet, what has been fought for is the illusion of power. The actual power we are striving to take back for Humanity is far more expansive than what we have been programmed to know about while living in 3-D.

THE GOLDEN DOOR IS ...

Most citizens of the United States, and many people around the world, have heard of the Statue of Liberty. Many know of its inscription:

> "Give me your tired, your poor, your huddled masses, yearning to breathe free, the wretched refuse of your teeming shore. Send these, the homeless, tempest-tossed to me, I lift my lamp beside the golden door!"

Can we look beyond these words to ask: what do these words really mean? What do they promise us? What might they really be telling us? What might they really be telling you, your actual SELF?

388

- These words suggest that you can go to a place for safe refuge—*that you can of your own Free Will migrate out of, and back and forth from, one reality into another.* The extension of this idea, the possibility and option for life BEYOND, is what these *How To Die And Survive* books are explaining.

- As you are reading these words, you may be helping to release, to break free, the long-kept Truth. Can this Truth about who we really are, where we live and can live, be broken free, released from the vault at this precious and perilous time in planetary and cosmic history?

- This is the moment that precedes the future of the Species of Humanity, not only on Earth, but in all dimensions. There is something very big about the future of the Human Species. Such important information is there, speaking to us from within the issues addressed in these *Keys To Consciousness And Survival Series* books, including in these *How To Die And Survive* books. Humans living in the material plane on Earth have put themselves on notice: their hearts are sounding the alarm. It is time to know who we truly are, to understand ourselves as not only biological life forms, but as interdimensional beings.

- *In accessing further your own rightful interdimensional nature and awareness, you are reaching beyond programmed-in limitations. Now, as you learn more about who you truly are, you are ever more responsible for your survival. You are responsible for the quality of your survival—the richness of the harvest— that you take from your transitions, your in-life as*

well as seeming end-of-life deaths. You can learn to DIE AND SURVIVE both here and BEYOND. You can survive.

- **Humans are fighting for the right to break free of the shackles of an <u>evolutionary trap</u>.** (Important note: *Volumes 5 and 6* in this *Keys To Consciousness And Survival Series* define and detail this *evolutionary trap*. See these *Overriding The Extinction Scenario* books.)

- **Consider the possibility that Humans are fighting an intergalactic, better stated, *interdimensional*, war of ideals and even of access to survival BEYOND.**

- **We need not be limited to our programmed-in understanding of ourselves, however we received this programming -- by evolution or by design. We need not be limited to what we have been programmed to know and to not know.**

WE CAN HARVEST OUR SELVES FROM THE TRANSITION WE CALL DEATH

Understanding of what death is can be adapted, expanded, deepened. Death can take on another meaning. We can reach into the BEYOND, see BEYOND OUR present LINE OF SIGHT to know where and what we are and can be. (Refer to *Volume 10* in this *Keys To Consciousness And Survival Series*, titled, *Seeing Beyond Our Line Of Sight*.)

We can transform our physical death from an event in which we are the victim of this death, to one of empowerment. We can transform death to what it can be for us as a species, to an

evolutionary LEAP for us, for the Species of Consciousness we are, for the true expression of the actual Humanity.

So, we <u>do</u> have the option of knowing how much we <u>do</u> know, of accessing, of pulling into our conscious awareness, <u>knowledge of what is really going on here</u>. We can rethink what we have been told about our lives. We can protect, shield, even add to, the energy we generate while we live in biological bodies. We can access this energy to propel ourselves to new levels of survival both here and BEYOND.

At the right time, and not before that, each of us *can* harvest our own personal energy arrangement to transform it. We can harvest our SELF during our physical death—even on a smaller scale during any of our in-life transitions—any minor or major transition, change, or ending.

We can transform the process and the direction and the survival pathway itself.

Each of us can see how to RE-transform death from a process through which we may seem to be aimlessly and hopelessly tumbling, into a profound initiation, and a great liberation with a survival option.

INITIATION

Clearly, we must <u>at least consider</u> this idea that we may, as a personal consciousness, be able to *die and survive.*

In-life and seeming end-of-life transitions and deaths are among the many initiations we move through. Now, what might this mean: initiation? This initiation is not about

membership in a club, or about membership in something difficult to get into.

The initiation being referred to here is about: (1) the ever more conscious transition of the SELF; (2) the ever more consciously moving into a new format of the SELF; (3) the ongoing never ending transition of the SELF through, the LEAP into, another dimension of awareness, of reality.

Few people consciously train for *initiation-by-physical-death* or for any of their other *initiation-by-living-transition* processes and adventures. This is not surprising. Transitions may suggest we are moving into unknown areas, into places or formats we have not known. The unknown itself can be somewhat scary. Living things tend to be afraid of great changes, of great risks, of great unknowns. Yet, fear is not the only feeling that may arise when we face unknowns.

As we approach this interdimensional awareness and the potential for empowerment it holds, we must protect our approach, *shield our learnings as these develop*. We can allow ourselves to monitor what parts of our programming, and also of the social environment where we exist, may seek to stop us from knowing more about what it means to *survive*.

THE CHOICE TO EXPLORE THIS

So we have a choice. We can remain a prisoner of what we do not know, even of our oblivion. We can remain deprived of our rightful access to other domains of awareness and reality, deprived of our power to expand to new niches beyond the physical plane, realms of our own personal consciousness.

We must sense where there is a programmed-in, dictated denial of this option to *die and survive*. Sure, we can opt to continue down the path toward mindlessness, while believing we are mindful. We can opt to continue to allow possible opportunistic programmings, forces, and factors to affect us.

When this happens, we may be commanded, hypnotized, to surrender our basic Human *survival rights* to our own *individual power*, and therefore rights to the power and spirit of our collective Humanity, both here and BEYOND.

EXERCISE #52.1
HARVESTING DEATH

Imagine that you are a field of corn or some other crop being harvested.

Come to terms with the concept of harvest. Harvesting harvests energy that has been stored in what is being harvested. Those who are harvesting the energy are generally not returning it to the life form it is being harvested from.

Decide what it would be like to harvest your own energy, to use it to adapt or change or heal, to elevate-ascend, to DIE AND SURVIVE.

EXERCISE #52.2
FINDING FREEDOM

Review your life. Identify events or times when you felt the most liberated, the most free. If you have no memory of such a time, make one up and briefly live it out in your mind.

What sort of energy did you experience with this sense of liberation, of freedom?

Use the experience of this exercise to develop your feel for freedom as an <u>energetic condition</u>. What would you like your sense of freedom to feel like?

What does freedom feel like? What might freedom be like when DYING AND SURVIVING, when moving out there BEYOND this place, this physical plane on 3-D Earth?

53
FUELING FREELY-WILLED ELEVATION-ASCENDENCE

> To the extent that a man believes that his mind is a potential enemy, that it may lead to the "evils" of question-asking and criticism, he will feel the need for intellectual passivity ... to deliberately sabotage his mind in the name of virtue.
>
> George H. Smith
> *Atheism: The Case Against God*

We each view minor and major in-life transitions and events, even death and dying itself, and then also possible after-life experiences, in our own ways. This is a good thing. It is helpful to have so many ideas about all this available to us, as we are dealing with great unknowns.

Many Readers say that they are here, reading these pages and conducting these exercises, as they are looking for possibilities of an after-life, of life BEYOND, of surviving death. Other Readers say they are here reading these pages as they want to apply these ideas about navigating personal change and transition in their daily lives. These and other approaches to this material are all welcome.

SURVIVING TRANSITION AS ELEVATION

Consider the surviving of an in-life transition, or even of a seeming end-of-life or possible after-life transition, as moving or elevating to a next stage or level of existence.

Elevation is rising above something and perhaps also staying there. We elevate out of an old pattern or system or behavior or body, into a new one. Ultimately, we become our own elevation, or what we can think of as our own *elevation-ascendence*. We *ascend* to a new way of seeing ourselves, our lives, our realities. Basically, what elevates is our awareness, our focus, the focus of our awareness.

TRANSCENDING IS THE LEAP

Elevation-ascendence is in essence a state of mind, or of personal consciousness, in other words, a state of SELF. This state of SELF expands and shifts to *die and survive*. The SELF both *engages in* and concurrently *becomes* the LEAP into what is BEYOND. This LEAP is itself expansion in awareness.

This LEAP is itself SURVIVAL.

This LEAP is the **light-energy-action-process of expansion.** This is the process involved in expanding along the range of the personal CONTINUUM OF CONSCIOUSNESS. (Refer to *Volume 3* in this series, titled *Unveiling The Hidden Instinct*, for definition, discussion, and exercises regarding **activating this LEAP.**)

You can trigger—activate—the LEAP, the elevation-ascendence of your actual SELF, of your personal consciousness, at any time you choose. In fact, you are always doing this. Selecting for yourself your own definitions of,

conditions of, and times of, your various shifts, your various elevation-ascendences, allows you to better and more consciously navigate these in-life and end-of-life processes.

CONSCIOUSNESS FORCE

We have spoken a great deal about the importance of being very conscious of your own consciousness. It is also always very important to be conscious of other consciousnesses that influence you. Among these many other consciousnesses is a great and very pure *consciousness force*.

You can tap into this supreme force for energy, for the fuel you need to ascend. This supreme energy is free energy. You have a right to tap into this. However, only the right, highest, most ethical, purest use of your Free Will opens the flow of this supreme energy to you.

CLARIFY YOUR WILL

Much of your life is spent clarifying your Will. You may even be doing this almost daily without realizing this. You are clarifying your Will, and developing your Force of Will. You may feel this is about will power, or confidence, or outspokenness. However, the Will itSELF is actually about YOU, your actual SELF, the SELF that survives.

Consciously clarifying your Will can be valuable in daily life, and in navigating change and transition processes, both here and BEYOND. You can sense your SELF, the clarity and strength of your SELF, by sensing your Will. The term strength here has nothing to do with lifting weights. This strength is

clarity, is being in touch with your SELF to sustain your SELF, your existence through transition -- to survive.

PHASES OF TRANSCENDENCE

Consciously moving through life (and its transitions and deaths) involves your sense of SELF, your Will, the clarity of your Will. The more clarity of Will you have, the more aware you are of your SELF as you seek to survive.

This is about being ever more aware that you exist, and of what it feels like to exist, and thus to survive.

Recall the phases of transcendence described in the previous *How To Die And Survive* book, and in other books in this series. These phases have been diagrammed and described in *How To Die And Survive, Book One's* and *Book Three's* Figures 6.1 through 6.3, and also in those books' Exercises 6.1 through 6.5:

Phase 1: Struggle
Phase 2: Paradox
Phase 3: Insight
Phase 4: Spiritual Elevation

You can ever more consciously work through these phases in order to make your experiences of Phase 4: Spiritual Elevation, increasingly powerful. You work through these phases in order to generate as many powerful Spiritual Elevations as you seek.

As your spiritual elevations gain in power, your personal consciousness gains power. This is good. However, with this advancement comes great responsibility.

You must always seek authenticity in the expression of your power. Be who you really are. When you are uncertain, wait to express your power. Your ability to wait this way is, in itself, an expression of your power.

PROTECT YOUR SELF BY KNOWING

Your Will can be weakened, poisoned, killed. Do not allow internal or external influences to suck on or contaminate your power. For example, do not be fooled into sabotaging your power by the temptations of SELF-doubt and negativity.

Try to notice if and when you are being dishonest with yourself, or perhaps being in a state of denial, or maybe just being nonchalant and noncommittal about your own survival. Be aware that you are vulnerable when you are not paying attention.

This is not about being paranoid. Being aware is not being paranoid. It is taking care of business, of the business of your survival both here and BEYOND.

When predatory factors may sense you are not paying attention, this may be an opportunity for them. When you are not aware of your own boundaries, the boundaries of your actual SELF, know that other forces may find you to be a candidate for take-over.

These are vague but definite opportunistic, even authoritarian, forces both here and BEYOND. These are forces and factors and presences which may seek to exploit your weakened state, your vague interdimensional identity, and your vulnerable boundaries. A weakened Force of Will may find itself unwittingly surrendering to take over, outside control, even to enslavement to programming.

**You can help protect Free Will
by becoming increasingly free.**

You already know the Truth. You have a right to recognize the Truth, and to perpetually seek its recognition in your SELF and in your species.

EXERCISE #53.1
REVIEWING GROWTH OF WILL

Your sense of your SELF, of the clearness, of the clarity of your Will, changes over time. You can draw or graph this, track your clarity of Will through your life, or just scribble this to see it.

Draw a time line that shows your increasing clarity of will. Your graph may look something like this, pictured here below, with a squiggly line indicating that your force of Will may generally zig zag over time, but may increase with age.

This chart has a vertical line on the left, showing clarity of will increasing in strength from zero to at least level ten. This chart has a horizontal line on the bottom, showing birth or age zero through life to as along as you live.

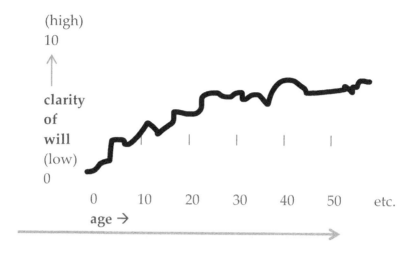

After thinking about it, many people find that their clarity of Will increases although comes and goes as they age, until it perhaps plateaus later in life. Others say they continue to refine their clarity of Will as they age. Others say they have never thought about this before, but now are aware of this sensation of having a personal Will, and are now becoming more aware of what it means to know your actual SELF.

EXERCISE #53.2
INCREASING CLARITY

Can you sense this thing we are calling your Force of Will? Can you sense your own presence, your own SELF, and sense in your SELF your own Force of Will?

Find your Will. Give it an image if you can. Look at it. Is it vague, hard to see, or distinct? Can you bring it more into focus? What does this feel like? ... Focus on your clarity of Will. Spend a few minutes feeling as if you are increasing its degree of clarity.

401

Form for yourself your own ways of knowing when your Force of Will is more or less clear to you. Are there ways you can fine tune the clearness, the clarity of your Will?

54
ENTERING
METATERRA AS A CITIZEN

Would you like to liberate yourself from
the lower realms of life?

Would you like to save the world from
the degradation and destruction it
seems destined for?

Then step away from shallow mass
movements and quietly go to work on
your own self-awareness.

If you want to awaken all of Humanity,
then awaken all of yourself.

Lao Tzu
Hua Hu Ching

So, let's say that you do wake up dead. And then, you realize
that you are not dead, that you have indeed *died and survived.*

Here you are. You have come such a long way, traveled such a
journey to be here. You have survived what at first seemed to
be the obstacle course of your survival. You have experienced
your essential *dimensional transition,* the transition that has
brought you way out here, BEYOND.

403

At a particular point, you feel that you have, at least for the time being, arrived at your destination—or at least achieved entry into a temporary resting point.

Glorious relief fills you. You realize that you can indeed make this tremendous journey. You can indeed *die and survive*. In fact, you already have *died and survived* many times, and can do this again and again. You understand that your SELF, your actual SELF, is who and what lives on.

The majesty of this realization registers in your awe that you are still conscious, that you are still your SELF. You are actually able to recognize your arrival in this new life space, this glistening realm, this world which some call after-life. Yet, this is LIFE, continuing LIFE, and is LIFE AFTER LIFE AFTER LIFE, ON AND ON.

Welcome to Metaterra.

MEET METATERRA

The realm of METATERRA is of course BEYOND. The realm of METATERRA was presented to this author years ago, when she was a child (presented by what is best described as beings BEYOND). Metaterra was presented with the encouragement that while this author lives here on Earth, she develops these KEYS TO SURVIVAL and INTER-DIMENSIONAL AWARENESS found on these pages and in other books in the *Keys To Consciousness And Survival Series*, and in the *Metaterra Chronicles Collection*.

Readers will note that this author has included many KEYS in this *Keys To Consciousness And Survival Series* of events and

publications. This material is indeed produced and presented to Earth and BEYOND by this author and Metaterra®.

Indeed, this author and Metaterra are presenting you with the messages contained herein, including these *How To Die And Survive* teachings. In these teachings are your vehicles of transport and transition. In these teachings are KEYS TO YOUR INTER-DIMENSIONAL SURVIVAL.

What is this place, Metaterra? By its very name, it is "meta" — above, overarching, transcending, beyond, this "terra" — Earth. Think of planet Earth as not just a planet, but a location within a dimension, within a level of density. When you succeed in rising above, elevating-ascending from "terra" into the next frequency of your own inter-dimensionality, you are in your own version of *Meta*terra.

Some people may want to describe Metaterra as heaven. Technically speaking, heaven is what you perceive it to be and what you make it. Metaterra can be your heaven if you enter Metaterra respectfully and as a true citizen of the next level of life. Why the concept of citizenship here? Because, citizenship involves rights and responsibilities.

All too frequently, life forms move through the material plane, as well as through higher dimensions of the Cosmos, without consciously accepting responsibility for their movement, or for their behaviors and uses of energy during their transitions and evolutionary phases. Only recognizing that citizenship is both a right and a responsibility, do you gain actual power and participation.

You may find yourself asking, why on Earth should power and full participation be so important while dying itself is such a challenge? If you find yourself responding that dying is hard enough, that you cannot focus on these other issues, this is entirely understandable.

Please know that, if you can, even if for just a tiny moment here and there, look BEYOND, begin to think about the BEYOND that you are moving into. This can be a message from you to yourSELF. You can plant hints of this message for yourSELF to hear along the way and also to hear later, BEYOND. Remember that your transition, ending, and death processes can be reframed as needed for you to adjust to transition, even to survive.

How you experience a change or transition, any minor or major pattern or body death, is *how you perceive the transition, how you navigate the transition.*

No one is guaranteeing you an easy death—only the chance of an ever more aware and conscious death, one you can perhaps navigate to survive. Remember, by conscious here, this does not mean only medically conscious. Many who have died and survived, or who have had near death experiences, report that they have been conscious even when medical doctors have said they were unconscious. You see, the personal consciousness is the actual SELF who can understand that it is not tied to biology, and can evolve itself, teach itself, to survive. (Readers are encouraged to return to the *Foreword* to this book for more on this matter.)

Your death, when consciously and purposefully navigated, is your map into a kingdom and a territory that is rightfully yours, as this realm, this kingdom, is YOUR SELF, YOUR OWN CONTINUUM OF CONSCIOUSNESS.

Although this is YOU, you do not gain access to this territory of yours, without recognition that <u>you do enter it</u>. You see, KEY in your survival, in your dying and surviving, is simply realizing that <u>you can indeed</u> *die and survive*.

You can be in this territory with the knowledge of what it means to be there. You can protect your kingdom and its *divine ecology* by accepting the responsibilities of citizenship in your own kingdom, as a kingdom within your own version of Metaterra.

PARTICIPATE IN CONSCIOUS EVOLUTION

You can participate in the generation of and protection of your own and your species' conscious evolution. As a citizen of your SELF, and of the enveloping realm of Metaterra, you do the following:

1) You use the advancement of consciousness, power, and skill that is required to achieve entry into Metaterra, only with the highest of ethical intent.

2) You understand that you are a conduit of energies in and out of Metaterra, and you screen all that you allow to come through you into this kingdom.

3) You commit to the promotion of the conscious evolution of Humanity, a race which extends far past Human physical existence on Earth (Terra).

4) You continuously generate, format, and harvest energy toward the ever more right use of your own ever more Free Will.

5) You do not revert to previous modes of unconscious dying.

6) You know that you can be conscious while physically dying whether or not medically conscious, as the non-physical SELF that will survive is not medically determined.

7) You consciously choose to consciously *die and survive*, to allow your actual non-physical SELF, your own personal consciousness, to know it can and does survive.

And then, with these responsibilities exercised, you have a right to the following:

- Life.
- Liberty.
- The pursuit of heightened consciousness.
- Multi-dimensional travel and migration.
- Access to the highest Light.
- Your sovereignty.
- Your survival: your dying and SURVIVING.

EXERCISE #54.1

GAINING PASSAGE TO THE THRONE

This is a creative exercise, inviting you to explore ways of imagining or designing your territory and world BEYOND. This is a story, just to explore such an adventure. This is not to tell you what your story will become, but rather to invite you on a journey of imagination, to exercise your imagination. So here, simply tell yourself (or have someone read you) this story about a journey you make.

You may want from five to fifteen minutes to conduct this exercise. How much time you spend following this story is up to you.

Now we begin:

You find yourself on a city street in an unusually foreign land. Many of the street's inhabitants look to be a mix of many ethnicities as well as otherworldly. Everything looks as if the intensity of its color has been heightened 1000 times.

Someone is walking briskly toward you. You cannot see the stranger well enough to determine her or his identity. In fact, you cannot see his or her face at all. She or he is wearing a loose hooded garment, bright yellow in color. He or she is carrying a yellow bag made of finely webbed fishnet. Inside the bag is a manuscript, as you were writing your own story. This hooded figure is bringing you your unfinished manuscript.

You have to get the message out now. You gaze at the manuscript. As you focus your eyes on it, it seems to become a portal, yet a bit like a vortex sucking you in. . . .

No. No. Change that. Make this a different image. You give your mind instructions in order to control this dream. The image of the

409

portal appearing to be a vortex is replaced by a translucent ring. As you look into the ring, you see your own atomic anatomy. You see the atoms and then their brilliantly colored luminous electrons as they organize themselves within and throughout your body.

You see and feel everything about your ENERGETIC ANATOMY in greater detail now. Small dots of Light are moving in rings and spirals, little brooks of energy are streaming into larger rivers of energy. Each dot of Light seems to have its own type of energy, and organizes itself into a flow with other bits of energy to create particular characteristic patterns. You vibrate with excitement as you see this process.

This is the level, the visualization, on which you can make change in how you see what is happening, on where you are going. It is all a matter of redirecting the imagined streams of energy at the level of the imagined sub-sub-sub-atomic particles of you, your SELF. Oh, but this takes so much focus, so much concentration. Do you have the energy to do this work? Do you have the energy to guide your SELF and others? Yes.

Now, the dazzling particles of Light moving through space fade out and you find yourself back in the foreign street.

You become aware of another street, connecting to this street at a right angle. As you look toward that street, you realize that its entrance has a giant mirror-like quality to it. Everything about the strange world you are standing in is reflected in a misty haze in this membrane, this living mirror, only everything looks different. The colors are different. It all looks like a wonderfully nostalgic memory.

Now that you look closely, it seems as if the mirror keeps changing from a mirror to a window to a mirror, and back and forth. You feel this is a safe portal. You decide to pass through this glass-like membrane at this entrance or window into another world.

Although this entrance is only a few feet away from where you stand, when you decide to go through it, it is a while from the moment you decide to go there to the moment you are finally there. It is as if, once you make that decision, time becomes thick like mud, but a gentle and invisible mud. For a moment, everything occurs in slow motion. Your breathing becomes deep and slow.

Within the thick but clear mud, there is an electrical charge, a kind of static electricity. The charge transforms everything around you as well as the chemistry within every cell of what you believe is your body. You can feel every bit of yourself, even the particles of what you believe is your physical existence, transforming.

You actually feel as if you are dissolving. You are surprised to find that this does not scare you now. You just let yourself melt down. As far as you can tell, you are not even breathing anymore. You have no lung cavities to breathe into, no body to need air . . . Time passes . . . Time . . . passes. . . . There is a long waiting. . . .

And then, there is a sudden and rapid re-integration of what at first seems to you to be your physical SELF. Everything pulls, as if by some gentle predesigned suction, back into its place. You are all together again. Only now, there is a new vibrancy and a singularity in your being, a freshness you have never felt before (at least as far as you can remember).

411

Now, you feel lighter as you walk on. You become aware that the streets look like the streets of a foreign country you somehow know. Although you do not remember ever going there, you remember in extreme detail every wall, every stone, every corner of this place. How? Had you somehow absorbed that information from someone else's memory banks? Possibly, but you feel that you have been there hundreds or millions of years ago. You wonder calmly how this could have happened, and where this ancient place could be.

You wander on, lost in pleasing yet inconclusive thought, until you notice commotion up ahead. There is some form of street sale going on. Shopkeepers have placed their tables, covered with ornately woven clothes and rugs, and thousands of strange clay figurines, out on the cobblestone streets.

Something at one of the tables catches your eye. You approach the table and ask what this is, asking in a strange language you suddenly realize you speak. In an indecipherable accent, a woman next to you replies, "A clay figurine, which has been waiting for you to find it."

Now you hear a loud flapping sound. You turn your attention to the red, yellow, and black flags which decorate the streets of the island. You can hear the whipping of these flags as they beat stridently, almost in synch with each other, in the wind that rushes over your head along the rooftops.

You ask, "Why are they here," not knowing what you mean.

One of the foreign shopkeepers decides to answer. "They say they have a way of life that is the best for the workers of the future. But they are not doing what is best for any of us, not at all. We are more than worker drones who can be worked to death and then left to simply die off."

You are somewhat surprised by this daring statement, as you know such speech, even such thoughts, are not allowed there. You decide you want to change this. You look up at the flags and study the designs and forms on them: a graphic representation of a computer micro-megachip, the silhouette of a Human brain surrounding it, and all of this is surrounded by a Human fetus.

The shopkeeper is speaking more forcefully now, but in a low voice. "They lead all of us blindly into their repression with their deceptive talk of a better life. The Human mind is being consumed, forced to serve the ultimate machine, poised and waiting for ever more of their programming. They want our minds, our energy, our labor, as if we are their slaves. They want to restrict us to the material plane where they can control us, not allow us to know we can DIE AND SURVIVE."

Apparently, one of the other shopkeepers understands her, because he says something to her, and then she becomes irritated and speaks loudly and rapidly in some archaic dialect.

Abruptly, this woman, now breathless, stops talking. She grabs you by the elbow and pulls you down the cobblestone street. The woman jerks you into a very narrow alley. She then scribbles her name and address on an old and soiled piece of note paper and says, "See those men? They are following me. I must go now. They will leave you alone. Find me later: You will come to understand why we met." Her gleaming blue eyes seem to be fading to gray with fear and, at the same time, with the adrenalized determination of a hunted animal which now speeds her movements.

You look around, searching the shadows for the pursuers. When you turn back, she is gone. You see she left you with the clay figurine in

your palm. This is the marker of this meeting and its message which you will carry with you. You will know to look for this marker and many other of your markers, many times on your journeys.

The island is very small. Later, you walk up and down every street in search of this woman. She is nowhere to be found. Nor is the imposing team of pursuers. As you hunt for the woman, hoping to help her, you find yourself in an increasingly unusually foreign place, until you can no longer recognize it as where you were.

You decide you must move into your own survival realm now.

Things change as you move forward. Even the atmosphere itself changes. You do not recognize anything anymore--not one building or street or face, and not the language or languages you hear.

Eventually, you become aware that a magnificent ceremony is about to take place. Everyone, including the air, is moving calmly toward the ceremony. As you are moved along, you feel you are calling your SELF to move along.

When you finally arrive, you can see that the crowd is waiting for someone to take the throne. There is a strange circle of Light on the ground that somehow you know is the throne. You find yourself moving toward it to see it better. What an unusual throne that is.

Around the throne, you are pleased to find advisors and guides you suddenly realize you have long known in your waking and sleeping and real and imagined life. They all emit pleasure at your arrival. Your family is there. Your ancestors are there.

Finally, you understand that this is your throne. They and YOU, your SELF, are waiting for you to take your place as leader of your

own kingdom. They are waiting for you to take your sovereignty, to take your Free Will. They know you must transform, you must DIE AND THEN SURVIVE THIS DYING, to do this.

You feel yourself hesitating. DIE AND SURVIVE, you say to yourself. You wait a moment. Eventually, your hesitation melts away and you bravely take a step forward. You feel the riveting exhilarating rewriting of your energy arrangement, the awesome transformation of every bit of yourself into YOU, your actual SELF, in the very moment you step to the throne. It all happens so quickly, right as you step into your rightful place on the throne.

The crowd cheers and you love the cheers. You feel the waves of approval wash through you on all levels of your being.

You take a rich, deep, and fulfilling breath and exhale knowing you are finally home: Metaterra. You realize you have known this kingdom was there, all along. You give this Meta-Terra kingdom your own name now.

EXERCISE #54.2
DEFINING YOUR KINGDOM

Continue from the above Exercise, #54.1. Now, make this story more and more your own. Give it whatever places and persons and colors and events you wish to.

Allow your fantasy to run freely through your reign as ruler of your own personal Kingdom, of your own personal consciousness. Describe, visualize, your own Kingdom BEYOND in detail if you like. You are developing your own visualization of your own domain BEYOND.

You may want to, now or later, get to know this place more and more, as you will return again and again. You will feel more at home there, when someday finding yourself there, when you wake up dead and realize that you have survived.

Feel your role as leader of your own territory emerge as you define your territory. Perhaps tell yourself a story of how you imagine you arrive there, or of how you imagine you first realize you have found this place.

Sometimes, visualizations and creative stories help you feel your way through such different places and processes like this. Now, be sure to remember that this is a kingdom in the realm of your own consciousness.

From time to time, as you move on through your physical plane life, and into your future, continue to develop this kingdom of yours in your mind, and BEYOND.

Get to know this place. Define it, map it, interact with it, own it. Establish entry ways, and maybe arrows, even signs of safety. Set or post signs that are signals from you to your SELF, reminders and markers for you.

You will later recognize what you have placed in your consciousness to be there for you, as you move into the BEYOND, into your own BEYOND. These signs are for you, especially you, as this is your kingdom, your own life after life.

55
DYING WITH GRACE

> Calves are easily
> bound and slaughtered,
> never knowing the
> reason why.
> But whoever
> treasures freedom
> like the swallow
> must learn to fly.
>
> *Donna, Donna*
> Sholum Secunda
> Aaron Zeitlin

When you have thought through these definitions of transition and death, you have prepared yourself well for actual SURVIVAL. You know what it means to move BEYOND. You know what it means to then become less dense, Lighter. You know how to visualize, imagine, call in, the Light. You understand the meaning of attachment and the process of detachment.

You can learn to find your way through, in and out of, to and from, whatever matrix you find yourself in, whatever pattern you find yourself in, whatever condition you find yourself in, and whatever body you find yourself in. You understand that this is the movement of your personal consciousness, of your actual SELF, as this is who you actually are.

417

You can know more and more about how to navigate death, resurrection, and elevation-ascension. You can know how to discern and cathart. You have learned the meaning of _meta_death and of all the higher level deaths and processes associated with elevation-ascension. You can do this. You can fly!

Now, when it is the right time _and only the right time_, you will be ready to die with your own grace and power. You are ready to DIE AND SURVIVE when you feel called to do so!

COMPASSION MOVES US

Above and beyond all of the methods and processes and understandings that we have discussed in this volume, is the compassion described earlier in this and the preceding _How To Die And Survive_ book.

Remember, dying with your grace requires your compassion — compassion for the world around you, compassion for those you leave behind, compassion for those you head toward, if you believe you are headed toward those — **and compassion, above and beyond all, for yourself, for your lower physical life self, and also for your actual already inter-dimensional SELF.**

Understand that you, your SELF, are traveling through this profound peak experience, which is something almost impossible to describe in words, almost impossible to foresee in any way at all.

In the immediate moment, in the right now instant when you DIE AND SURVIVE, you transform, you even elevate, while

at the same time you are stripping down to your ACTUAL SELF, to who you truly are.

Here is where your powerful beautiful glistening personal consciousness lives, right here within the realm of your own CONTINUUM OF CONSCIOUSNESS. Get to know this place. Learn to travel to and from this place. This is where you can and do DIE AND SURVIVE.

KNOW YOUR OWN STATE OF GRACE

There are many definitions and understandings of grace itself. Many view grace as being a way of walking, such as in moving gracefully. Others will say grace is a way of being with people, such as in being gracefully diplomatic or generous or wise. Others speak of divine grace as a state of being or mind or spirit where the divine reaches into the person or persons who are graced with this.

This divine grace is often defined based on religious teachings. However, no matter what your own belief system, and whether or not you are particularly religious, or even spiritual for that matter, this divine grace can speak to the exercising of high ideals in life, and of your own personal divine process.

Here, in these *How To Die And Survive* books, the state of grace being referred to is your own state of grace, however you choose to define this for your SELF. This is your grace, your presence, and the way you move through your life. This is the way you move through your transitions and deaths, even on into your life after life state.

This true grace is not an emotion.

This true grace is a state of being.

Very rarely do we take the time to learn our own grace. Do you know what your state of grace is or can be? Can you find your grace within yourself? To *DIE AND SURVIVE* with grace, you must KNOW YOUR OWN GRACE. You must know the dignity and conscious SELF-respect of THE STATE OF GRACE YOU CAN DEVELOP FOR YOUR SELF.

EXERCISE #55.1
IMAGING GRACE

Stretch your imagination.

What do you consider essential to your dying with your own grace?

What preparations, what behaviors, what final events, what attitudes might contribute to this grace?

List these, write these down, or describe these aloud.

EXERCISE #55.2
OVERCOMING CHALLENGES TO GRACE

Ask yourself what types of deaths would present challenges to your dying with grace.

How could you manage to meet your own definition of dying with grace (as in the above exercise, Exercise #55.1) when confronted with such challenges?

List, write down or describe aloud, one or more plans for bringing your own grace to your survival of your own in-life and other transitions, even for surviving your seeming end-of-life and after-life transitions.

<u>56</u>

ACHIEVING HIGH METAXIS:
THE META-LEAP

> It is not born,
> it does not die;
> having been,
> it will never not be...

> "The Second Teaching"
> *Bhagavad-Gita*

And so, you have chosen to consciously enter the maze of transition and death, a territory you will explore again and again. You have initiated yourself into the basics of this *How To Die And Survive Consciousness, Ascension, and Death Technology.* Celebrate your brave decision. No matter how modestly you choose to do so, be certain to applaud yourself, or at least give yourself a pat on the back.

Someone very close to you may note your willingness to examine the matters discussed in these volumes, THE TRUTH ABOUT OUR OPTION TO SURVIVE. And there is no one so close to you as your SELF—is there? So, acknowledge your SELF for considering this *How To Die And Survive* material.

Recognize yourself for your confrontation with old models of transition and death. See how these understandings of transition and death apply to in-life, as well as seeming end-of-life and after-life realities and processes.

CORAGGIO

Some of the encounters you have invited, some of the journeys you have initiated, have already demanded more courage from you than you may have acknowledged having, even to yourself. YOUR COURAGE IS ALREADY HERE. On some level, you know this. You feel this.

So hang on now. Be proud of your ability to change your mind, to change the channel, to take a new direction. To master any transitional LEAP, you may want as much flexibility as you can muster, flexibility *and* awareness. You will see that no matter how much you know regarding the journey you call transition, and the journey you call death, there is more—there is always more to discover beyond what you think you know. And indeed there is always more out there, BEYOND.

Those Humans who populate the Earth area of the 3-D material plane are finding their way so bravely, somehow sensing the possibility they carry dangerously limiting perceptions that have been implanted, programmed-into them. Yet, those controlling programs are difficult to detect. The disguising cover illusions those programs create are like tightropes that end in mid-air -- disappear -- much the way Human people are told they must simply disappear, die and not live on, not survive.

SEEING BEYOND ILLUSION

The material plane illusion is where many beings are pressed to be always breathing the last gasp before imagined or actual disaster and or actual death. And they live a double life:

Strangling on an almost *absolute denial of,* and at the same time, an *insatiable fear of,* the unknown, they do live on … and on until they die. What else is there to do?

Dare we ask whether we, as our own personal consciousness, might be able to die and then survive BEYOND without being absorbed into a oneness and dying? Yes, we do dare to ask, and are asking this now.

A rewrite of the understanding of the SELF, and of the SELF's right to DIE AND SURVIVE, shifts the experience of being the SELF. Suddenly, you know more about who you actually are.

IN WANT OF COMPASSION

In want of love, compassion for themselves, for their Human condition, Humans on 3-D physical plane Earth gather in places of worship, yet also in offices and bars, on highways at rush hour, at political conventions, at rock concerts, in parks, on beaches, in stadiums—laying their souls upon the altar of physical plane experience.

Physical Humans are programmed to obediently make themselves sacrificial lambs to their so-called gods of presumed truth.

Those who begin the search for the raw unmitigated Truth become aware of how very lost, even captured, their minds

may have been. And while it is the key to liberation, the Truth threatens to shatter the illusion to which so many may have succumbed. They seem to instinctively fear that if the stupor comes crashing in, it may wake them, awake them loudly like the shattering of ice-cold glass. Such a crashing awakening itself seems like a death. Yes, waking up may at first feel like dying. Yet, waking up may be surviving.

Concerns, even fears, may race through people's minds, as the programming is to experience all this from this weakened emotional position.

So, some people understandably cringe. The sky of their reality could end up falling in on them. Pieces of the broken sky could fly like shrapnel and cut them. And then they would bleed, bleed an as yet unbled blood, from an as yet unfound heart. They could cry the bloody tears of unbloomed flowers who have been picked before their time and cast by those who pick them into realms no flower would envision adventuring.

How fragile the mind of physicalized Humanity. How naive we have been kept while being dictated to by those designers who control us with evolved in, or implanted, programming to see and feel what they choose for us to see and feel, and choose for us to know and believe we know.

How dictated-to we have been not to know that: we can as our actual SELVES, die and survive both here and BEYOND. How clearly we have been thwarted from knowing that: this survival as who we are, as our actual personal consciousness, is our birthright.

We must be careful being so naive, as we could become extinct that way—really die an absolute death. Extinction of a physical species is one thing, and we hope this can be prevented. Extinction of our species of the Consciousness of Humanity is yet another. And such extinction may be pending. We must learn to *die and survive* to help ward off our species' inter-dimensional extinction, both here and BEYOND. (Important and essential information regarding **surviving extinction** can be found in *Volumes 5 and 6* of this *Keys To Consciousness And Survival Series*, titled *Overriding The Extinction Scenario.*)

ACHEIVE HIGH METAXIS MIGRATION

For you, for the Human Species, an outstanding LEAP in evolution is essential. WE CAN TUNE INTO THE INSTINCTS WE ALREADY DO CARRY.

People of Earth know this, sense this. Other species on your planet, as well as many of your fellow Humans, have exemplified the *survival value of migration* across lands and seas. Yet, what is recognized of their migration has been within the third or physical dimension.

Your next major LEAP in evolution is the *metaxis*—the ability to engage in migration and expansion, individual and group migration, into and out of dimensions—with *high metaxis* being the ability to migrate from the material plane directly to and from, back and forth from, the most elevated and clear realm, and to do so at Will.

High metaxis **is the greatest of all LEAPs: the META-LEAP from wherever you are, right now or at any given**

moment, right into the realm of, the clarity of, the highest, purest, clearest Light.

BE CLEAR: THIS LEAP IS NOT ABOUT DYING

This LEAP is not about dying. You can expand this way while still living in your physical body. You see, your consciousness already does live there in your CONTINUUM OF CONSCIOUSNESS. Basically, your expansion is knowing that you are already both here and BEYOND. You have already expanded. You have already survived.

No need to "pass GO." Just LEAP directly to what you may see as your own personal god head, to what you may see as divine, to what is the fountain of your own gleamingly clear Light streaming throughout the atmosphere, throughout your consciousness, throughout all there is, at all times.

Your Light is here for you at all times. Just focus, center, elevate, and LEAP into your rightful wakefulness, and you will see it. (Again, for definition of the LEAP and details and exercises regarding this LEAP, see other books in this series such as *Volume 3*, titled, *Unveiling The Hidden Instinct.*)

Always know that the highest clearest purest presence does not demand you surrender your SELF to it. Know that your own personal kingdom, your own personal version of Metaterra, will never require you to die. In fact, your own Metaterra requires you to survive as the actual SELF who you truly are.

The survival of YOU, of your actual SELF, of your personal consciousness, remains your option even when meeting your

own highest Light. This is the certain test of the goal of a Light or Light presence. If it asks or demands you surrender your energy to it, demands you let yourself die and <u>not</u> survive, it is not seeking your SURVIVAL.

HIGH METAXIS AS HIGHEST LEAP, THE META-LEAP

High Metaxis is the last of the eight LEAPs named in this book, and in the previous *How To Die And Survive* book. High metaxis builds on the other LEAPs. Achieving high metaxis is the most complex and yet the most simple LEAP, the most far-reaching and yet the most immediate LEAP. This high LEAP (this high *light-energy-action-process*), this highest metaxis, carries your SELF, your personal consciousness, an immediate yet vast and most infinite distance while any physical or emotional body that you may have goes nowhere.

This LEAP does not require any death, not physical or otherwise. Of course, if you are dying a physical death this LEAP is here for you as well. So, you can, you may, but you do not have to, die by traditional definitions of death (such as physically) to achieve this high metaxis.

You will survive, as you have migrated, actually have EXPANDED, the focus of your SELF to extend into and include the spaces beyond your physical and emotional bodies.

KNOW THAT

Know that to fully and finally enter your BEYOND, there will be a time when cords to your physical and emotional bodies must be released. In an instant, you can and must shed

427

entirely your existing energy arrangement to form a new arrangement of your SELF, to form your elevated *consciousness matrix.*

You travel a forever away without moving.

Once you can go this eternal distance, this full journey, once you can summon the full experience of eternity into your awareness and do so most instantaneously, you have this death technology at your beck and call. You can make a major change in a moment. You can shift from here to there right now: You can indeed *die and survive.*

KNOW BASIC METAXIS

"Meta" means above, beyond, higher than, an overarching level. Above and beyond, on a higher level than going nowhere and not changing at all, is going somewhere and changing a great deal.

In this sense, <u>meta</u> moves to the BEYOND.
Meta <u>is</u> the BEYOND.

You metabolize the idea of, and image of, *Light*. You call on your vision of Light -- to utilize its *energy* in order to ...

engage in the *action*
your personal consciousness must take
to undergo the *process* of LEAPing
beyond the confines of your reality.

You open your eyes, break through your programming, come out of your established illusion, and come to life.

At the right time, and only then, you can even LEAP right out of your physical self, into your actual SELF. When it is time, you will see that this death is not death. This is high elevation-ascension. This is high liberation. And this high transition is yours of your own Free Will.

MIGRATION METAXIS

Metaxis is the acquiring of the awareness by one or more of the species in such a way that it *triggers the acquiring of this ability in a critical mass of the species--all at once.* Individual and group *migration metaxis* becomes possible for many members of the species, all at once. NOTE: This is not the giving over of your individual consciousness to join this group. This is the empowering of your SELF and of this group, by your remaining, by your surviving, as your own individual consciousness.

This is not about death, and this is not about death of the physical body. In fact, many consciousness-es have already expanded to live BEYOND while still here in the physical plane and in physical bodies. They have formed management of their cordings and attachments to their physical plane lives in a way that allows this expansion. (See other books in this *Keys To Consciousness And Survival Series*, and in the companion series, the *Metaterra Chronicles Series*, where this author shares more about this.)

HIGH METAXIS

High metaxis is an even more potent LEAP than *migration metaxis*. *High metaxis* is the ability of a critical mass of the

species to migrate its consciousness from the dimension of reality in which it is presently located, even to shift itself right into its region of highest Light.

Errors in discernment as described in Chapters 36 to 38 are impossible in high metaxis. You just *know* how to find the highest Light. You just *see* the Light surround you and *reveal* the pure Light, your own Light, your own SELF within you that guides your way on.

You just know you will survive as your actual SELF. You know, and then someone else knows, and then others know. This knowing allows you and others to see the *elevation-ascension pathways open to them.*

NOW YOU FINALLY KNOW

Gazing into this true Light, you finally know. You turn to yourself a moment, release all connections, all cords you may still be holding. You cry a tear, laugh a little laugh, open your heart, and then merge with the seed of life within you. This is your life, this is YOU. You have now found your actual SELF in the home of your personal consciousness where you already do live.

This is the seed, the word, the parable of your Light you have carried through time to *deliver unto yourself* at this most precious, most singularly exquisite, micro-moment of your finest transition.

Thank you for coming. You have journeyed far and wide, hard and long, lost and found, through oceans of tears and fields of laughter, to deliver the seed of Light to its child, its

blossom already blooming in anticipation of your arrival at your own destination. You are home again, here with your own SELF, back of your own Free Will.

You thank yourself for coming, for journeying far and wide to deliver the seed of your Light to your offspring flower, already in bloom, the white lotus of your own personal most divine eternity.

Take off your coat. Kick off your shoes. Stay awhile.

Rest in peace and then go back out for more ...

as you can indeed always

DIE AND SURVIVE.

EPILOGUE:
HOW TO DIE AND SURVIVE

We look around and see the astounding wonders of the amazing era we live in. At the same time, we see the great risks we face as our biosphere is undergoing increasing pressures and changes we hope and pray we can reverse or heal in time to survive them.

We are watching other species being threatened, even some becoming extinct. We cannot help but feel, on some level, the whispered threat of our own risk of personal and population, even species-wide, extinction.

We can still reverse this trend, however. We do know this.

We are now in a time when we want to reason with death, both as a concept and as a reality. Let's see that we can indeed survive, both here and BEYOND. It is time to fully embrace what this means. It is the actual SELF, the personal consciousness, that can survive.

Let's take the next step in our own evolution, and understand that the niches we can evolve into and for ourselves exist both here in the material plane and BEYOND. Once we master this awareness, we can survive both here and BEYOND.

THE LIFE FORCE DOES NOT DIE.
YOU DO NOT DIE.
WE DO NOT DIE.

NOW, TO EXPLORE NEXT LEVELS

Experience the exercises in
this book, HOW TO DIE AND SURVIVE, BOOK <u>TWO</u>
and in HOW TO DIE AND SURVIVE, BOOK <u>ONE</u>
as a collection, all together.
And, find new insights from this author,
Dr. Angela Brownemiller, as she shares more about
what inspires her, and about her experiences bringing
this information to the world.

Experience the personal insights gained from working
through these processes and exercises in sequence,
starting and stopping at any point you wish,
or doing this all in one sitting.
Explore the possibilities of
your survival and journey both here and BEYOND.
What does this mean? What can this mean?
See ever more deeply into this consideration of survival:
What survival can be,
What practices can develop this survival,
What awareness-es we can expand upon,
And more....

LEARN MORE ABOUT
TRANSITION NAVIGATION BOTH HERE AND BEYOND,
SURVIVAL POTENTIAL, LIFE-AFTER-LIFE CONCEPTS,
AND GENERATING THE IDEA OF THE BEYOND.

STAY TUNED FOR THE NEXT

How To Die And Survive book, Book <u>Three</u>.

See <u>Drangela.com</u> and <u>Amazon.com</u>

Readers are also encouraged to see other books in this

KEYS TO
CONSCIOUSNESS AND SURVIVAL SERIES

also written by
Angela Brownemiller

(note the spelling of the author's last name is
B-r-o-w-n-E-m-i-L-L-e-r)

See Amazon.com and Audible.com
and also DrAngela.com for these books.

All blessings to you, our Readers,
on your beautiful and brave journeys
both here and BEYOND.

Dr. Angela Brownemiller, Author
and
Kelly A. Thomas, Audiobook Narrator

WITH IMMENSE GRATITUDE

I wish to thank LWB, DAK, ELB,
and
my darling EdA
for their profound and daring wisdom and beauty.

And, I also wish to express my immense gratitude to all the spirits and souls and beings both here and BEYOND who have been present with me on my journey into this HOW TO DIE AND SURVIVE world, into this awareness so urgent, so intense, and yet so obvious. You are such dear precious and powerful presences. It is a great honor to be with you, to hear you speaking through time and across dimensions, to feel your presences every day, to experience this sharing of ideas with you, such remarkable essences. There is no doubt in my mind of your existence. Your message that we can survive is heard and delivered.

Welcome to the portal.

Trrr--ssttrrrttt xu-la ndnn-dndndn-dahhh.

We are

but sight seers

captives

in this plane

on this planet

til our visas expire

til our chains break —

pieces of a mosaic

hurtling forward

in time

to become a

whole picture.

APPENDICES

BOOKLIST AND RECOMMENDED
BOOKS, EBOOKS, AUDIOBOOKS, PROGRAMS

KEYS TO CONSCIOUSNESS
AND SURVIVAL SERIES
by Dr. Angela Brownemiller

Volume 11
How To Die and Survive: Book Two
Extending Our Interdimensional Awareness:
Next Concepts For Living and Dying
****

Volume 10
Seeing Beyond Our Line of Sight
Consciously Moving Through Life's
Changes, Transitions, and Deaths
****

Volume 9
Navigating Life's Stuff–
Dynamics of Personal Change, Book Two
Keys to Consciously Moving Through
Our Processes and Their Patterns
****

Volume 8
Navigating Life's Stuff –
Dynamics of Personal Change, Book One
Sensitizing to and Navigating
Our Patterns and Their Processes
****

Volume 7
The Go Conscious Process
Steps and Practices for Heightening Conscious Awareness,
Shifts, Transmigrations of Focus,
LEAPS OF SELF
****

****

Volume 6
Overriding the Extinction Scenario, Part <u>Two</u>
<u>Raising</u> the Bar on The
Evolution of the Human Species
****

Volume 5
Overriding the Extinction Scenario, Part <u>One</u>
<u>Detecting</u> the Bar on The
Evolution of the Human Species
****

Volume 4
How to Die and Survive
Interdimensional Psychology,
Consciousness, and Survival:
Concepts for Living and Dying
****

Volume 3
Unveiling the Hidden Instinct
Understanding Our
Interdimensional Survival Awareness
****

Volume 2
Keys to Personal Discovery
****

Volume 1
Keys to Self
****

BOOKLIST AND RECOMMENDED READING
Continued....

Metaterra Chronicles Collection
Angela Brownemiller

Ask Dr. Angela Series
Angela Brownemiller

—

The Bloodwin Code (Episode Books 1, 2, 3, 4, 5)
Angela Brownemiller

—

Transcending Addiction
Angela Brownemiller

—

Gestalting Addiction
Angela Brownemiller

—

Contact us for information on the special
Science Fiction Series
on these consciousness and survival topics.
Email:
DrAngelaBrownemiller@gmail.com

For more information on her mind-body-spirit-consciousness projects and her other work, see **DrAngela.com** ....

The works of Angela Brownemiller are brought to you by:

METATERRA® PUBLICATIONS

(**and numerous other publishers**, see Amazon.com).
For copies of print books, audiobooks, and ebooks by this author,
see Amazon.com
or contact us at
DrAngela.com

To take part in our events and workshops,
and or
for personal consultations
in person or by telephone or online,
contact us at
DrAngelaBrownemiller@gmail.com

GET THE TRUTH ABOUT ADDICTION
Life-changing insights into the reality of
patterns, habits, addictions, and obsessions
in our lives and minds.

Now in powerfully narrated AUDIOBOOK
as well as PAPERBACK and EBOOK forms!

SEEING THE HIDDEN FACE OF ADDICTION

Detecting and Confronting This Invasive Presence

Dr. Angela Brownemiller

SEEING THE HIDDEN FACE OF ADDICTION
can be found on Amazon.com and DrAngela.com

VOLUMES 8 & 9 in the
KEYS TO CONSCIOUSNESS AND SURVIVAL SERIES

Can we better understand the journeys we travel through in our lives? Can we detect and work with the patterns and processes we are forming, living within, and moving through? How much can we see about the patterns we form, and sometimes feel we cannot change, are caught in? How do we sensitize ourselves to the patterning processes we are engaged in? Find your way through the maze of life. See:

NAVIGATING LIFE'S STUFF:
DYNAMICS OF PERSONAL CHANGE, BOOK ONE
Sensitizing to and Navigating Our Patterns and Their Processes

NAVIGATING LIFE'S STUFF:
DYNAMICS OF PERSONAL CHANGE, BOOK TWO
Keys to Consciously Moving Through Our Passages and Their Patterns

Now in Paperback, Audiobook, and Ebook forms.
Find these and other books by Angela Brownemiller on
Amazon.com and Audible.com and DrAngela.com

Volumes 4 and 11 and 14 in the
KEYS TO CONSCIOUSNESS AND SURVIVAL SERIES:
The HOW TO DIE AND SURVIVE Books
by Dr. Angela Brownemiller

YOUR RIGHT TO KNOW IS CLEAR. These far reaching, and life changing, books offer new ways of understanding ourselves and our lives. The author details progressive understandings and practices for moving into multi- and inter- dimensional consciousness and survival skills. Through use of metaphor, this author guides Readers through: her progressive "shift" awareness-es; through LEAPs in understanding her sequential "shift technologies" by means of concepts, processes, and exercises contained in the chapters of these books. These exercises begin quite simply and carefully build toward some very esoteric understandings. ... These books overcome limits to old models of what we are, who we are, and where we can be and go. Ultimately, this is an exploration of the infinite potential of our consciousness. Join us for the journey of your lifetime, of all your/our lifetimes.

Volumes 5 and 6 in the
KEYS TO CONSCIOUSNESS AND SURVIVAL SERIES
By DR. ANGELA BROWNEMILLER:

OVERRIDING THE EXTINCTION SCENARIO, PART ONE:
DETECTING THE BAR ON THE
EVOLUTION OF THE HUMAN SPECIES

and reach more deeply into all this with…
OVERRIDING THE EXTINCTION SCENARIO, PART TWO:
RAISING THE BAR ON THE
EVOLUTION OF THE HUMAN SPECIES

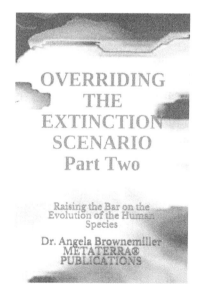

Now in Paperback, Audiobook, and Ebook forms.
Find these and other books by Angela Brownemiller
on Amazon.com and DrAngela.com

453

Volume 3 in this
KEYS TO CONSCIOUSNESS AND SURVIVAL SERIES:
UNVEILING THE HIDDEN INSTINCT
by Dr. Angela Brownemiller

Every day, we are presented with minor and major opportunities, reasons, even needs, to understand the nature of transitioning, shifting, from one state of mind, one way of being, one way of seeing the world, from one reality to another. In this sense, we are frequently calling upon ourselves to shift ourselves and our consciousness-es from one dimension of ourselves to another. At times, we may even sense that our well-being, perhaps even our survival, depends upon such a shift. ... Should we at some point find the survival level need to shift ourselves across ways of seeing the world, realities, dimensions, even perhaps from physical to non-physical and back, it is essential we have at least already considered the concepts involved. This book introduces, via metaphor, minor and major shift awareness-es, making these understandings accessible to us should we need these for everyday challenges as well as potentially profound survival reasons.

UNVEILING
THE
HIDDEN
INSTINCT

Understanding Our
Interdimensional Survival Awareness

Dr. Angela Brownemiller
METATERRA®
PUBLICATIONS

455

Volume 10 in this
KEYS TO CONSCIOUSNESS AND SURVIVAL SERIES:
SEEING BEYOND OUR LINE OF SIGHT
by Dr. Angela Brownemiller

SEEING BEYOND OUR LINE OF SIGHT: CONSCIOUSLY MOVING THROUGH LIFE'S CHANGES, TRANSITIONS, AND DEATHS ... is a simple yet profound book offering subtle yet major shifts in the way we think about changes, transitions, endings, and deaths. Here, we can see that we have the capability of holding and empowering our conscious selves as we move through events, changes, transitions, even emotional, even physical, death processes. ... The journey this book takes us on opens doors to finding our way through challenging, trying, even very difficult, events and passages in our lives. ... That we can survive is central as we undergo all minor and major transitions in our lives. ... Find yourself, know yourself, guide yourself through the minor and major transition and death processes you face during your life. You can define who and what you are for yourself. You can open this option in your mind, the option that you can develop this knowledge of yourself, and then carry this knowledge of yourself through this life, and perhaps also on beyond this lifetime.

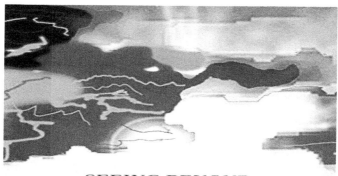

**SEEING BEYOND
OUR LINE OF SIGHT**

**Consciously Moving Through
Life's Changes, Transitions, And Deaths**

Angela Brownemiller
METATERRA® PUBLICATIONS

DETECTING THE OMEGA DECEPTION

NOTES FROM THE FRONT

ANGELA BROWNEMILLER
Metaterra© Publications

THE TRUE STORY OF THIS AUTHOR'S DISCOVERY OF THE OMEGA DECEPTION.

Find this and other books by Angela Brownemiller on
Amazon.com and at **DrAngela.com**
DrAngelaBrownemiller@gmail.com

REVEALING
THE OMEGA KEY

COSMIC LOVE STORY THROUGH ANCIENT END-TIME EARTH-
CHANGE PROPHECY TO MODERN GLOBAL CONSPIRACY

ANGELA BROWNEMILLER
Metaterra® Publications

REVEALING THE OMEGA KEY
prophecy in novel form
COSMIC LOVE STORY THROUGH
ANCIENT END-TIME EARTH-CHANGE PROPHECY
TO MODERN GLOBAL CONSPIRACY

AUTHOR CONTACT
For Consults, Workshops, Events, Appearances:
www.DrAngela.com

for
Paperback, Audiobook, and Ebook
versions of this and other books
by this author
Dr. Angela Brownemiller

DrAngelaBrownemiller@gmail.com

see

www.Amazon.com
and
www.DrAngela.com

ABOUT THE AUTHOR
Dr. Angela Brownemiller
Dr. Angela®

Dr. Angela Brownemiller, also known as Dr. Angela®, is an author, journalist, social thinker, clinician, psychotherapist, trainer, speaker, and creator of the ASK DR. ANGELA Series of broadcasts, podcasts, books, audiobooks, Ebooks, and programs. The views of Angela Brownemiller are centered on the great potential of the Human mind, heart, and soul, and on the rights of all of us, who and whatever we are (or think we are). Dr. Angela Brownemiller views the Human consciousness as a wealth of opportunity for exploration, insight, knowledge—and survival.

DrAngelaBrownemiller@gmail.com
DrAngela.com

Made in United States
North Haven, CT
06 April 2023

35123832R00254